Jeremy Black offers a much needed re-balancing of the history of eighteenth-century warfare. Taking a truly global approach, his account is as concerned with military forces in Asia, Africa and the Middle East as it is with Western military history.

Beginning in 1700, Black chronologically surveys a century of global warfare, synthesising a broad range of literature along the way. This book is ideal for those seeking an accessible and authoritative account of eighteenth-century military history.

Jeremy Black is Professor of History at the University of Exeter, UK. He is an authority on early modern British and continental European history, with special interest in international relations, military history, the press, and historical atlases. His books include *War in the World*, *Beyond the Military Revolution*, *Eighteenth-Century Europe* and *Eighteenth-Century Britain*.

D1440820

War in the Eighteenth-Century World

Jeremy Black

palgrave
macmillan

First published 2013 by
PALGRAVE MACMILLAN

Palgrave Macmillan in the UK is an imprint of Macmillan Publishers Limited, registered in England, company number 785998, of Houndmills, Basingstoke, Hampshire RG21 6XS.

Palgrave Macmillan in the US is a division of St Martin's Press LLC, 175 Fifth Avenue, New York, NY 10010.

Palgrave Macmillan is the global academic imprint of the above companies and has companies and representatives throughout the world.

Palgrave® and Macmillan® are registered trademarks in the United States, the United Kingdom, Europe and other countries.

ISBN 978-0-230-37002-9   hardback
ISBN 978-0-230-37001-2   paperback

This book is printed on paper suitable for recycling and made from fully managed and sustained forest sources. Logging, pulping and manufacturing processes are expected to conform to the environmental regulations of the country of origin.

A catalogue record for this book is available from the British Library.

A catalog record for this book is available from the Library of Congress.

10   9   8   7   6   5   4   3   2   1
22 21 20 19 18 17 16 15 14 13

Printed in China

For David Allen

Contents

Preface

This is an account of the eighteenth century that is as concerned about the Chinese conquests of Tibet and Xinjiang, the Afghan overthrow of the Safavid rulers of Persia (Iran), the campaigns of Nadir Shah of Persia, and the Ottoman (Turkish)–Persian war of the 1720s–40s, as it is of warfare involving Western forces.[1] In India, the dramatic Afghan victory over the Marathas in the Third Battle of Panipat (1761) plays a greater role than the smaller-scale, but usually more prominent, battle of Plassey (1757) in which the British defeated the Nawab of Bengal.

At the same time, there is an effort to fit the West into the account, while not destabilising it by suggesting that the West was necessarily dominant. We might end in 1798–9 with Napoleon crushing the Mamluks of Egypt and the British totally defeating Tipu Sultan, their leading opponent in southern India. However, to indicate the problems with charting trends, within a decade the French and British were out of Egypt, being defeated there in 1801 and 1807 respectively, the French had lost in Haiti, and the British were under serious strain in India in the latter stages of the Maratha War.

Thus, this book is to be written without any teleology focused on eventual Western success later in the nineteenth century, important as that was to be for global history then and subsequently. The book is also written from a twenty-first-century perspective of a decline in relative Western, and certainly European, power and a rise of non-Western military fortunes. This perspective provides a salutary way of re-considering earlier trajectories of military history, whether geographical, organisational or cultural in character.

The core organisational and analytical nature of this book is one of devoting relevant attention and consideration to non-Western parts of the world, and notably in light of over half the world's population then being in Asia: China alone had *c.* 300 million inhabitants in 1800, whereas the British Isles had about 15.5 million and Europe, as a whole, about 187 million. Although the Indian subcontinent, where British power had become significant by 1800, had about 200 million inhabitants then, other areas in which, like China, Western military pressure was, as yet, of scant significance, including Persia and South-East Asia, also contained appreciable numbers of people, although not at this scale. The contrast between North Asia (Siberia), a vast region with a low population, where Russia had become the dominant power in the early seventeenth century, and populated East Asia, where Western powers lacked sway, is readily apparent.

This book therefore follows on from my *War in the World: A Comparative History, 1450–1600* (2011), and *Beyond the Military Revolution: War in the Seventeenth-Century World* (2011), in offering a much-needed rebalancing of the history of eighteenth-century warfare in non-Western-centric and non-teleological terms. A simple goal, however, is neither a simple nor an easy task. The range of military activity round the world poses the problems of mastering often disparate scholarship, and confronting limited and patchy knowledge, as well as deciding what to include and exclude, the last a particularly difficult issue. Finally, there are serious difficulties in deciding the themes that should be employed to shape the material.

The significance of evidence is a key issue. For example, Turkestan (in Central Asia) and South-East Asia, both large and very varied areas, were among the regions in which there was not a shift from matchlock to the more effective flintlock muskets seen in the West. Yet, that does not inherently mean that warfare there was in some way primitive. More generally, there is the danger of assuming that, because Western forces and military models were dominant across the world by 1900, that means that the eighteenth century should be judged in terms of their development and of signs of the weakness of other military systems.

Reviewing battles, there are particular problems with determining what actually happened in most. Established accounts can be flawed and contradictory. In part, these faulty reports reflect the limitations of individual observers, but they also tend to simplify what were often lengthy and complex engagements.[2] Furthermore, for some battles, participants provided few or no accounts. This problem is particularly true for conflicts and developments in certain parts of the world, such as the Horn of Africa (modern Ethiopia, Somalia, Eritrea, Djibouti).[3] Conflicts involving Western forces tend to be better covered but, even so, accounts of them often feature some confusion and there can be considerable difficulty in establishing the chain of events. This difficulty then feeds through into problems in assessing relative capability.

I have taken guidance from two sources. The first, and most important, is reading the work of other scholars. I am very fortunate in its quality, and, if I can position my own study to support this scholarship, I will be pleased. At the same time, it is important to note the major contrast in the amounts published on Western and non-Western military history, both on land and, even more, at sea. Nevertheless, despite this contrast in quantity, there are, alongside the first-rate work on Western military history, excellent studies on many other parts of the world, studies that those working on Western military history would profit from reading.

Secondly, each of my books is designed to take a place in a wider intellectual architecture. This book is both the sequel to the two titles above and the culmination to a move from a Western focus seen in successive works I have written on the period, especially *European Warfare 1660–1815* (1994), and *European Warfare in a Global Context, 1660–1815* (2007). As I cannot expect that all of my books will be read, while, anyway, they are each designed to be independent, there is, where appropriate, a degree of repetition, but this is a new book, designed to consider eighteenth-century military history from a global perspective.

In offering truly global history, I break from the usual practice in works on global military history of offering a unitary argument tying seemingly disparate military events, settings and cultures into a coherent theme, or superstructure. However helpful such a practice may be for pedagogic reasons, notably for providing coherence and clarity, I have always been sceptical of thematic accounts, such as the gunpowder empires, the Rise of the West, the Military Revolution, the advent of the 'fiscal–military state',[4] and so forth. Instead, I draw the reader's attention to events and processes that can undermine storylines of technological determinism, Western global dominance, and bureaucratic centralisation. The rejection of simpli-fied, overarching models means that events will necessarily appear more confusing and ambiguous than would otherwise be the case, especially as many of them will be unfamiliar to Western readers. History, however, is a messy process. We need detail to comprehend it; hence the need to include narrative sections outlining campaigns and battles.

Moreover, my accounts of military conflicts around the globe offer important correctives to the well-established, but overly simple, narrative of modernisation, with its stress on the decline of cavalry and the rise of infantry, artillery and fortifications. For example, the continued impact of cavalry is shown repeatedly in this book, while episodes demonstrating the efficacy of fortifications are balanced by episodes that reveal them to have been counterproductive. More generally, instances of success or failure are presented as responses to local conditions and demands, rather than as reflections of the 'inherent' benefits of certain technologies or formations.

There are several possible ways of organising the book: chronologi-cal, geographical, and thematic by types of warfare. The former has the disadvantage of leading to a degree of repetition – China occurs in each section, while the discussion of particular areas is broken up. The chrono-logical approach can also be criticised for resulting in a misleading empha-sis on the simultaneity of events as if that simultaneity was the key issue. Comparisons across time can also suffer.

However, I favour this approach as, without necessarily implying that this is the only context for consideration, this very simultaneity enables the reader to grasp the relative significance of developments, and also lessens the standard Western teleology. China *should* occur in each section. Moreover, this approach is that taken in the 1450–1600 and 1600–1700 books for which this book is a sequel. Lastly, as in those books, there will be a use of the chronological framework to put an emphasis on particular areas when they are especially prominent. Thus, Persia (Iran) takes the leading role in chapter 3, but a far smaller part in chapters 2, 5 and 6; while China is more prominent in chapters 2 and 4 than in chapter 3.

Across the century, it is necessary to consider how wars were won. As in other periods, victory in battle was not necessarily a condition of winning a war, but it was a key element, in part because most wars ended with a compromise peace rather than a total success. To this end, victory in battle proved important in registering strength and success, and thus encourag-ing the defeated power to accept that it had lost or was losing, and therefore to compromise. However, the extent to which this strategy was defined is a matter of some uncertainty.

As ever, it is important to appreciate that academic discussion of war can seem bloodless in contrast to the savage and cruel realities of death and destruction, fear and suffering. These affected civilians, a term that was not in use until the 1790s,[5] as well as the military. In 1713, when a large Russian amphibious force appeared off Helsinki, the greatly outnumbered Swedish garrison burned the town to the ground and ordered the population to leave. In turn, the Russian occupiers of Helsinki from 1713 to 1721 built forti-fications, desecrated the graveyard, and seized people for Russian service, leading to the period being known as the Great Wrath.

Maps are important for locating places mentioned in the text. These days, maps can readily be found online, while, for atlases, it is useful to consult the *DK Atlas of World History* (1999) and the works referred to in its bibliography, notably Joseph Schwartzberg's *Historical Atlas of South Asia* (2nd edn, 1992), the *New Cambridge Modern History Atlas* (1970), and J.D. Fage's *Atlas of African History* (1958).

During the course of reading for this book, I was particularly struck by differences in the literature, not only drawing on contrasting national emphases, but also relating to the very chronology of events and discussion of their causes, course and consequences. This issue is scarcely unfamiliar to historians, but proved especially notable in this topic when it came to considering Asian developments, specifically the conflicts between China and both the Zunghars and Burma. For example, in the former case, there are very different accounts of the warfare of the 1730s, while, in the latter case, aside from contrasting accounts of the campaigning in the late 1760s, there are significant differences in the discussion over both outcome and aftermath.

These points underline both the more general difficulties in establishing relative capability and the need for more fresh work in the subject. The latter is particularly required for South-East and Central Asia, for Persia after 1750, and for sub-Saharan Africa. In some cases, there are serious problems with the availability of evidence, but there are always opportunities for more work.

Pradeep Barua, Paola Bianchi, Guy Chet, Brian Davies, Wayne Lee, Jürgen Luh, Davide Maffi, Ciro Paoletti, Kaushik Roy, Rick Schneid, Eugene Van Sickle, Peter Wilson and three anonymous readers kindly commented on an earlier draft, and Virginia Aksan, Michael Axworthy and Yingcong Dai on particular sections. I have profited from advice from George Bournoutian, Ted Cook, Rudi Matthee and Tim May. None is responsible for any errors that remain. I have also benefited from the opportunity to give lectures at Appalachian State, North Georgia, Longwood, Southern Mississippi, Richmond, Eastern Tennessee and Waseda universities, the Institute of Historical Research, the Virginia Historical Society, the Citadel, and at the 2006, 2008 and 2011 Gunther E. Rothenberg Seminars in Military History at High Point University. Visiting historical sites can be inspiring: I certainly found scrutinising the harbour defences of Havana taken by Britain in 1762 instructive.

Jenna Steventon has proved a most helpful editor, Jocelyn Stockley a wonderfully effective copy-editor.

It is a great pleasure to dedicate this book to David Allen, a key member of the university community who has proved a constant support for the academic values I hold dear.

1 *Introduction*

The West and the Rest

History is at once what happened in the past and the varied accounts we tell about it. As such, history reflects scholarly advances in what we know about the past, as well as current changes in interest and concern. The latter are germane to this book because of the rapid rise in relative prominence of China and India, and the apparent decline, at least relative decline, of the West, and certainly of Europe. In 2012, Asian military expenditure passed that of Europe, although the latter remained higher at the per capita level. This perspective poses a number of questions in the coverage of the eighteenth century. First, how far should more attention than is conventionally given be devoted to China and India in that period because of the situation today? Secondly, should there be more attention because trends in that period can be linked to the situation today, notably the Chinese conquest of Xinjiang and Tibet in the eighteenth century and opposition, sometimes violent, in each now to Chinese rule? Thirdly, if the latter two approaches are rejected as misguided, then how should attention be apportioned between areas and developments in the eighteenth century? However, the very use of the term 'development' presupposes a clear pattern of improvement and improvability.

Fourthly, what form should the attention to China, India and the non-West as a whole take? As an aspect of this question, how will it be best to counter what Patrick Porter has recently termed 'military Orientalism'? This phrase means a misleading stereotyping, indeed primitivisation, of Asian warfare, and, notably, a tendency to argue that it is/was more primitive (and thus inexorable) in character than Western counterparts.[1] Instead of such stereotyping, it is instructive to note parallels in human behaviour as demonstrated through warfare. This study will show that the nature of warfare arose from a dynamic mix of available technology, geographical factors, human skills and political circumstances, generating essentially similar situations despite cultural differences. In short, we face many of the familiar conceptual, methodological and historiographical problems of military history as a whole.[2]

Again, if long-term significance is the issue, then should the focus be on the build-up of Prussian power, when Prussia in the event was rapidly brought to total defeat by France in 1806–7 only two decades after Frederick the Great, a focus of conventional attention, died in 1786; or on the French military, when it similarly totally collapsed in 1812–14 and, again, in 1815, two decades after the spectacular successes of 1792–5.[3] This question reflects the degree to which, in the Western-centric view, there is not only a question of the predominance of the West as a model. There is also an emphasis on the experience of certain countries in constructing the narrative, for example France rather than Spain, as well as a preoccupation with 'great captains', such as Marlborough and Frederick the Great; with battles, rather than other kinds of operations; and with regular rather than non-professional forces.

Again, how far should the focus be on the growth of the British empire, which itself disappeared from 1947 when India and Pakistan became independent? The last point is of particular relevance for Indian history. The standard account of military history there in the eighteenth century focuses on British successes, notably Robert Clive's striking victory over the Nawab of Bengal at Plassey in 1757, which began the process by which Britain became dominant in Bengal by 1765 and thus became a key territorial power able to draw on the resources of one of India's wealthiest regions. Similarly, the conquest of Mysore in 1799 brought Britain dominance in southern India, which again lasted until 1947.

These successes were central to the development of the British empire in South Asia, but that is now in the past. Therefore, it is pertinent to consider whether other themes should be pushed to the fore when considering the military history of South Asia. To take a modern theme, how far is the struggle in the eighteenth century between Indian rulers and successive invaders, first the Persians (Iranians) in the late 1730s, and then the Afghans from the 1750s to the 1790s, from across the Khyber Pass relevant or, at least, deserving of more attention than the rise of British power there?

These points are introduced because readers need to know that there is no clear standard by which relevance, and still more, relative relevance, can be determined. To pretend otherwise is not only to insult their intelligence but, moreover, to downplay the role of the historian in moulding our view of the past. Without sinking into the mire of postmodernism, the issues of relevance and relativism need to be handled.

Topics other than geographical emphasis are also pertinent. There are major questions about which themes to include and, in particular, how much weight to place on each. These questions range from the necessary degree of attention to naval history, a topic dominated by Western states, to those subjects covered by umbrella titles such as 'statebuilding' or 'war and society'. These, and other, methodological issues and conceptual questions will be returned to across the book, and should also be considered as at play throughout.

Much historical analysis centres on the question of change or continuity; and war in the eighteenth century is no exception. The tradition in Western historiography is to look for change and to see it in terms of development, through greater proficiency, towards modernity; the latter generally presented in terms of a stereotypical view of the present and of recent years. However, this analytical approach, with its emphasis on modernisation, is not only deeply flawed in itself, but is also seriously contingent, in that the condition of the present changes radically, with consequent alterations in how both modernisation and the 'turn' or move into modernisation are perceived, as well as in the significance understood for recent years.

As with the shift in relative power across the world in the early twenty-first century, there has also been a major change in modern warfare. The idea of 'total war', in terms of the mass-mobilisation and industrial basis of the two world wars and the nuclear arms race of the Cold War[4] (a situation that was contrasted with the earlier, supposedly more limited war, in goal and means, of the *ancien régime* West), has been replaced today by a more diffuse situation. In this, the major states rely on professional militaries that are relatively small in terms of population size, while the range of insurrectionary warfare and terrorism raises questions about the governability of large areas and puts the emphasis for many states on counter-insurgency warfare.[5]

The implications of this shift for considering past ages are unclear, other than leading to an understandable interest in areas that have recently been and/or currently are centres of conflict, notably Afghanistan and Iraq. Considering the eighteenth century less in terms of conventional state-to-state warfare, often misleadingly described as limited, and more, instead, with regard both to asymmetrical conflict (that between forces that are differently armed and, often, have contrasting purposes) and to (the generally related) insurrectionary and counter-insurrectionary warfare,[6] is certainly instructive. Such a consideration also matches current interests in moving away from assessing rivalry between Western states and, instead, focusing on conflict between such states (as well as their counterparts elsewhere, such as China) and opponents with dissimilar governmental systems that were reliant on what, to conventional militaries, appeared as irregular warfare.

There has been a linked change in ideas about the significance of Western warfare, although the impact of this in the literature is still limited. In place of a familiar focus for international relations and warfare on French expansion in Europe, traditionally the dominant theme for the late seventeenth century, or the *ménage à trois* of Austria, Prussia and Russia, conventionally the dominant theme for the eighteenth prior to the French Revolution, with the effectiveness of powers assessed accordingly, comes a greater concern, as in this book, with Western conflict with non-Western powers. In part, this attention rests on a larger interest in warfare with the Turks than hitherto and, in particular, on an approach that is not predicated on inevitable Turkish failure. Russia and Austria thus rate more attention as opponents of the Turks,[7] rather than as opponents of Frederick the Great of Prussia. Russia spent more time fighting the Turks than waging war with Prussia, although the situation was different for Austria. To downgrade the Russian achievement in repeatedly defeating the Turks is to fail to place due weight on the strength of non-Western military systems and the difficulty of defeating them.

In part, there is also an engagement with trans-oceanic Western warfare, both without an assumption that the Western forces would necessarily win and because this warfare is seen as significant for non-Western areas and for discussion of military capability and development. It is mistaken automatically to assume that Western military progress was set in the Western European core: that, with his linear formations and emphasis on firepower, Robert Clive in India in the 1750s was simply enacting the methods of John, 1st Duke of Marlborough in Europe in the 1700s or of Frederick the Great of Prussia in Europe in the 1740s and 1750s. Instead, it is pertinent to consider the view that warfare on the Western periphery represented a melding, both longstanding and more recent, of practices; and, in some cases, could influence the core. The last is particularly the case with the Russian use in the West of attack formations, tactics, operational methods and command experience that were developed to fight the Turks.

Moreover, conflict with the Turks provided a common practical school for Western cadets. They volunteered there as Venturers and normally came back with a remarkable and commonly-shared fighting experience which was reapplied in the West. The consequence, however, could be a stalemate, as happened on the right wing of the Allied front at the battle of Blenheim in 1704, because both the opposing commanders fought using the same tactics. Prince Eugene, the leading Austrian commander against the French in the War of the Spanish Succession (1701–14), was criticised for doing war 'in the hussars' way' due to the tactics he learned in Hungary against the Turks in 1683–8 and 1697–9, which were based on raids, speed and, in some way, guerrilla activity. Moreover, in 1744, at Madonna dell'Olmo, Piedmontese infantry repelled Franco-Spanish cavalry simply by firing from behind a line of *chevaux de frise* (obstacles placed on the field of battle). Such field fortifications were not used in the West from the start of the century, but were employed by the Austrians against the Turks. In 1744, Austrian units took part in the battle on the Piedmontese side.

Rather, however, than being learned from conflict with the Turks, guerrilla warfare was a sort of instinctive tactic focused on ambushes and based on the weakness of one side and its own knowledge of the ground. The Piedmontese used Waldensian militia in small units with remarkable results against the French, notably in the War of the Austrian Succession on the Alpine front in the 1740s, and guerrilla attacks affected French operations by cutting supply lines. The same tactics were applied in the County of Nice by the local population against the occupying French from 1792 to 1796.[8]

There has also been discussion of the idea that 'small war' techniques developed for conflict in North America were then applied in Europe. However, the latter thesis underplays the continued importance of these techniques throughout. This importance is usually neglected due to the focus, instead, on battles. More generally, there is a misleading insistence in much Western scholarship on defining a single way of war, as well as the undue influence in military academies of 'staff' histories which also seek to explain Western dominance militarily in such a fashion.

The conceptual and methodological context within which the question of military change or continuity in the eighteenth century is to be assessed is problematic and, indeed, unstable, not that that situation prevents bold and confident statements about significance and consequence based on the notions of modernity and of revolutionary change towards modernity. Indeed, for historians of warfare, the psychological impact of concepts spurred on by the American and French revolutions, and advanced with these revolutions as the major topic and evidence, is considerable. So also is the tendency to discuss the eighteenth century in terms of the alleged precursors or lack of anticipation of these revolutions, and of the apparent consequences of the revolutions.

For many scholars, this tendency has defined and, I would argue, distorted our understanding of the period. In addition, leaving aside the locating of supposed revolutionary change, there is also the wider issue, in discussing change and much else, of the problematic nature of an aggregation or lumping that integrates myriad cultural and technological processes and settings into one account.

The number of supposed military revolutions, moreover, becomes an issue. As far as the eighteenth century is concerned, there is the problem that, although the period is usually presented in Western scholarship in terms of the (new) revolutionary challenge that, in its last quarter, was posed to the Western *ancien régime* by the American and French revolutions, it is also necessary to address the argument that the century witnessed the last part of a putative early-modern military revolution focused on Western Europe and, indeed, that this century is important to this latter thesis, notably with the success of Western methods against non-Western powers.[9] This thesis has been extremely influential and, although most of the discussion of it, and the related concept of gunpowder empires, relates to the period 1450–1650,[10] nevertheless the thesis influences the treatment of the eighteenth century.

However, as this book will make clear, a focus on the alleged early-modern military revolution distorts the understanding of war around the world as it leads to an excessive attention not only to the West but also to initiatives stemming from it. Moreover, the assumption that there had been a fundamental shift in military power towards the West by then works much less well for the Old World than it does for the New. This assumption also leads to a failure to devote due attention to what does not fit into the thesis,[11] for example the continued role of cavalry and the significance of developments in South Asia that do not match the narrative or analysis of growing Western power and proficiency.

From the global perspective, it is unclear how far to incorporate standard discussion of the American and French revolutions in an assessment of military history in which due weight is given to Asia, other than by emphasising variety in place of the standard teleology. Furthermore, it is symptomatic of the disproportionate emphasis on the conflict in North America during the global stage of the War of American Independence from 1778 to 1783 that the literature poorly covers the warfare in India from 1778, in which Britain fought both the Marathas and Mysore while France eventually participated. American scholars, moreover, are especially apt to underrate the Indian Ocean dimension (both on land and at sea) to the struggle between Britain and France. In addition, contrasting problems posed by the different spheres of military operations highlight the problematic notion of any argument that this era saw a 'typical' state of conflict. For example, in India, unlike America, the British suffered because their opponents enjoyed greater mobility thanks to the role of their light cavalry. The far greater population of India, as well as its territorial divisions, also promoted military developments that were not present in America.

More centrally, the question of change and continuity in the established teleology appears misplaced. There had been developments in warmaking by 1800, for example the increased use of flintlock rifles in Atlantic Africa and the new use of firearms in Hawaii; but, across most of the world, there was relatively little difference in warmaking between 1700 and 1800.

Certainly, the period, both in the West and on the global scale, did not see changes in warmaking comparable to those in the nineteenth century.[12]

Indeed, from this perspective, that of relatively little development, the eighteenth century has value as a period, and is not simply an artificial unit selected in accordance with the Christian calendar, a unit therefore that has scant meaning for much of the world. The 1690s and 1700s see a divide in the West with the replacement of pikes and matchlocks by flintlock muskets equipped with bayonets. Thereafter, there was scant change in weaponry until the nineteenth century. In Asia, the defeat of the Zunghars by China and the failure of Aurangzeb in India in the 1700s mark major transitions. The eighteenth century can be separated from the nineteenth because the latter saw crucial changes, notably the crisis of China, the conquest of much of the world by the West, and the application of steam power and steel technology to warmaking. These changes represent a clear contrast to the eighteenth century, although the divide occurred during the nineteenth century and not at its outset.

That, however, does not mean that the warfare of the eighteenth century was without consequence. Leaving aside the important argument that, in the eighteenth century, we are prefiguring the present by returning to a period not dominated by Western colonialism, there were central themes in the period that were significant for global history. The most important was in Eurasia, namely the closing off of the steppe world by the expanding sedentary imperial powers, China and Russia. At the same time, the vitality of non-sedentary peoples, most of whom were pastoralists, was shown in the overthrow of the Safavid empire of Persia by Afghan invaders in the early 1720s, and in the Afghan invasions of northern India in the late 1750s and early 1760s under Ahmad Shah.

Bellicosity, culture and rulership

International rivalry was one of force and power, with warfare, here and more generally, linked to state-forms, governmental development, and the culture of majesty. Tensions between tribal and state forms of government were significant, although, alongside contrasts between the two, there were also overlaps.[13] Across the world, *gloire*, loosely translated as the pursuit of glory, was important in causing conflict and setting military objectives. Military success brought exemplary purpose and fame, and acted as a lubricant of obedience in Crown–élite relations.[14] Military heroism played a major role in the representation of states,[15] and this role affected literature and the arts.[16]

War offered the possibility of strengthening the dynastic position, both domestically and internationally, and also of enhancing territorial control.

This element was important to major rulers pursuing large-scale goals, but also to lesser princes, such as Max Emmanuel, Elector of Bavaria during the War of the Spanish Succession (1701–14), seeking to sell his participation in the conflict for gains in territory and status.[17] In the event, his support for Louis XIV of France led to defeat and the conquest by Austria of his territories, which he only regained as part of the peace settlement.

Military command could be separated from rule, as was demonstrated by the great success and considerable importance of Prince Eugene, the Duke of Marlborough and Marshal Saxe, leading generals for Austria, Britain and France respectively. In addition, George Washington and the Marquis of Lafayette, both heroes of the American Revolution, were to offer a model of modern military celebrity in which political dedication to a cause they did not control was a key aspect of their appeal.[18] In the Turkish empire, military leadership on campaign was increasingly by Grand Viziers (leading ministers), and not by sultans. Ahmed III accompanied the army in 1715 and 1717, but remained far behind the front line, and in 1730 did not even set out on campaign, helping precipitate the rebellion that led to his overthrow.

Nevertheless, military command was generally a key aspect of rulership, a situation encouraged by the view that waging a lawful war required a declaration of war and that only true sovereigns could declare war.[19] John Campbell's comment on Frederick William I of Prussia (r. 1713–40) – 'he made his troops his delight, and led all his days rather a military than a court life' – could have been repeated for other rulers. The wearing of uniform was important for monarchs in some Western states.[20] So also were military reviews. Thus, in 1777, Ferdinand I of Naples spent much time exercising his troops, including taking part in a mock campaign he had planned that entailed constructing a camp and staging mock battles and a siege.[21]

Moreover, many of the key commanders of the period were also rulers. Most, such as Peter the Great (I) of Russia (r. 1689–1725), Frederick the Great (II) of Prussia (r. 1740–86), and the Qianlong emperor of China (r. 1736–96), inherited the right to rule, and then used war to enhance their assets. Peter, in particular, transformed both army and state in order to increase Russian military effectiveness and win territory and prestige. In contrast, having become crucial to military success against the invading Turks, Nadir Shah of Persia took over a failing empire in the 1730s, declaring himself Shah in 1736, and gave Persia a military dynamism, until his assassination in 1747.

War and military activity played important roles in a culture of power to which honour and prestige were significant, let alone such related issues as insecure and provoked masculinities.[22] Concern for personal honour was particularly apparent in the case of officers, and greatly affected command practices and issues.[23] The effects, however, varied. No Western ruler matched 'Alaungpaya of Burma (r. 1752–60), who judged men largely by the number of heads they could produce after a battle. Moreover, unsuccessful Burmese officers were executed; a practice also seen with the enforced suicides of commanders in China. With the prominent exception of Admiral Byng, shot in 1757, after a court martial for failing to relieve the British garrison on the Mediterranean island of Minorca the previous year, the execution of commanders was rare in the West until Revolutionary France, from 1792, treated failure as a demonstration of treason. The American revolutionaries had not followed this course, which was a prime instance of the less radical path followed there than in the case of France.

The cultural dimension extended to the aesthetics of warfare, with rulers placing particular value on a good-looking army. This preference played a role in recruitment, encouraging the acceptance of tall men over short ones, notably by Frederick William I of Prussia. For the same reason, many Western rulers designed their soldiers' uniforms, with an emphasis on having the army look good, as well as seeking to assist local textile industries. Military activity also fulfilled narratives and models of imperial and royal destiny and role. The repute of rulers and the fame of ancestors were echoed.[24]

The willingness of rulers, commanders and combatants not only to kill large numbers, but also to accept heavy casualties, was an important feature of military culture, although the latter acceptance varied. Preserving the army was the first priority, but there was a greater willingness to take casualties than with much, although by no means all, modern warfare, and certainly in so far as regular forces are concerned. Based on the cost of training modern troops and their relative rarity, a functional explanation of this current unwillingness can be advanced, contrasting it with the situation in the eighteenth century. However, social, cultural and ideological factors are, and were, more significant, not least of which is the contrast between modern individualism and hedonism, and, on the other hand, earlier concepts of duty and fatalism in a much harsher working environment. The extent to which this sense of duty and fatalism can be related to levels of habitual violence in society[25] is unclear.

The acceptance of casualties was crucial to the bellicosity of the age. Enlightenment individuals in Christian Europe and North America might criticise all, or much, of this belligerence, presenting it as a pointless and indeed dishonourable bloodlust, but these views had scant impact on the goals and means of waging conflict. Instead, the continued normative character of resorting to warfare was more notable, and across the world. Wars were believed to be not only necessary, but also, in at least some respects, desirable. This conviction proved a key context for the eighteenth century, and also for those that preceded and followed it. The belief in necessity also helped explain the attitude in combat zones to those who would later be called civilians, including the response to conventions that restricted violence, at least within cultural zones, such as Christendom and the world of Islam.[26] In practice, these conventions were frequently ignored.

The nature of rule was a central element in the military history of the period. Military systems with political continuity and stability, and administrative strength, notably China, Britain and Russia, proved more able to sustain a projection of their power than monarchies on horseback such as those of the Zunghars, Nadir Shah in Persia, Ahmad Shah in Afghanistan, and Napoleon, or, with the exception of their not using horses, 'Alaungpaya in Burma, and Tamsin in Siam (Thailand). Ultimately, therefore, military history is an aspect of the other histories of the period, as well as contributing greatly to them. Environmental history was one such. The dependence of operations on the weather and climate was a key element, as 'the present scarcity of corn and all other provisions'[27] could delay or prevent moves, or be believed likely to do so. Harsh winters and springs delayed the appearance of grass, affecting the moves of cavalry. Nevertheless, governmental development was significant to military capability, notably in helping produce, deploy and sustain the necessary resources for war,[28] but, moreover, as an aspect of a system of rule that also provided the political stability valuable for military activity.

Possibly linked to this emphasis on strong states as the key players, there has been a tendency, as, misleadingly, with work on the twentieth century,[29] to downplay civil warfare in the central narrative and dominant analysis of military history. Crucially, such warfare was not an important feature of Prussian military history, and notably not in the eighteenth century. Yet, it is mistaken to ignore this element. In particular, the last quarter of the eighteenth century saw major insurrections and civil wars across Europe, including in Russia, Transylvania, Hungary, Belgium, the Netherlands, Ireland and the Turkish Balkans; as well as in British North America, the Andean chain, Haiti and China, especially the huge and very costly White Lotus rebellion of 1796–1805 in China. Each insurrection was very different, and it is harder in these cases to draw common themes for the nature of conflict or military capability than it is when considering conflict between regular forces. Partly for this reason, but also owing to the relative lack of research, and to the prejudices of military establishments that saw (and see) internal policing and the suppression of rebellions as less prestigious tasks, this type of warfare has been relatively neglected in the literature.

Aside from serious issues in the coverage of warfare in this, and other, centuries, there are concerns about standard explanations. As a reminder, for example, of the need for care in drawing clear causal conclusions in the sphere of international conflict, governmental systems of continuity, stability and strength were not invariably successful in war, as the Chinese discovered in Burma and Vietnam, the Russians in Persia, the Afghans in Persia and the Punjab, and the British, eventually, but more centrally to their military effort than in the Chinese and Russian examples, in North America. In each case, failures can be regarded as those of imperial over-stretch, albeit in very different contexts, the last example, the American Revolution, having an element of civil war not seen in the other examples cited in the previous sentence. However, although the thesis of such an over-stretch appears seductively clear, its application is not readily inherent to particular circumstances. Instead, far from being readily obvious,[30] over-stretch emerged through the warfare of the period, warfare that helped define imperial limits and, more generally, mould, as well as register, the politics of the period.

A common requirement of the ruler-leaders in this era was the demon-stration of both political and military skill, with the latter closely asso-ciated with the former. Thus, it was necessary to divide opponents, to create tensions in their alliances, and to fight them in sequence. This was a practice at which Frederick the Great was adept, as, in more propitious circumstances given his far greater power, was the Qianlong emperor. It was also important to hold together constituencies of interest, be they international alliances or the groups within countries backing a war effort.

This political dimension to conflict is also captured in the stress in the literature on statebuilding, but there is a danger that that dimension of causes and consequences is approached in an overly schematic and modern fashion, and without giving due weight to other political aspects of warfare and the related military aspects of politics. The notion that war makes states and states make war is seductively clear, but also begs a lot of questions about both the processes involved and the extent to which war also fulfils other purposes, as well as frequently undermining states as a result of the burdens, both resource and political, incurred. In addition, it is important to emphasise the degree to which rulers, in making war, called upon non-bureaucratic processes to raise and support forces. These processes had significant consequences for the way in which war was pursued. Moreover, the extent to which states make war was (and is) neither automatic nor consistent. Rather than viewing this question in terms of a model, whether of war, the international system, or of statebuilding, that takes precedence over particular circumstances and individual decisions, it is more pertinent to focus on these circumstances and decisions.

These circumstances and discussions are of particular significance when considering choices made between possible challenges, for these choices indicate that geopolitical factors also played through specific issues. For example, by turning east against Afghanistan and India in the late 1730s, each a different military environment, Nadir Shah reduced the pressure on his former opponents, the Turks. By doing so, he enabled the latter to concentrate on war with Russia and, more successfully, Austria, and to great effect in 1739 when the Austrians, as a result, lost Belgrade. Governments could also be divided over policy, as was the Chinese one over going to war with the Zunghars in the 1750s, the British over war with Spain in 1729, 1738–9, and 1761, the French over war with Britain in 1770, 1778, and 1790, and the American over policy towards Britain and France in the late 1790s.

The role of ideology also has to be assessed. If religious differences played a part in rivalry between Shi'ite Persia and Sunni Turkey, they did not prevent peace between the two for most of the second half of the century; although, in the Punjab in north-west India, religious hostility between Sikhs and Afghans led, in the 1760s, to sustained and eventually successful opposition to the latter. Tension over the radical plans of the French revolutionaries may have led to war with Austria and Prussia in 1792, but Britain, the Dutch and Spain did not enter the war with France until 1793, while Prussia and Spain left it in 1795. In the early 1790s, Russia was more concerned about controlling Poland than about opposing French radicalism, and crushed Polish opposition accordingly in 1794.

Far from there being any fixed relationship between war and politics, it is the flexible nature of the links that helps explain the importance of each to the other. Military activity certainly altered the contours and parameters of the politics that helped cause it, and sometimes of the states involved in conflict. In some cases, military activity had a comparable impact on social structures. The centrality of war as a basis of change, however, does not mean that there was a consistent pattern of cause or effect.

The variety of military goals is a theme of this book. As a result, diverse forms of conflict arise, as do different measures of capability. The issues of variety, diversity and difference make it difficult to arrive at an overall conclusion, but one of the most significant is that these very contrasts created problems for military systems. Those systems that focused on symmetrical warfare tended to assume that it could subsume asymmetrical conflict, both with foreign foes and with domestic opponents; but this focus could lead to their militaries being poorly prepared for different circumstances. This situation was exacerbated when training for commanders was limited, on the job, and without any real doctrinal consideration of other types of conflict. Yet again, the emphasis is on variety rather than on assuming any necessary pathway.

2 1700–1720

The themes outlined in the introduction can be readily seen in this chapter. The variety of conflict across the world emerges clearly. The first two decades of the century witnessed a high level of conflict across the world, in many senses continuing the wide-ranging and sustained warfare of the 1690s.[1] In East Asia, the expansion of Manchu (Qing) China, which had already led to victory in Mongolia over the Zunghar Confederation in 1696–7, was continued into Tibet. In India, the conflict between the dominant ruler, the Mughal emperor Aurangzeb (r. 1658–1707), and the Marathas persisted. In Europe, the protracted warfare of the 1640s–90s between the Ottoman (Turkish) empire and at least one of its Christian neighbours resumed in the 1710s, with conflicts with, successively, Russia, Venice and Austria. The last denoted the Habsburg empire, which also ruled Hungary, the modern Czech Republic, Slovakia and Slovenia, and parts of northern Italy and Yugoslavia.

Within Christendom, the extinction of the line of the Spanish Habsburgs in 1700, with the death, without children, of Carlos/Charles II, led to a war for dominance of an inheritance that included, besides Spain, much of Italy (Sicily, Sardinia, Naples, Lombardy), Belgium, and most of Central and South America excluding Portuguese-ruled Brazil. This War of the Spanish Succession (1701–14, although with different years for other combatants) saw a resumption of the Nine Years' War of the 1690s between France, whose ruling Bourbon dynasty inherited Spain in 1700 in the person of Philip V (r. 1700–46), and an alliance focused on Austria, the Dutch and Britain. France was ruled from 1643 to 1715 by Louis XIV, the Sun King, and his ambitions appeared to dominate Western Europe. However, the Nine Years' War (1688–97) and, even more, the War of the Spanish Succession represented a falling off from the diplomatic and military success achieved by France in the 1670s and early 1680s.

Although extensive, these were not the sole rivalries and/or conflicts to span the century divide; far from it. Conflict was frequent across the world, including in many regions that tend to be ignored in military history and which, aside from issues about the sources, therefore pose the question of how far and how best they should be considered. For example, Iyasu I (r. 1682–1706) of Ethiopia had, throughout his reign, fought the raiding nomadic Oromo, who played a role similar to those of the nomadic peoples who pressed on their sedentary counterparts in Eurasia. Although Iyasu developed support from Oromo tribes who had converted to Christianity, he found it very difficult to gain lasting success in his protracted warfare with the other Oromo.

However, as a reminder of the interaction of warfare with what may be termed 'domestic politics', Iyasu was assassinated in 1706. The interrelated importance of dynasticism and monarchical leadership helped ensure that the fate of rulers was important and their killing frequently a goal of conflict whether domestic or international.

China

Continuity in conflict does not establish priority, but this chapter begins with East Asia because the eventual Chinese victory over the Zunghars of the steppe, in warfare in the 1690s, 1710s and, finally, 1750s, is a prime instance of one of the key themes of the book, the importance of East Asia, and one of the central topics, the relationship between settled people and semi-nomadic peoples. This victory was also more complete than those that tend to attract attention for the century, especially the triumphs of Frederick II, 'the Great' of Prussia (r. 1740–86), over Austria, and of Britain over France, notably in the War of the Spanish Succession and the Seven Years' War (1756–63).

Moreover, the victory over the Zunghars helped ensure the shape of modern China as a state that incorporated not only the Han Chinese of the heavily-populated regions of what is now eastern China, but also the non-Chinese peoples in the more lightly-populated areas further west. Defeat over the Zunghars led to Chinese rule of Xinjiang and helped consolidate Chinese dominance of Tibet, which was otherwise challenged by the reality or prospect of Zunghar intervention. As a result of Manchu expansionism, China became both a contiguous empire of great size, and also a state where the heavily-populated core in eastern China was given considerable strategic depth other than from attack by sea, which was, in fact, to occur, principally from Britain and, later, Japan between 1839 and 1945.

Considering China also indicates the value of breaking the eighteenth century down into smaller chronological units, a process that undercuts the tendency to pursue long-term schematic interpretations or, at least, encourages a chronological specificity that aids analysis. At the level of the entire century, or if there is discussion of East Asia as a whole, then the theme becomes simply one of Chinese success, and there is a danger that this success appears inevitable, and is treated as a simple building block in a wider analysis of military activity. In particular, the struggle between settled and semi-nomadic peoples appears foreordained, and is rapidly summarised in terms of the closing of the steppe.

On 12 June 1696, the army of the Zunghar ruler, Galdan Boshughtu, was destroyed at Jao Modo by the Chinese under the personal leadership of the Kangxi emperor (r. 1662–1722). Developing the policy of his predecessors, the latter had successfully integrated the military system of the Han Chinese with that of the Manchu forces and their (eastern) Mongolian allies who had conquered China in the 1640s and 1650s. After another effective Chinese campaign in the winter of 1696–7, Galdan died of smallpox, although Chinese propaganda claimed he had killed himself by taking poison. The Chinese benefited from Galdan's failure by extending their control in Mongolia and intervening in Tibet. This success then looks towards the campaigns of Kangxi's grandson, the Qianlong emperor, who, in the late 1750s, wiped out most of the Zunghar population and conquered the Zunghar heartland in Xinjiang.

The situation appears less clear-cut, however, if the century is segmented chronologically, because Zunghar resilience emerges as an additional theme, one, indeed, that helps underline eventual Chinese success and makes it appear more impressive. An emphasis on the Zunghars also ensures attention to the continued importance of cavalry armies. Kangxi's success did not in fact end the conflict, which had become a bitter battle for mastery over a broad swathe of inner Asia stretching from the arid plains of Mongolia to the high mountains of the Himalayas, a great distance.

In Kangxi's later years, there was a struggle for dominance in Tibet, a large area which was not then part of China, and control over which would affect the loyalty of the eastern Mongols to China, a loyalty that was a key element in the rivalry between the Manchu and the Zunghars. The Manchu used Lamaist Buddhism to influence the Mongols, and, therefore, needed to control the Tibetan centres of Buddhism. In 1706, Lajang Khan, a Mongol who was a Chinese protégé, defeated the Tibetan army outside Lhasa and stormed the fortified Drepung monastery where the sixth Dalai Lama had taken refuge.[2]

In 1717, the Zunghars mounted a significant response. A 6,000-strong force, under Tsering Dondup, the brother of the Zunghar ruler, Tsewang Rabtan (r. 1697–1727), crossed into Tibet from Khotan by a very high and arid route over the Kunlun range, losing many men as a result of the harshness of the terrain, but pressing on. Lajang Khan's advisers were divided over the best way to respond: Aka Taiji recommended fighting on an open plain, while P'o-lha-nas suggested taking up a strong defensive position, the tactic adopted by the Chinese at Jao Modo. The former reflected a cultural and social preference for cavalry warfare, the latter pressure to use firearms.

In the event, Lajang's army remained in the pastures that fed his animals, and it was attacked there by the Zunghars. A general musketry volley was followed by fighting at close quarters, particularly with swords and knives. After a number of similar battles, Lajang was driven back to the Tibetan capital, Lhasa, which, thanks to the gates being treacherously opened and/ or ladders being dropped down the walls, was successfully stormed after midnight on 21 November 1717. Trying to escape, Lajang was killed. Over a three-day period, all the real and supposed adherents of the Chinese party were slaughtered and the temples were looted.[3]

The Zunghar campaign was no mere raid, which would be of no consequence except to the victims. Instead, it was a conquest that was part of the wide-ranging struggle for primacy with the Manchu rulers of China. The campaign indicated a number of points that are of wider relevance for the period. They both offer little-known instances of widespread processes and also demonstrate the importance of avoiding the tendency to simplify, and commonly primitivise, steppe and, more generally, non-Western warfare. First, the crucial role of politics emerges anew. Chinese success in 1696 had owed much to support from Galdan's rebellious nephew Tsewang Rabtan, which was an aspect of China's longstanding strategy of trying to play off steppe forces and utilise steppe allies, a strategy carried forward by the Manchu. Rabtan subsequently became an opponent of China. Similarly, disunity on Lajang's side was important to the result in 1717. His regime rested on force, his army was divided and lacked coherence, and the attack on Lhasa was greatly assisted by traitors within.

Secondly, the 1717 campaign suggested the transience of much military achievement. As earlier in Mongolia in the 1690s, the Kangxi emperor responded to problems by fresh efforts, a psychological trait of his that rested on the massive strength of his military system and the great resources of his state. Nevertheless, both strength and resources could be difficult to apply, and did not lead to automatic success. The Chinese launched counter-attacks in 1717 and 1718 via Kokonor, but their preparations were insufficient, and the expeditions failed. The troops were hit by food shortages and bad weather. In 1718, an expedition under Erentei, a Manchu general, met resistance, ran out of food, and was routed on its withdrawal, with the general and most of the troops killed. As a result, the emperor cancelled plans for an expedition in 1719 and, instead, deployed more troops to the frontier.

Concerted operations by two armies under Yinti, the emperor's four-teenth son, and General Nian Gengyao, advancing on different routes, led to the conquest of Lhasa in 1720. The unpopularity of the Zunghars in Tibet contributed to this result: taking a sectarian position in its divided politics, they had violently turned on many of the monks. As a result of this stance, there was no Tibetan opposition to the Chinese advance. The army advancing from Sichuan took Lhasa on 24 September without as much opposition as the troops advancing from Kokonor encountered, as the Zunghars had moved south to face the latter. This second army arrived in Lhasa on 10 October. Meanwhile, to prevent Rabtan from intervening from Xinjiang, two other Chinese armies were sent to attack him.[4] The ability of the Chinese to deploy so much force underlines the benefits that could be gained from plentiful manpower.

This transience of Zunghar success opens up significant methodological points, as well as illuminating Chinese strength. The difficulty of achiev-ing lasting triumphs underlines the problem, for contemporaries and subsequently, of assessing military capability and effectiveness, both in contemporary terms and over the *longue durée*. Which battles and campaigns are important and worthy of study, and how are armies to be judged? For example, also in 1717, the Austrians under Prince Eugene defeated the main Turkish army outside Belgrade before capturing the city. This victory attracts much attention, and the battle was certainly far greater in scale than that at Lhasa. Moreover, the Turkish loss of Belgrade appears to fit into a clear pattern leading to the eventual collapse of the Turkish empire in the 1910s. However, again by introducing narrow chronological bands, the situ-ation appears less clear-cut. In 1739, the Turks regained Belgrade after defeat-ing the Austrians, while, having lost it in 1789 to Austria, they regained it in the subsequent peace negotiated the following year. The Turks did not finally lose the city for good, and then to an autonomous Serbia, until 1817, and the Austrians did not conquer it again until 1915, and then only until 1918.

Turning to the successful Chinese response in Tibet in 1720 raises the question whether the Zunghar invasion of 1717 had revealed that centuries-old patterns of military behaviour, in the shape of attacks by steppe raiding forces, were still valid; or, conversely, whether the eventual outcome, Chinese success, indicated the superior power of imperial sedentary states, answering the question the historian Edward Gibbon was to pose later in the century as to whether the 'barbarian' invasions of Europe could recur. The Chinese successfully intervened in Tibet again at mid-century (see p. 72), and essentially remained dominant there.

Thirdly, the 1717 campaign demonstrated the continued importance of cavalry, and yet also raises questions over steppe warfare and cavalry as a whole. In part, these questions arise because the struggle in Tibet witnessed the interaction of steppe and Chinese understandings of victory. These understandings entailed a continuum of conflict in which it was necessary to determine what was most important and viable: holding territory or defeating an opposing army in the field. The tactical and operational aspects of cavalry warfare on the steppe had profound effects on the strategic understandings of what constituted victory. Conditions were extremely fluid, the enemy could always ride away, there were few strongholds to capture; and, therefore, it was difficult to achieve and impose a sense of victory, and hard for those opposing steppe forces to control the situation. In this context, gaining some kind of hold over a population without the regular application of force was far from easy. Subsidies and genocide were two possibilities, both, but especially the former, employed at times in Chinese relations with their neighbours.

At the same time, it would be seriously mistaken to see China as an unchanging entity with a consistent strategic culture and military style, an approach that is encouraged by the use of the language of strategic culture. Instead, Manchu conquest in the mid-seventeenth century helped to make the position in China both dynamic and volatile. Political considerations played a key role in that the emperors regarded their bannermen, a major element of the regular forces, as more reliable than their more numerous Han Chinese Green Standard troops. The bannermen included Manchus, Mongols and Chinese, the last, the so-called Hanjun, recruited before the Manchu conquest in the mid-seventeenth century. The bannermen were stationed in northern China, around the centre of authority, the imperial capital of Beijing, and down to the River Yangzi, and the garrisons lived in segregated walled compounds. The first permanent banner garrison was not established in the south-west (below the Yangzi) until 1718, and this development reflected the severity of the Tibetan crisis for China. The Green Standard troops were stationed all over the country, but with many in the south.

There was also a difference in function, with the Green Standard troops focusing on dealing with rebellions, while the bannermen were the vital troops in confronting challenges from the steppe. Their stress on cavalry and experience of steppe warfare were important to this function. The bannermen did not have a tradition of infantry warfare to match that of the Green Standard troops, most of whom were armed with matchlock muskets by 1700. These remained the major weapon throughout the century, and many were made in the garrison cities for use by their garrisons. The Chinese use of Western artillery experts, notably Jesuits, in the seventeenth century had provided effective cannon,[5] but these cannon were essentially an add-on and did not transform the nature of Chinese warmaking. Moreover, the Chinese did not match the major Western advances in gunfounding and ballistics during the eighteenth century.

Great care was taken with the choice and loyalty of military commanders, as the army was the principal support of the Manchu dynasty against rebellion. Other than when appointed to command expeditions, commanders had direct control over only a relatively small number of troops. Moreover, the authority of the emperor over the military was carefully maintained. Furthermore, senior commanders were bound to the imperial family, not least by marital links, but also by giving them remunerative civil positions in peacetime. Most senior commanders were Manchu. Thanks in part to this system, the emperors did not face any rebellion by the army during the century and there was no comparison with the dangerous dissidence of the Turkish *janissaries* (infantry).

Related to subsidies to steppe peoples came the effort to lessen potential opposition on the steppe by winning allies. This policy was also seen with the Spanish treatment of Native American tribes in the south-west of what is now the USA. However, the Spaniards had a much weaker hand than the Chinese, both because they lacked the resources and the traditions of intervention on the steppe that might serve to help win allies, and because they did not have the powerful army that the Chinese were repeatedly able to deploy in advance of their fortifications.

The 1720 operation against Tibet was a major success for the Chinese, and a formidable triumph of force-projection in a difficult and distant environment. The establishment of the seventh Dalai Lama was made with Chinese backing, helping the latter ground their position in Tibet. A 4,000-man-strong Chinese garrison was established, an important extension of power, as there had been no Chinese garrisons when Tibet had earlier accepted tributary status. Moreover, much of eastern Tibet was added to neighbouring Chinese provinces. This success looked toward the increase of Chinese control over Tibet later in the century. In 1730, the Chinese assumed suzerainty over Bhutan, a Tibetan vassal in the Himalayan mountains.

There was also conflict to the north of Tibet, with the Chinese and Zunghars contesting the oasis settlements that were crucial bases on the trade route to the west and vital supply-points in the corridor along which invasions by one or other would be conducted. In 1715, the Zunghars failed to take the town of Hami from its Chinese garrison. The Chinese then took the initiative, capturing Barkol in 1716. The shortage of forage in the region led the Chinese to adopt the new tactic of establishing a number of permanent military colonies linked by outposts. This method provided a new military capability and threatened the Zunghars.[6] It was also a method used by the Russians as they expanded southward into the steppe, and by the Spaniards as they sought to protect Mexico's northern frontier.

The Chinese pressed on to take the distant oasis of Turfan in East Turkestan in 1720, again a formidable logistical achievement and one not matched since the Tang dynasty a millennium earlier. Chinese operations were helped by a rebellion by the Muslims of Turfan against Zunghar control.[7] The oasis of Urumchi in Turkestan was occupied in 1722. Like the Manchu dynasty, the Tang (r. 618–907) ruled a cosmopolitan empire. They also faced both external challenges and rebellion. The Tang were confronted by an expansionist Islam.[8]

At the same time as China expanded, the Zunghars remained a potent force on the steppe, able, from their base in Xinjiang, itself a very large area, to exert force on their neighbours, not only in China but also elsewhere on the steppe. This capability gave the Zunghars a strategic depth that made them potentially a particularly difficult opponent for China, with the Manchu dynasty's sensitivity increased by its origins as an attacking force from the north-east of China.

The Chinese government also faced opposition as the result of the policy of imposing central control in peripheral, often highland, regions in place of relying, as hitherto, on native chieftains. This process was linked to the expansion of settlement by the Han Chinese. Non-Han peoples resisted, as in the regions of Guangxi and western Hunan where opposition was suppressed in the early 1710s.

Meanwhile, the Zunghars were also confronted by Russian activity: relations were exacerbated by the Russian advance into the upper reaches of the valley of the River Ob. Biysk was founded as a base in 1709, but the Zunghars responded by destroying it and by besieging the fortress of Kuznetsk, albeit unsuccessfully. This attack led to a standard Russian response: expansion and consolidation through fortification. A series of fortresses was built on the River Irtysh, including Omsk (1716) and Ust'-Kamenoorsk (1719). Moving from the fortresses, however, proved less successful for the Russians, a frequent problem which indicated the limitations of fortresses as a tool of policy. A Russian expedition sent to discover gold sands in the Zunghar lands was forced to retreat in 1715 in the face of superior forces that threatened its communications. A second expedition sent in 1719 was clearly defeated in spite of Russian superiority in firearms. The Zunghars stopped the Russian attempt to take over the basin of the Zaisan river.[9]

Further west, Prince Cherkasskii, who had established two Russian fortresses on the eastern shores of the Caspian Sea in 1715–16, was less successful when ordered to persuade the Khan of Khiva (in the valley of the Amu Darya in what is now western Uzbekistan) to accept Russian suzerainty, and thereafter, to investigate the route to India. His force was attacked by Khivans, Uzbeks and Kazaks in 1717, and, although protected within their camp by firepower, the army was annihilated when it left camp.

Helped by divisions among their opponents and by the inroads of disease, Russia had found it far easier to expand across lightly-populated Siberia to the Pacific in the early seventeenth century than subsequently to advance southwards, whether against Manchus (Chinese), Zunghars or toward Central Asia. This contrast provides an instructive instance of the variations involved in conflict between Western and non-Western forces. These variations included the character of the armies that posed difficulties for the Russians. Most notably, the Manchu forces that pushed them from the Amur Valley in the 1680s had a greater infantry component than Russia's opponents further west.

The Russians also faced continued opposition in eastern Siberia from indigenous peoples. Resistance by the Itelmen of Kamchatka was to be overcome. Relying on bone or stone-tipped arrows and on slings, the poorly-armed Itelmen were brutalised in the Russian search for furs. They rose in 1706, but were suppressed. When they resisted in 1731, the Itelmen had some firearms obtained from the Russians and were able to inflict many casualties as a result, but they were eventually crushed, while their numbers were further hit by the diseases that accompanied their adversaries. Largely-isolated communities proved especially vulnerable to disease as their immunity was low. Another rising in 1741 was defeated.

However, the Koraks of Kamchatka proved more formidable than the Itelmen, and were effective with bows and captured firearms. The Russians responded brutally and were willing to kill as many Koraks as possible, not least in the war of 1745–56. The Koraks then submitted. As a reminder of the value and problems of comparison, this success can be compared with that of the Chinese over the Zunghars, but the scale of opposition and operations was very different, and the Koraks lacked the mobility that cavalry offered the Zunghars. The Chuckchi of north-east Siberia posed greater problems for the Russians than the Koraks (see p. 189).

Cavalry and environments

The important role for cavalry seen in the Eurasian interior is not the impression that emerges from warfare in Western Europe or from Western operations elsewhere in the world. In these, especially the latter, infantry predominated, and thus their recruitment, deployment, tactical capability, and morale were key elements. Cavalry was of particularly limited value in amphibious operations, given the difficulties of transporting and landing horses without injuries, notably broken bones, that rendered them worthless. Moreover, the availability of forage was an issue, not least because it was bulky to transport. The emphasis on infantry can be seen with two successful Spanish operations, the invasion of the island of Sardinia in 1717 and the attack on the North African city of Oran (in modern Algeria) in 1732. Trans-oceanic operations by Western forces classically relied on infantry, with any cavalry usually coming from local allies, as in India. Thus, the British forces in North America, whether operating against French, Spanish, Native American or Patriot American opponents, were essentially infantry.

Infantry also predominated in areas outside the Western military tradition. This was true of regions that lacked the horse, notably Australasia, Oceania, those parts of the Americas to which the horses brought by the Europeans had not yet spread, and the bulk of sub-Saharan Africa to which the horses brought by the Moors had not spread. No other animal had been so effectively domesticated for military service, although elephants were used in India and Burma, and camels in desert regions. Oxen could also be important for pulling cannon (as were horses), while mules could play a role in logistics.

In the regions without horses, men fought on foot, which, anyway, was the most appropriate means for forested areas, such as coastal West Africa, Amazonia, Ceylon (Sri Lanka), the Himalayas and South-East Asia. Far more of the world was covered by forest and woodland than is the case today, and less of the forest and woodland was managed (and thereby accessible) than today.

However, cavalry still dominated warfare in many areas, such as Central and South-West Asia, India (apart from Kerala in the south-west, the forested valley of the Brahmaputra river, and the waterlogged Ganges delta), and the *sahel*, the savannah belt of Africa south of the Sahara. Cavalry was also important in Eastern Europe, where its presence indicated the pressures of opportunity and need. Cavalry was multi-functional, significant in combat but also on campaign. Its mobility, especially across open plains, provided an operational as well as a tactical value, and, under both headings, it was also important for resisting others who had plentiful cavalry. Thus, the Polish and Russian armies had large numbers of cavalry for fighting the Turks and, notably, their allies the Crimean Tatars, who provided the Turks with much of their cavalry for operations in Europe. As a result, the Russian annexation of the khanate of the Crimea in 1783 was a serious blow to the Turks, and, indeed, affected them in their war with Russia in 1787–92. In northern India, cavalry was important both against rival Indian powers, such as the Marathas, and against cavalry forces invading from Afghanistan: Nadir Shah of Persia in 1739 and, in a more sustained fashion from the 1750s, Afghan forces.

Cavalry remained important in Western Europe where, indeed, Frederick the Great of Prussia built up his cavalry during his reign (1740–86), while his ally Duke Ferdinand of Brunswick did so as well during the Seven Years' War (1756–63). In both these cavalries, the dragoons and hussars became multi-functional, serving as heavy cavalry during battle and as light cavalry during small war deployment. Ferdinand even mixed up dragoons and hussars with his light infantry.

Cavalry also became more significant in some other areas, especially the wide expanses of the Great Plains of North America where the horse and its use spread northwards from Spanish-ruled Mexico. In both North America and South Asia, the horse proved reconcilable with the use of missile weapons, not only the bow and arrow, but also pistols and even muskets. The continued role of the Afghans in north-west India until the end of the century provided a clear demonstration of the significance of cavalry, and calls into question accounts of military progress in India (and more widely) focused on the rise of infantry. Far from cavalry proving anachronistic, the combination of horseman and missile weapon remained a major threat to infantry and other cavalry, offering tactical, operational and strategic capabilities. The ability of cavalry to respond to the need to control wide open spaces was also significant.

Environmental factors, nevertheless, acted as a constraint on cavalry, as they had done for centuries, affecting both the range and impact of Eurasian cavalry forces and the more general use of the horse. In much of Africa south of the *sahel*, the tsetse fly acted as a fundamental constraint; while in South-East Asia dense tree cover was a serious issue. Linked to the presence of large water bodies, this tree cover encouraged a reliance on elephants.[10] In India, the Ganges plain below Patna was very rich, but, with its numerous waterways and waterlogged fields, it was not good cavalry country, thus providing a measure of protection against cavalry attack for Bengal that was lacking across most of Hindustan. This was even more true of east Bengal, which, like Assam, was swampy and malarial.

In short, environment was an important constraint on the effectiveness of particular weapons systems, both limiting the global impact of technological developments and affecting the evolution of distinctive types of warfare in different regions. The role of environmental factors had an important regional dimension, and this was true of terrain, vegetation and disease. The last was also significant on the global scale, in particular affecting both outside forces and local communities without immunity. Western troops were badly hit in the Tropics, notably in Africa and the West Indies, with yellow fever proving particularly deadly, as the British discovered when attacking Cartagena (on the Caribbean coast of modern Colombia) in 1741 and Havana in 1762, and when operating against Spanish-ruled Nicaragua in the early 1780s. Yellow fever and malaria had become endemic in the Caribbean by the 1690s, and local forces knew how to use this advantage, as when the slaves who successfully opposed the French in Saint-Domingue (Haiti) in the 1790s and 1800s chose to attack in the wet season, when disease was more prevalent, and, conversely, were more cautious in the dry season.[11]

The Chinese were similarly affected, probably by malaria, in Burma in the late 1760s, while the troops returning at the close of the 1740s from the First Jinchuan War in Sichuan spread epidemic diseases. Conversely, the Chinese did not face comparable problems for men and horses from disease when campaigning on the high, arid steppe against the Zunghars. Instead, the availability of food and water were key issues there, not least because of the significant numbers of troops deployed by the Chinese.

The impact of the human environment was very varied. For example, unlike India, Burma depended on conscripts (peasant levies) because South-East Asia's population density was lower than that of India, and it was therefore harder to recruit soldiers by paying them. Moreover, rice cultivation in Burma permitted the maintenance of a large army.

However, a typology of warfare based on adaptation to environmental factors is limited. First, no uni-dimensional explanation and typology of warfare is adequate,[12] and secondly, other important factors may be omitted. A crucial one, indeed another form of environment, is political context, which helped explain the very varied determination of combatants to fight. For example, the determination of the Kangxi and Qianlong emperors to overcome the Zunghar challenge on the steppe proved far greater than the concern of the Manchu with expansion into South-East Asia. This political dimension took precedence over the environmental contrast between areas of commitment, and notably because the identity of the Manchu dynasty rested in part on its steppe origin, while its control over the Khalka (eastern) Mongols was challenged by Zunghar expansion. Furthermore, as demonstrated repeatedly over previous centuries, the centre of Chinese government at Beijing was highly vulnerable to attack from the steppe, as it was not from Tibet, Nepal, Burma or Vietnam.

As another aspect of the political context, it is appropriate to contrast areas of the world with limited state development, such as Patagonia,

Amazonia, North America, Australasia, the Pacific, the areas in eastern Siberia still outside Russian control, and parts of South-West Africa, with others where government was more developed and society more differentiated, such as China, Japan, Burma, Siam, India, Persia, the Ottoman empire, Kandy (the interior of Sri Lanka), and much of West Africa. It would be mistaken to treat either group as an undifferentiated whole. Nevertheless, there was a contrast, one that was captured by Western writers, such as Adam Smith, who advanced a stadial (stages) thesis of human development (see p. 188). In the former group, there was no specialisation of the military, and fit adult males were all expected to act as warriors. As the economies of these regions were also limited, and mostly dependent on pastoral or shifting cultivation, they supported only relatively small populations, primitive governmental systems, and a resource base that could carry neither a large army nor what later would be termed a 'military-industrial complex'.

In contrast, more developed societies had evolved more specialisation, had permanent armies which, therefore, required support, and could generally field and maintain larger forces than the regions in the former group. More developed societies were also able to support wars of expansion, although not all did so. Continuing the pattern of the previous century, Japan, for instance, did not engage in war at all during this period. There was no attempt by Japan to intervene anew in Korea, as had been done in the 1590s, a lack of effort which was an appropriate response to the strength of Korea's Manchu overlords. Japan also made no attempt to challenge the Western powers in the western Pacific, notably Spain in the Philippines, and the Russians as they expanded in the eighteenth century from Siberia to the Aleutian Islands and then Alaska. This failure to act accorded with Japan's quiescent stance from the early seventeenth century, rather than emerging as a necessary consequence of environmental factors.

India

The role of political contexts and circumstances was amply displayed by the contrast between China and India. The Mughal emperor Aurangzeb (r. 1658–1707) was a dynamic ruler who overcame a host of opponents. Moreover, just as the Kangxi emperor dealt with a major problem that the previous Ming dynasty had failed to surmount, that of defeating the challenge of the steppe, Aurangzeb overcame the longstanding opposition by the sultanates in the Deccan (south-central India) to rule from northern India. In the 1680s, the sultanates of Bijapur and Golconda were defeated and annexed, a major achievement and one that can be rated alongside the territorial expansion that decade by Louis XIV of France, an expansion that tends to receive far more scholarly attention.

The logistical challenge facing Aurangzeb in the Deccan was formidable, albeit not as significant as for Kangxi because it was possible for Aurangzeb to draw on nearby and local agricultural resources. However, Aurangzeb had to support large numbers of troops and to move resources from northern India, while, unlike Kangxi, he confronted the problem of large-scale and lengthy sieges; the Zunghars did not pose this challenge for the Chinese. Indeed, the lack of a need for siegecraft was true for Chinese operations as a whole, although in the Jinchuan wars they faced the serious problems of confronting resistance based in a large number of stone towers built in difficult terrain (see pp. 75, 110).

Aurangzeb had less success with the Marathas than Kangxi did with the Zunghars or the Qianlong emperor in the Second Jinchuan War. The Marathas were a Hindu warrior caste that (like the Zunghars, but not the Jinchuans) had particularly effective light cavalry, although they also deployed numerous infantry (a point that tends to be forgotten), as in the battle of Dabhoi in 1731.[13] The Maratha cavalry relied on harassing tactics, an operational preference for cutting opponents' supply lines, and a related strategy of exhausting them by devastating territory rather than risking defeat in battle. Aurangzeb achieved successes against the Marathas in the late 1680s, but their resistance continued. The mobile and decentralised style of the Maratha fighting system was crucial in enabling them to resist Aurangzeb effectively, and accentuated the Mughal problems of relying on preponderantly heavy cavalry, which was slower-moving than the light cavalry of the Marathas, and therefore required more supplies. Aurangzeb was also affected by the agrarian problems of his territories.

It is pertinent to contrast Aurangzeb's failure with Kangxi's success, as this difference underlines the mistake of assuming that the key contrasts were those between Western and non-Western forces, or, more plausibly, between the forces of settled societies and more pastoral opponents, significant as the latter certainly were. The Mughals sought battle, but won no equivalent to Kangxi's success at Jao Modo (see p. 15). Only so much can be made from discussing relative capability in terms of individual battles, and the political context was important to Kangxi's triumph, notably Zunghar disunity, which was even more of a factor in Qianlong's eventual victory in the 1750s. However, military comparisons are still instructive, notably the challenges posed to both Aurangzeb and Kangxi by opponents able to focus on mobility, and the tendency to respond by fielding larger forces. These forces both exacerbated the problem posed by the lesser mobility of major armies and, due to the logistical burden, drove up the already high cost of campaigning. The Marathas did not defeat the Mughals in decisive battles, but, like the Crimean Tatars in response to Russian invasions in the 1680s and 1730s, rather denied the Mughals safe control of territory. By engaging in battle with the Manchus, the Zunghars failed to do the same.

Nevertheless, the Maratha belief that forts were necessary for the symbol and reality of power provided the Mughals with clear targets. Similarly, the American attempt, during the War of American Independence, to hold major cities in 1776–80 (New York, Philadelphia, Charleston), or to regain those that had been lost (Philadelphia, 1777; Savannah, 1779), gave the British successive opportunities to engage their opponents in battle and to try to defeat them. Position warfare was different from its manoeuvrist counterpart.

Aurangzeb was able to conquer a whole series of these Maratha forts, most of which were hill fortresses, frequently of considerable antiquity. In part, Aurangzeb was successful thanks to his siege artillery. It was not particularly sophisticated by Western standards (a comparison that could also be made of the muskets), and was made of wrought iron, as opposed to the less rigid cast iron of the West from which cannon could be made that were capable of taking more powerful charges of gunpowder. Nevertheless, there were improvements in artillery in India, notably a switch to iron in place of stone cannon balls. However, exploiting the weaknesses and divisions of opponents proved more useful, notably the bribery of fortress commanders. Success in this method reflected the fissiparous character of competing forces, and also the degree to which commanders needed triumphs in order to reward their followers. As a consequence, adversity, in contrast, could lead to a ready and rapid shift of sides.

The Mughal campaign against the Marathas continued until 1704, when the fortress of Torna fell to a surprise night storming. Moreover, Maratha forces were not strong enough to break sieges which Aurangzeb covered with field armies. Nevertheless, despite his successes, Aurangzeb failed to conquer the Marathas, while the war was very costly and the impression of failure it created was damaging and helped sustain opposition in the Mughal lands in north India. In India, as elsewhere, the impression of success was one of the most significant attributes both of generalship and of rule.

The sense of Mughal failure, indeed decline, strengthened after Aurangzeb's death in February 1707, providing provincial potentates in India with the opportunity, and also the need, to grasp power. Aurangzeb's ineffective successors were unable to maintain cohesion at court, and this failure helped make it impossible to maintain the support of the regional viceroys and, indeed, the effective backing of the army. In contrast, although France was weakened when Louis XIV was succeeded in 1715 by his infant great-grandson Louis XV, and the latter's divided Regency government faced political and ecclesiastical dissension and serious financial problems, the crisis was surmounted and France was able to act in war as a major power in 1719 and, more decisively, in 1733–5.

Bahadur Shah, the Mughal emperor from 1707 to 1712, was an experienced military figure and was able to defeat his brothers in the war of succession that followed Aurangzeb's death. A similar war had led to Aurangzeb gaining the throne. Bahadur also crushed a rebellion launched by the Rajput ruler of Jodhpur in 1708, while a Sikh insurrection in 1709 was limited (though not crushed) the following year. However, Bahadur did not have comparable success against the Marathas, while his response to the Rajput rising was to break with the long-established Mughal practice of seeking to woo Rajput support, a practice that had been very important to Mughal success. Like his counterpart Shah Husain of Persia (see p. 52), Bahadur's successor, Jahandar Shah (r. 1712–13), proved weak and pleasure-seeking. Jahandar Shah was overthrown in 1713 in a coup by his nephew Farruksiyar.

The viceroys increasingly asserted their independence. The key loss was that of Nizam ul-Mulk Asaf Jah, who essentially took over as Subahdar (Viceroy) of the Deccan from 1712. He was to establish the basis of what was to become the nizamat of Hyderabad. So also in 1712, with S'aadat Khan, the Viceroy of Oudh (Avadh) in the Ganges valley between Delhi and Bengal.[14] The fluid state of Indian politics ensured serious problems in determining how best to negotiate and to define legal settlements between Indian potentates, not least as the latter were developing new political and governmental practices.[15] The centralising policy of Aurangzeb had alienated many of the key groups, and they did not rally to the throne as the Mughal empire came to face potent challenges.

Ironically, but reflecting similar processes, there was also a collapse in the cohesion of the Marathas. In 1707–8, there was a struggle for control between Shahu, the grandson of the key Maratha king, and Shahu's aunt, Tarabi. Shahu (r. 1708–49) defeated Tarabi, but then had to face a more profound dissolution of authority, as successive *peshwās* (chief ministers) became the real power, not the king. Moreover, *jagirs* (land grants) were used to reward *sirdars* (military leaders), who became, in effect, autonomous. As in the Ottoman empire, the nature of military reward interacted with key questions of political stability.

Ottoman empire

The dangers of hindsight emerge clearly in comparison. That the Mughal empire was to decline greatly in the eighteenth century, notably from the

1740s, helps make it tempting to treat the decline as inevitable and to write the Mughals out of the picture as far as eighteenth-century developments and warfare are concerned. The comparison with the Ottoman empire (Turkey), however, indicates the danger of jumping to such conclusions. Important Turkish territories were conquered by Austria, Poland, Russia and Venice in 1684–97, and the peace treaties of 1699–1700, notably the Peace of Carlowitz of 1699, saw the Turks make major territorial cessions, including Hungary (bar the Banat of Temesvár) to Austria. These cessions enhanced the resources at the disposal of the Habsburgs and also lessened the danger of opposition to them by the Hungarian nobility.

Furthermore, as so often, defeat in war helped lead to political crisis. Sultan Mustafa II (r. 1695–1703) was seen as compromising Muslim honour by accepting Carlowitz, which was a peace entailing recognition of Christian Europe, rather than merely a truce. These terms contributed to the crisis of authority in 1703 when there was a mutiny in Constantinople by troops, already facing pay arrears, and now ordered to suppress a rebellion in far-off west Georgia, a troublesome frontier region. The range of factors involved in the crisis underlines the danger of only citing one as the key element. In the resulting crisis, a rebel army was formed, and, on 19 August at Havsa near Edirne, it defeated the far smaller army of the unpopular Mustafa. Five days later, he was replaced by his brother Ahmed, who became Ahmed III (r. 1703–30).

Nevertheless, despite these serious problems, it is necessary also to note Turkish strengths. In the warfare of the 1680s and 1690s, the Turks had resisted attempted knockout blows, mounted counter-offensives, and retained most of their territories, thwarting hopes that their empire might collapse. Moreover, in 1700–1, a Turkish expeditionary force defeated Sulayman Baba, an expansionist Kurdish chieftain. He was executed. In addition, the Turks showed considerable resilience when war resumed in the 1710s. Encouraged by the clergy, by Devlet Giray II, Khan of the Crimean Tatars, and by Charles XII of Sweden who had fled to Turkey after being defeated by the Russians at Poltava in 1709, Ahmed III declared war on Peter the Great of Russia in November 1710.

The Turks had lost the fortress of Azov, near the mouth of the River Don, to Peter the Great of Russia in 1696, a step that threatened the Crimean khanate, and, indirectly, Turkey's position on the Black Sea; but, in 1711, fast-moving Turkish cavalry outmanoeuvred Peter when he invaded Moldavia, modern north-eastern Romania. This was a rash step on Peter's part as, unlike in 1696, the Turks were not facing any other foe, while Moldavia was closer than Azov to the centres of Turkish power. Finding less local support than anticipated, Peter advanced slowly and lost the initiative. His strategic and situational intelligence was inadequate. Moreover, by advancing as a single force, the Russians increased their already serious logistical problems and made it easier for the Turks, under the Grand Vizier, Baltaci Mehmed Pasha, to encircle them. Surrounded on the banks of the River Pruth, short of food and water, and under fire from the Turkish cannon, Peter was forced, on 22 July, to accept humiliating terms including the loss of Azov.[16]

In addition, in 1715, the Venetians were driven from the Morea (the Peloponnese in southern Greece) by the Turks in one of the most decisive and rapid campaigns of the century, and one that reversed the Venetian conquest of the region from the Turks in the 1680s, a conquest that had been recognised in the peace negotiated in 1699. In their campaign, the Turks benefited from taking the initiative, from greater numbers and effective logistics, and from expertise in siegecraft. The Venetians had 7,000 men scattered in six fortified cities whereas the Turks had 100,000 troops. Looking forward to the opportunity to regain the Morea, the Turks were also angered by the refuge granted by Venice to Montenegrins who had unsuccessfully rebelled in 1711, in part in response to Peter the Great's encouragement. The Turks were also encouraged by the absence of comparable problems elsewhere. They had settled with Peter the Great and did not face war on their eastern frontier with Persia. Indeed, the two powers had been at peace since 1639, while, in the 1710s, Shah Husain of Persia was confronted with a major rebellion by his Afghan subjects.

As a reminder of the difficulties of drawing up a score-card of relative effectiveness, the Turks then failed when they attacked the Venetian fortress of Corfu on the island of that name in 1716. Had they succeeded, then the Adriatic Sea and the Apulian coast of Italy would have been vulnerable to Turkish attacks. Moreover, in 1716–17, the Austrians achieved major successes at the expense of the Turks. The Emperor Charles VI was concerned about Turkish successes against Venice and no longer anxious about a weakened France, his opponent in 1689–97 and 1701–14. As a consequence, in April 1716, Charles concluded an alliance with Venice. Austrian forces were concentrated against the Turks.

On 5 August 1716, under Prince Eugene, a victor over the Turks in the 1690s and the French in the 1700s,[17] the Austrians smashed the Turks at Petrovaradin (Peterwardein), an Austrian base on the right bank of the River Danube north-west of Belgrade. The Turkish army, about 70,000 troops plus auxiliaries, established a camp which was attacked by Eugene on 5 August. Initially successful in driving the *janissaries* (permanent Turkish infantry) back, the Austrians faced a counter-attack that, in turn, was beaten by a successful cavalry attack. Underlining the importance of cavalry conflict, the Austrian cavalry drove their opponents from the field, leaving the exposed Turkish infantry to be decimated. Probably about 8,000 Turks, including the Grand Vizier, Damad Ali Pasha, were killed, although far greater numbers slaughtered were claimed.

Eugene then marched on the mighty fortress of Temesvár, which had defied the Austrians in the 1690s and which controlled or threatened much of eastern Hungary. Well-fortified and protected by river and marshes, Temesvár, nevertheless, surrendered on 16 October after heavy bombardment. The defeat at Peterwardein was all-important in conveying a sense of relative strength and encouraged the Turks to abandon the siege of distant Corfu.

In June 1717, Eugene crossed the Danube by pontoon bridges east of Belgrade, which was surrounded by 18 June. It was then besieged and its fortifications greatly damaged by Austrian cannon. A Turkish relief army under the Grand Vizier, Haci Halil Pasha, arrived on 27 July, but it lacked many regular troops and the Grand Vizier preferred to rely on artillery fire rather than attacking Eugene. Instead, the Austrians were launched against this new army. On 16 August, Eugene mounted a surprise attack that heavily defeated the Turks, capturing their cannon and forcing them to retreat. Unexpected fog made the battle especially confusing.

On the 17th, short of ammunition, the garrison of Belgrade, now denied the chance of relief, surrendered, and Eugene occupied it on 22 August. Thus, the campaigns of 1716 and 1717 suggested that, however well fortified, the fate of fortresses was likely to be settled by battle, as defeat denied the possibility of relief and therefore exposed defenders to the prospect of unremitting supply problems. In addition, defeat in battle entailed a crucial loss of prestige, which also encouraged surrenders. Siege warfare therefore takes its place within a pattern of conflict in which engagements in the field were also very important.

The battle of Belgrade was a confused engagement, not a matter of neat formations exchanging fire. It, and the campaign as a whole, can be seen as indicative of a shift in warmaking. Although the Austrian victory cannot be simply attributed to the character of Western firepower, the battle revealed the quality of some units in the face of greater numbers. However, the Turkish numbers involved were not much greater, maybe 80,000 men to 55,000 Austrians; and other factors played a role, not least Eugene's ability to respond to the disorientation caused by the fog. Moreover, the first Austrian campaign in the Balkans that was logistically well organised was that of 1716, reflecting an improvement in government resources and bureaucratic mechanisms since 1703, although, in 1717, Eugene was affected by a shortage of money. This problem tended to occur after opening campaigns when there were usually some reserves to spend. Once these reserves were exhausted, problems mounted.

The Turks made peace at Passarowitz on 21 July 1718, ceding south-east Hungary (the Banat of Temesvár), Belgrade, northern Serbia, and south-west Romania (Little Wallachia), and abandoning their plan to free Transylvania (north-west Romania) from Habsburg (Austrian) control by supporting Francis II Rákóczi, who had already rebelled against the Austrians in the 1700s. However, before too great a change in fortune is read into this war and treaty, it is important to note that the Austrians did much less well in their next two wars with the Turks, those of 1737–9 and 1788–90, particularly the first, which proved disastrous, both militarily and politically (see pp. 68–9). A declining power, exhausted by the Great Northern War (1700–21), in which it was overrun by Charles XII of Sweden, Poland did not take part in the conflicts of the 1710s with the Turks, although it continued to play a role in transmitting Turkish military practice to Western Europe.

In the eighteenth century, each combatant was changing, the Austrians enhancing their firepower by adopting flintlock muskets and dispensing with pikemen, while the Turks increasingly put their emphasis on the infantry rather than on the *sipahis*, the feudal cavalry. The Austrians abandoned the pike in the Balkans in about 1691 when Marshal Caprara changed pikemen companies into musketeer ones. In the West, pikes remained in the Austrian ordinances until 1703, but were not used against the French from about 1690.

The *sipahis* had once been a dynamic force, but, increasingly, acted as a repository of conservative military practice. Moreover, the challenge posed by the Turkish cavalry to infantry was diminished by the enhanced firepower of Austrian units. Raimondo Montecuccoli, the leading Austrian commander in the 1663–4 war with the Turks, observed that, when fighting the Turks, it was necessary to use cavalry against their infantry and infantry against their cavalry. In turn, Austrian units benefited from the extent to which the ratio of officers to rank-and-file was much greater than in the Turkish army, thus ensuring that the Austrian army was better controlled and more agile.[18] In addition, the Austrians profited from better leadership overall, which reflected Eugene's tenure as President at the Court War Council from 1703. He was the representative of a new managing group.

The Sultan's inability to pay the army reduced his control and, alongside political tensions, led to rebellions, notably in 1717–19 and, more seriously, 1730. This problem in part reflected the lack of pillage and fresh land to distribute, as well as a loss of prestige stemming from the absence of new conquests. Desertion affected the number of Turkish troops and there was an increased need to turn to provincial militias as well as to forces raised by local strongmen. This tendency was linked to a lack of discipline and to an absence of consistent quality. This absence was especially marked at the edges of the Turkish world, notably if, as in Algiers and the Crimea, authority and power were shared with polities with a different fighting style. Indeed, Joseph Pitts, an Englishman captured by Algerian privateers who, after slavery, had become a soldier in the Algerian army, recorded of the siege of Spanish-held Oran in 1687 that it was ineffective 'for the Turks in Algier are nothing expert in firing [mortar] bombs'.[19]

More generally, however, the Turks were a settled society and developed state, and no longer the apparently inexorable people that had terrified Westerners in the fifteenth and sixteenth centuries. Moving onto the defensive created serious problems for the Turkish empire, both structurally and in terms of ethos. There was a marked deficiency in preparations for defence. A shortage of funds affected the fortress restoration that was encouraged by the external threats to the empire. Nevertheless, key fortresses, such as Ochakov, which controlled the mouth of the rivers Dnieper and Bug into the Black Sea, were not only repaired but improved, in part in order to make them more appropriate for resisting artillery. Older-style castles were superseded by thick earth ramparts.[20]

The greater strength of fortresses, the determination to secure territorial gains, and the need to dominate supply routes ensured that sieges were very significant in campaigning north of the Black Sea, as in the Danube valley where they had for long been to the fore. Cities like Temesvár and Belgrade were important because they controlled both the river and land routes necessary to deal with the shortage of available supplies in Hungary. Moreover, the increased emphasis on firepower in warfare in the region ensured a stress on artillery and infantry, rather than cavalry. The Austrians used cannon in large numbers from the second half of the seventeenth century. In 1716, Eugene had 90 field cannon and about 100 siege guns. Artillery helped make armies slow-moving, which enhanced the importance of supplies. In addition, on the steppe to the north of the Black Sea, the limited amount of food available underlined the significance of logistics. Large supply trains were necessary there, as was the use of river routes to move food.

Russia

The Turks defeated the Russians in 1711, but this was a success on the defensive. The Russians were one of the most dynamic military powers in Eurasia, while the Turks were no longer able to launch advances into the Volga valley, as they had unsuccessfully done in the 1560s, nor to contest the Ukraine with Poland and Russia, as they had successfully done in the 1670s and early 1680s. The attempts made in the sixteenth century by the Turks to develop military and political links with the Islamic states of Central Asia were no more.

As a result of the failure on the Pruth in 1711, Russia under Peter the Great (r. 1689–1725) did not achieve the gains at the expense of Turkey that were to be seen in the second half of the century under Catherine the Great (r. 1762–96). However, Peter greatly strengthened Russia's position, by considerably enhancing its position within Christian Europe, reforming the army and creating a navy (see p. 180). Russian victories over Sweden and dominance of Poland were not achieved in order that Peter should be better able to campaign against the Turks and further east, but they had that impact. Indeed, the unsuccessful Pruth campaign followed the crushing defeat of Charles XII of Sweden at Poltava in 1709,[21] while the successful end of the Great Northern War with Sweden in 1721 was to be succeeded in 1722–3 by Russian campaigning in the eastern Caucasus and northern Persia.

Peter responded to failure by resolutely pursuing improvement. He was aware that success was necessary in order to maintain power. Indeed, the humiliation of the leading minister Golitsyn's unsuccessful advance against the Crimea in 1689 had resulted in the fall of the latter, and Peter's overthrow of his half-sister Sophia (r. 1682–9). Peter's inability to take Azov in 1695 ensured a greater and successful effort the following year. The major Turkish base on the Sea of Azov, Azov controlled the route from the Don valley to the Black Sea. The more serious defeat at Narva by Charles XII in 1700 led Peter to re-build his army. Large numbers of troops were recruited, training improved and the new War Chancellery, established in 1701, enhanced Russia's logistical capability. A number of victories were won over the Swedes from 1701.

In a reminder of the need to look at the evidence carefully, to distinguish between intentions and outcomes, and to avoid reading back from the results, it is unclear how far these victories can in fact be attributed to Peter's military reforms. Indeed, simply greater numbers of men certainly played a major role, as they also did for other powers. About 300,000 men were recruited to the army during Peter's reign, while large numbers joined the navy. Many of the Russian troops, especially in the battles of 1701–4, were not new-style regiments. Furthermore, although impressive, the developing Russian metallurgical industry could not meet the army's need for muskets until 1712, so that, in 1707, the proportion of pikemen to musketeers was actually increased, while infantry firearms were not standardised until 1715.[22] The Russian military administration was dogged by confusion, expediency and opportunism.

Yet, Peter succeeded. With his Table of Ranks, he extended the notion of state service to include the élite. The greater resources of Russia were mobilised by force and due to the creation of *gubernii*, super-provinces under governors close to the Tsar, that permitted the establishment of an effective governmental system at the regional level. Alongside the impact of the Swedes advancing a great distance, the role of resources was shown in the contrast in the number of cannon at Poltava in 1709: Charles XII had four, Peter 102, with 21 of them heavy pieces. The Russians, in addition, had plentiful ammunition and their cannon fired 1,471 shot during the battle. Annual military expenditure rose from 750,000 roubles in 1680 to 5.4 million in 1724.

Peter introduced best Western practices and had a Russian work – *Noveischeye Osnovaniye I Praktika Arteleriy* edited by General James Bruce, Peter's artillery chief – published in Moscow in 1709. One of four works on artillery published in Russia at the time, it was the only one to reach a second edition. The first edition's thousand-copy print run signalled the rising potential of print. The text contained many new military terms that entered the Russian language. The Moscow-born son of a Scots officer in Russian service, Bruce had studied in London under those who would subsequently be seen as key figures in the Scientific Revolution. As Director of the Artillery Chancellery from 1704, Bruce standardised gun calibres and introduced the use of a linear measure to show ball diameters, as well as a calibre scale, and special curves and compasses for ballistic calculation.[23]

Russia offers a comparison with China, and certainly in terms of state effort and governmental direction, although China did not look to foreign models as Russia self-consciously and extensively did. The Russians were engaged against more opponents than China, although Turkish backing for Charles XII, who took refuge with the Turks after Poltava, was such that those struggles with Peter can be linked, just as those with the Zunghars and Tibet were linked for China. Other Eurasian powers could not match these efforts. Whereas Aurangzeb, as a Mughal prince, had campaigned (ultimately unsuccessfully) into Afghanistan in the 1640s, he focused, as a ruler, further south in his later decades; and no other or later Indian ruler, until the British in the 1840s, changed this focus. Nor did the Persians repeat the campaigning to the north-east against the Uzbeks they had followed in the sixteenth and early seventeenth centuries until Nadir Shah did so (successfully) in 1740, and his short-term effort was not repeated.

In contrast to the range of opponents faced by Russia and Austria, the Kangxi emperor focused on the Zunghars. Alternative opportunities were not pursued. Whereas the Mongols, after they conquered China in the thirteenth century, had (unsuccessfully) pursued maritime expansion against Japan and Java, Manchu goals by sea were restricted to nearby Formosa (Taiwan), gained in 1683. There was no attempt to invade Japan as a counter to earlier Japanese expansionism into Korea in the 1590s, nor any wish to expand or extend the brief frontier war with Russia in 1683–9, although the latter's expansion to the Pacific in the seventeenth century had brought them close to areas of Manchu concern, whereas the earlier Ming dynasty had not focused attention on the Amur Valley and nearby lands.

Austria

Austrian campaigning against the Turks can be related, at least in intention, to Russian and Chinese expansionism. Allowing, however, for the many difficulties in comparison, both militarily and politically, Austria, which greatly expanded territorially as a state between 1683 and 1720, into Hungary (1699), Italy (1714), Belgium (1714) and the Balkans (1718), still did not match Russia, even more China, in the resources it could expend.[24] Moreover, the heavily-fortified nature of the major Turkish positions, such as Belgrade, delayed Austrian advances. There was also a lack of soldiers both for multiple sieges and for garrisoning conquered places. Nevertheless, alongside successful sieges, the fate of these positions was often (speedily) settled by success in battle.

In the case of Austria and Turkey, politics again came to the fore. In 1718, the Austrians abandoned the war with the Turks when it had appeared very promising, indeed leading optimists to hope, as had been expected in 1689–91, that it would be possible to drive the Turks from the Balkans. In the earlier case, war with Louis XIV of France had led to the abandonment of these hopes. In 1718, it was the crisis created in Italy by Spanish expansionism, which both posed problems and provided Austria with opportunities for its own gains. Spanish forces captured Sardinia (from the Austrian ruler, Charles VI) in 1717 and Sicily (from Victor Amadeus II of Savoy-Piedmont) in 1718. As a result of intervening against Spanish forces in Italy, and of the successful supporting Anglo-French attack on Spain itself in 1719, Charles VI was able, in the peace settlement of 1720, to acquire Sicily in place of the less prestigious and less profitable island of Sardinia.

Africa and Australasia

The major developments of the first two decades of the eighteenth century were related to the Eurasian interior already covered and to the naval–colonial world which will be discussed in chapter 7. However, it is also instructive to consider warfare elsewhere in the world. Population levels and related governmental development were significant for military attainment and activity there. Areas of low density and limited development, such as the Kalahari Desert of south-west Africa, had a different level of military preparedness and warfare from that of states able to deploy armies of considerable size, for example Ethiopia in north-east Africa.

The same was true across the Pacific. In some island groups, such as Hawai'i and New Zealand, higher population density and more developed social and political systems enhanced the possibilities of large-scale military action, although there were also contrasts. In New Zealand, as in Tahiti and the Marquesa islands in the Pacific, there were many warring tribes, whereas in Hawai'i and Tonga dominant rulers could deploy large forces. In contrast, in the vastness of Australia, small migratory hunting groups formed the population. This different context ensured that the absence of horse and gun, also seen in Hawai'i and New Zealand, played out on another scale.

Where military transformation occurred, there were interactions between environment, trade and politics. In the forest zone of West Africa, muskets replaced the bow and javelin in the armies of states, such as Dahomey on the Slave Coast and Asante on the Gold Coast, that were able to obtain arms. In part, they were gained from trading with Western Europeans, notably by selling the slaves that were the product of the high levels of warfare between African states. The control over people represented by slavery thus linked warfare to global trading patterns, money proving a crucial medium of power and influence that was interchangeable, through trade, with force. As in many aspects of warfare, there was also a prominent role for private enterprise, as well as an overlap between it and state authority. This process was seen in the European–Native networks of trade that brought slaves to the coast, as well as the chartered trading companies, such as the British Royal African Company, that ran the coastal forts, for example Cape Coast Castle, where slaves were kept before shipping them to the Americas.

As a result, West Africa provides an instance of the impact both on military activity of participation in wider commercial and geopolitical networks and of such activity on these networks. In contrast, there was no such participation as yet in Australasia. The use of firearms in the forest zone in West Africa led to the development of more dispersed fighting formations and techniques. However, in the *sahel* (savannah) zone further north, the adoption of muskets by cavalry made relatively little difference to tactics. These muskets were obtained from Islamic traders from North Africa. Clashes between cavalry-centred and infantry-dominated armies occurred along the ecological borderline between savannah and forest.

The emphasis on cavalry in the savannah was not the only restriction on the development of infantry–firearms combinations. In the kingdom of Kongo (in western Angola) and on the Slave Coast of West Africa, musketeers largely replaced archers during the course of the eighteenth century, as they had done on the Gold Coast in the seventeenth; whereas, further away from the Atlantic coast and its European influences, there was greater reliance on the traditional military system of forest Africa: shield-carrying, heavily-armed infantry, operating in densely-packed formations and fighting hand-to-hand, especially with swords. In so far as there were missile weapons in support, they were generally bows and javelins, not muskets. This was true of such armies as those of Matamba, Kasanje, Muzumbo a Kalunga, and Lunda (in modern eastern Angola). Lunda expansionism is a reminder of the mistake of assuming that Western-style weaponry and military organisation were necessary to military success.[25]

A similar range of weaponry was found in Japan and South-East Asia. In India and China, there was a greater emphasis on firearms from the start of the century, but other infantry weapons were also used.

Native America

The military history of the New World, and notably of South and Central America, is generally discussed in terms of the European invaders. The Native Americans are presented as responding to their moves, and as being dependent on the diffusion of European means, in the shape of guns, gunpowder, shot and horses. Although such diffusion could be effective,[26] it faced problems, for example in the supply of gunpowder, and it would be misleading to suggest that acquiring European arms was responsible for Native resilience. In South and Central America, the *conquistadors* of the sixteenth century had overthrown the developed states, but they did not rule all of the area. As a result, in part, of this factor, the Europeans had taken only a fraction of the territory, and, in succeeding centuries, conflict between Spanish and Portuguese colonies and Natives continued.

In the eighteenth century, the Spaniards made minor advances south in both Chile and Patagonia (modern southern Argentina); but in Chile expansion was limited and warfare with the Araucanians, who themselves attacked in 1723, 1766 and 1769–70, decreased. The Araucanians also advanced across the Andes to challenge the Spanish position in Argentina where most of the pampas was not to be conquered until the nineteenth century. Attracted by discoveries of gold and diamonds, the Portuguese advanced into the interior of their colony of Brazil, notably into Minas Gerais. However, much of the interior of Brazil remained under Native control.[27] Aside from conflict between Europeans and Natives in South America, there were rebellions in the European colonies and warfare between Native groups.

This situation was even more the case in North America where, in 1700, the European presence, especially at any distance from the Atlantic seaboard, was limited. Moreover, in places, such as the new French colony of Louisiana, this presence was weak. In 1710, the wood of the fortress at Fort Louis (later Mobile), which had been built in 1702, was so rotted by humidity and decay that it could not support the weight of the cannon. The garrison suffered from an absence of fresh meat, from an insufficient supply of swords, cartridge boxes, nails, guns and powder, from demoralisation and desertion, and from the lack of a hospital.[28] Similar comments could be made about many of the European positions in West Africa. The survival of Louisiana at this stage rested on its acceptance of the Native population, for European imperialism in many places can be described as much in terms of mutual benefit and consensus as of the coercive cutting edge of military superiority. Trade was the key element of this mutual benefit.[29]

Florida is commonly depicted in historical atlases as a Spanish colony, but the Spanish presence was largely restricted to the two coastal bases of St Augustine and Pensacola and to nearby settlements occupied by Natives who had been converted to Christianity. Much of Florida, notably the south, was outside the Spanish sphere of influence, and, indeed, the Spaniards knew little about the interior.

To defend the northern frontier of New Spain in northern Mexico, the Spaniards relied on Cuera cavalry and on *presidios*. With their leather armour providing protection against Native arrows, the Cuera were a good example of adapting to conditions. Moreover, their use in combination with outposts was a common response of settled societies to the threats from nomadic or less settled populations on 'wild' frontiers. The *presidios* were more than just forts. They were part of an ideological, economic and demographic response in that they provided Catholic missions, trading posts and settlers. The combination of small, mobile forces and outposts was broadly similar to the Habsburg (Austrian) military frontier and to various systems used by the Russians and Turks.[30]

The Western idea of civilisation developing in stages, the stadial theory, allocated Native Americans a primitive status as tribes (rather than states) heavily dependent on hunter-gathering, instead of settled agriculture and industry. Irrespective of this theory, there was certainly no comparison with the bureaucratic mechanisms of Chinese or Western armies. Numbers were far smaller among Native Americans, as in Australasia, and, as a result, there was more emphasis on the individual prowess of warriors. Yet, warfare also reflected and sustained social roles. In particular, aside from building up tribal cohesion, men hunted and fought, while women were responsible for agriculture. Furthermore, conflict was in some respects not unlike hunting, both because opponents could be regarded as akin to animals, and because emphasis was both on the masculinity of the individual, who was pitted against other individuals and against the environment, and on the group, which was also important in hunting.[31] Thus, the half-moon tactic, employed in hunting, was also successfully used in warfare.

The absence of large armies did not entail any lack of organised and deadly conflict.[32] Instead, Native Americans had developed effective tactical formations, and a form of warfare well-attuned to the forested nature of much of the eastern half of the continent, with ambushes, rushes and feints, and a combination of accurately-aimed fire and an astute use of cover. These tactics were more important than the weapon which was used, whether bow and arrow or musket, although musket shot was less likely to be deflected by vegetation. Moreover, offensive warfare against fortified villages developed, notably with the growing use of indirect assault tactics rather than the more costly direct assaults.[33]

The Europeans held no monopoly on fortifications. Eastern Native Americans had many palisaded villages and, with the introduction of firearms, European-style bastions appeared to provide defence against cross-fire. For example, changes in Iroquois fortifications and siege warfare transformed the power ranking in the North-East. These changes were an instance of application of Western martial practices, but can also be seen within a wider context of more traditional Native practices that remained viable in wars against Natives and Europeans.

Nevertheless, the vulnerability of fortified villages to European fire-power encouraged their abandonment when hostile forces approached, especially when the latter had cannon. The Natives had learned that forts could be death traps.

Warfare between Native groups was affected by the spread of muskets and horses. In about 1730, the Comanche became the first tribe to equip an entire people with horses. In any conflict, the side which acquired muskets and horses first dominated, but, once both sides in a conflict had them, the nature of warfare altered. The arrival of the horse brought a far greater mobility, allowing the Native Americans to follow herds of bison or deer for hundreds of miles, and the resulting improvements in diet led to a larger and healthier population. Requiring much organisation and planning, these animal drives served as preparation for human conflict.

More generally, tribal warfare was affected by trade and animal movements, and by competition for hunting grounds. At the beginning of the century, the Cree fought the Chipewyans, and the Comanche fought the Penxaye Apache, while the Assiniboine were defeated by the Blackfoot. Raids and ambushes played major roles in conflicts, which lasted for considerable periods, for example between the Navajo and the Southern Ute from the 1710s to the 1750s.

Across the century as a whole, the Europeans made major advances in North America. However, the general impression of European military superiority and territorial expansion has to be supplemented by an awareness of the setbacks that were faced and of the often complex reasons for European success, part of which depended on Native support. These points are particularly apparent in the early years of the century, not a period of major European success. The British faced determined resistance in the Carolinas where the Yamasee, with Creek support, nearly destroyed the colonies in 1715.[34]

Such conflicts, however, look different from non-European perspectives. For example, both the Creek and Carolinians sought to influence the Cherokee during this war, and, in the end, the Cherokee hoodwinked the Carolinians into a war with the Creek.[35] As in India, European powers, and the goods and opportunities they provided, were fed into local antagonisms, helping to fuel them at the same time that the powers were affected, if not manipulated. The French vied with the British to win allies, while the French and Spaniards competed among the Alabama and Creek in the late 1710s, establishing a regional pattern that was to last, with important variations in participants, until the end of Spanish rule in Florida in 1819–21.

Western colonies

The politics of alliance were also important to conflict between Western powers, both in the colonies and in Europe. Conflict in the colonies was less intense and central to rivalry between the powers than it was to be in mid-century when substantial regular forces were committed, especially in North America and the West Indies, but such conflict was already important. Ministries in Europe were responsible for key steps, notably in 1711 when the Tory government in London sent a major expedition against Québec, the leading French base in New America. In the event, nine ships were wrecked with heavy losses in fogs and gales in the poorly-charted St Lawrence, and the expedition was abandoned.[36]

The contrast with success at Québec in 1759, yet again the surrender of a city following defeat in battle, indicates an increase in British capability, but it is also necessary to give sufficient weight both to the role of contingencies and to the significance of political support. Under the impetus of William

Pitt the Elder, the Pitt–Newcastle government had provided large-scale support for offensives in North America from 1757, and previous ministries had done so from 1755. Even so, the sequence of events did not automatically flow from the commitment of resources as the fate of the 1711 expedition had already demonstrated. The British came close to failure at Québec in 1759 and the French nearly regained it in 1760, besieging the city after defeating a British force outside it, only for French Canada to succumb later that year in the face of advances by larger British armies.

Bases were the targets of attack, not least because Western colonies were totally dependent on these intermediary points with the homeland, points that could also serve as the focus of commercial networks among the native population. This dependence was more the case for the French than the Spanish colonies, as the latter had a larger, more dispersed and longer-established population, in part because agriculture was more significant than in the case of the French colonies. As a result, the French colonies proved more vulnerable to British attack than their Spanish counterparts. However, other factors were also pertinent, notably the tropical location of many Spanish colonies and thus the inroads from disease faced by assailants, as the British discovered at Cartagena in modern Colombia in 1741 and (more successfully) Havana in 1762.

War with Spain in 1719 led to the French capture of eastern Texas and of Pensacola, the major Spanish base in West Florida, both to surprise attacks. Spain was vulnerable as a result of the heavy costs incurred in the recent War of the Spanish Succession (1701–14), as well as because Philip V (r. 1700–46) was more concerned about the conflict in Spain itself (attacked by British and French forces in 1719) and in Sicily (invaded by Spanish forces in 1718). Moreover, France had more military possibilities for overseas operations in 1719–20 than it had done in the War of the Spanish Succession as a consequence of the active encouragement and support of Britain, the world's leading naval power. The recent enemies were allies from 1716 to 1731, which provided both with military opportunities.

Pensacola was then recaptured by an expedition of 1,400 Spanish troops from Havana, a reminder of the hierarchy of bases and the important role of forces available in the colonies as opposed to having to face the lengthy voyage from the metropole. Pensacola was next retaken by the French and their local allies, the Choctaw. Colonial conflict, however, was generally dependent on European power politics, and Spain regained Pensacola as part of the peace negotiated in 1720. This return continued the pattern seen earlier with Louis XIV's willingness to cede French colonial claims to Nova Scotia and Hudson Bay to Britain by the Treaty of Utrecht in 1713. This choice reflected his focus on dynastic and Continental (European mainland) interests, and his relative lack of interest in colonial issues.[37] The last was more generally true of French ministries, although intervention in 1778–83 in the War of American Independence marked an important exception.

The West

The essential similarity in weapons and tactics was the most striking feature of warfare in the West, although, in Europe as a whole, there was a contrast between Western and Turkish forces. As an instructive indication, both for conflict between non-Western powers and between Western and non-Western powers, the similarity in weapons and tactics between Western forces did not make sweeping victory impossible. However, such victories were generally due not to distinctive tactics and weaponry but rather to numbers of troops, the experience and motivation of the soldiers, the exploitation of terrain, generalship, especially in terms of the retention and employment of reserves, and the chance factors of battle and, to a lesser extent, sieges. For example, in Peter the Great's most important victory, Poltava (1709), numbers and generalship played key roles. The Swedes suffered terrible casualties as Charles XII launched a brave and foolhardy attack on a well-defended Russian position which exposed them to the more numerous, and well-directed, Russian infantry, artillery and cavalry.

The introduction of the socket bayonet and flintlock musket at the close of the seventeenth century contributed to a major change in tactics, training and the face of the Western battlefield. In Western Europe, infantry had hitherto been divided between musketeers and pikemen, but the proportion of the latter fell during the seventeenth century.[38] Pikemen provided musketeers with protection from cavalry and from other pikemen, but the combination of pikemen and musketeers was complex and led to a degree of tactical inflexibility as well as a density of formation that limited the possibilities of linear deployment over an extensive front. Such a front was appropriate in order to maximise firepower.

In contrast, bayonets provided protection without lessening firepower, and in the 1700s the pike disappeared from Western armies (many have been discovered in the silt at Blenheim) leading to an increase in tactical flexibility. Halberds were retained but only used for ceremonial purposes, while swords were used by officers and cavalry.[39] Standardised infantry weaponry permitted more effective drill, and drill and discipline were essential to firepower.

Moreover, more linear and thinner formations were employed on the battlefield with the infantry close-packed and deployed over an extended front in order to maximise firepower. Battalions were drawn up generally only three ranks deep, and firings were by groups of platoons, in a process designed to maximise the continuity of fire and fire-control. Linear formations operating across a more extended front also accentuated the serious problems of command and control posed by the limitations of information and communication on the battlefield, and this situation put a premium on the availability of sufficient officers.

Soldiers fired by volley, rather than employing individually-aimed shot. Despite the bayonets, hand-to-hand fighting on the battlefield was relatively uncommon, and most casualties, both fatalities and wounds, were caused by shot. For those French troops wounded at the battle of Oudenaarde in 1708 and admitted into the Hôtel des Invalides in Paris, 65 per cent of the wounds were inflicted by musket shot.[40]

The nature of the weaponry was highly significant. The problems created by short-range muskets, which had a low rate of fire and, as a result of their recoil, had to be re-sighted for each individual shot, were exacerbated by the cumulative impact of poor sights, eccentric bullets, heavy musket droops, recoil, overheating, and misfiring in wet weather. As muskets were smooth bore and there was no rifling, or grooves, in the barrel, the speed of the shot was not high and its direction was uncertain which greatly compromised accuracy. Non-standardised manufacture of muskets and balls and wide clearance (windage) meant that, unless held in place, the ball could roll out if the barrel was pointed towards the ground, while, at best, the musket was difficult to aim or to hold steady. Balls were rough cast and the spherical bullets maximised air resistance, which, again, ensured a need to fire at short range.[41] The accuracy of muskets and cannon was limited, and training, therefore, stressed rapidity of fire, and thus drill and discipline. Musket fire was usually delivered at close range, as impact and accuracy markedly diminished thereafter.

Infantry was flanked by cavalry units, but the proportion of cavalry in Western armies declined during the century as a result of the heavier emphasis on firepower and the greater cost of cavalry. Cavalry was principally used on the Western battlefield to fight cavalry. In contrast, cavalry advances against unbroken infantry with their firepower were uncommon, although, due to its linear formations and the difficulties of regrouping rapidly during combat, infantry was vulnerable to attack in flank and rear.[42] Cavalry played a crucial role in some battles, for example the British victory over the French at Blenheim in 1704 where, having drawn the French reserves into resisting attacks on the French flanks, the British broke through the centre of their position. This victory by John, Duke of Marlborough showed the importance of being able to control the flow of a battle, the need to impose on, and profit from, opponents' decision-making, and, specifically, the value of cavalry–infantry co-ordination, or at least combination. Similarly, at Fraustadt in 1706, a Swedish army defeated a Saxon force twice its size, the numerous Swedish cavalry enveloping both Saxon flanks, while the relatively small Swedish infantry force held off attacks in the centre. In general, however, cavalry was less important than it had been in the past.

Fraustadt was one of the Swedish successes in the Great Northern War (1700–21), a major struggle that indicated the potential for tactical, operational and strategic decisiveness in Western warfare, as well as the significance of alliance politics. The war began when Frederick IV of Denmark, Peter the Great of Russia, and Augustus II of Saxony-Poland planned concerted attacks on the Swedish empire, which then included Finland, Estonia and what is now northern Latvia, as well as territories in northern Germany. This empire had largely been assembled over the previous 150 years, and the attempt to partition it reflected a general sense of the transience of territorial control, the inherent competitiveness of dynasties, and the possibilities of achieving major change through warfare.[43]

The nature of opportunity also emerges clearly. Poland and Russia had just emerged from their war with the Turks, while the Danes benefited from the end of the Nine Years' War in Western Europe in 1697. Resource issues helped ensure a marked preference for sequential (rather than simultaneous) warmaking, which was further encouraged by the need to keep armies active (and, hopefully, supplied by operating abroad and even financed by allies) if they were to retain their effectiveness.

The assailants assumed that their attacks would divide Swedish forces and ensure speedy success, but the young Charles XII responded rapidly, prefiguring, in a more difficult context, Frederick the Great of Prussia's use of a central position against Austria, France, Russia and Sweden during the Seven Years' War (1756–63). Very much a war-leader, Charles gained and used the initiative. A Swedish landing on Zealand in 1700, threatening Copenhagen, drove Frederick IV of Denmark out of the war; the strength of Swedish-held Riga's defences blocked Augustus; and Charles was able to move rapidly to Narva in Estonia, which was then besieged by Peter. Charles's moves in 1700 illustrated the operational and strategic importance of amphibious capability, which, in turn, demonstrated the significance of naval power. Advancing rapidly on the Russian positions outside Narva, the Swedes gave the more numerous Russians no time to deploy their cannon but, instead, stormed the Russian entrenchments in two columns, benefiting from a snowstorm that blew directly into the faces of the defenders. The Swedes quickly came to hand-to-hand conflict, proving adept with their bayonets, and the Russian position collapsed with heavy casualties.

Narva showed that, as with the Turkish defeat outside Vienna in 1683, a poorly-commanded and badly-deployed siege army was vulnerable to a relief attempt, but, more generally, demonstrates that there was little that was formulaic about the Western battlefield. The patterning of drill and related tactical formations, and their use and effectiveness, were dependent on the exigencies of circumstances. Command style was a key aspect of the latter, and Charles XII's bold, ever-advancing generalship was more similar to the style of the Kangxi emperor or Nadir Shah of Persia (see pp. 58–9) than to the cautious style of some Western European generals of the period. This contrast was not simply a matter of personality. Like the Kangxi emperor, Nadir Shah and Frederick the Great, Charles XII had an ability as sovereign to command that these generals lacked. In particular, rulers could direct resources and ensure a focus on the campaigning in which they were involved. Such a position offered greater opportunities for initiative and decisiveness, and notably at the strategic level.

In 1701, Charles decided to replace Augustus II in Poland with a more pliable ruler, a recognition of the need to ground military success in political change. The French readiness, when at war with Britain, to support 'James III', the Jacobite (exiled Stuart) claimant to the throne, was another instance of the same process, although France did not play a direct role comparable to that of Charles in Poland. His decision led to Charles being embroiled for some years in the unsteady complexities of Polish politics and diverted him from dealing with the growing power of Peter the Great. This example is another indication of the role of choice in policy and strategy, a choice of commitments that was political as well as military in character, and with military tasks and means shaped accordingly.

In the summer of 1701, under cover of a smoke-screen, Charles crossed the River Dvina near Riga, before successfully driving away the defending forces. Charles next overran Courland (modern western Latvia), before advancing into, first, Lithuania and, then, Poland. He captured the cities of Warsaw and Thorn, while Polish-Saxon armies were defeated at Klisów (1702), Pultusk (1703), Punitz (1704), and Fraustadt/Wschowa (1706), the frequency of battles serving as a demonstration both of the need to win victory in order to maintain the dynamic of success and of the difficulty of translating victory into political outcomes.

These battles, and Russian victories over the Swedes, such as at Eristfer (1701), Hummelshof (1702) and Kalisz (1706), receive far less attention than those in Western Europe during the contemporaneous War of the Spanish Succession (1701–14); but they underline the variety of battle, and thus the importance of flexibility, experience, command skills, and unit cohesion, to success. Victory at Klisów over a larger Saxon army was typical of Charles's daring generalship, his conviction of the value of the attack, and his willingness to take risks. A silent march through difficult terrain secured the element of surprise, the Swedish cavalry attacked at once without pausing to open fire, the artillery was quicker than the more numerous Saxon cannon, and the infantry advanced to attack with cold steel in the face of Saxon musket fire. The Saxons broke, as defending forces tended to do if they could not keep their attackers at a distance. Linear formations relying on firepower were not designed for close-quarter fighting. Saxon losses in dead and wounded were at least twice those of the Swedes.

Every case is different, but it is instructive to compare Swedish tactics, operations and strategy with those of the Jacobites in the 1740s (see pp. 93, 96), and the French Revolutionaries in the 1790s (see pp. 154–5). Despite increasing firepower, which was easier to employ by stationary troops as it was difficult to fire on the move, the continued value of the offensive is apparent. At the same time, it was necessary to consider how best to use this potential for shock, given the casualties that would be taken in any advance against defensive firepower, as well as the danger that shock action would be absorbed and/or countered by defence in depth, notably the availability of reserves.

Whereas Western Europe, like India, contained many fortresses, especially in the Low Countries, eastern France and northern Italy; in Eastern Europe, there were far fewer fortifications and no system of advanced fortresses, although, in Eastern Europe, there was also no equivalent to the situation confronting the Chinese on the steppe, namely a lack of fortified targets. The contrast with the situation in Western Europe ensured that it was easier for the participants in the Great Northern War than for their counterparts in Western Europe to make major advances, as when Charles XII invaded Saxony in 1706 and Ukraine in 1708. However, Charles's total defeat at Poltava in 1709 was followed by the collapse of the Swedish empire, again indicating the importance of the defeat of field forces. Short of supplies, the Swedes decided to attack the powerful Russian position, penetrating the redoubts at heavy cost. In the final engagement, though, the Russians advanced from their camp with their entire force, and their superior strength and firepower proved decisive. The Russians lost about 1,300 men dead and the Swedes 6,900 dead and 2,800 taken prisoner, a high ratio from an army of 19,700 men. The Swedes' defeat turned into disaster when most of the retreating army surrendered to their Russian pursuers three days later; however, Charles XII's escape to Turkey, which gave him shelter, ensured that this operationally-decisive battle did not end the war.

The collapse of the Swedish empire owed much to the inexorable nature of Russian pressure, which was responsible for the conquest of Estonia and Latvia in 1710, and of Finland in 1713, the latter a conquest greatly assisted by Russian naval power in the Gulf of Finland. Moreover, Sweden's problems brought in Western cormorants who competed for and conquered her German possessions: Denmark anew and both Hanover and Prussia.

Sweden was not to regain its empire, and the Great Northern War was therefore decisive. In contrast, the War of the Spanish Succession was better matched in terms of resources and strategic strength. Louis XIV's France had a relatively secure home base protected by the largest army in Western Europe and by excellent fortifications designed and improved by Sebastien le Prestre de Vauban (1633–1707). These efforts rested on the largest population in Western Europe, a sound agricultural base, and a political culture and governmental system able to mobilise resources. As such, albeit at a smaller scale, France was similar to China.

The fortresses which provided defence-in-depth on the vulnerable north-east frontier of France indicated the effort deployed. For example, 1,200–1,500 men worked daily from 1698 to 1705 on the still-impressive fortress of Neuf-Brisach, which was part of the French system in the Upper Rhineland. Moreover, the supporting infrastructure was formidable. A forty-kilometre canal, including three aqueducts, was constructed to bring materials for the works from the Vosges mountains. As a result of its fortifications, France avoided many of the consequences of successive defeats by Marlborough, at Blenheim (1704), Ramillies (1706), Oudenaarde (1708), and Malplaquet (1709). The efforts of the victorious Allies were dissipated in sieges, notably of Lille in 1708.[44] The French fortified system also proved effective in 1707 when the Allies invaded Provence and unsuccessfully besieged Toulon, the fortified base of the French Mediterranean fleet. However, Allied failure there was not only due to the fortifications. The French had had time to concentrate forces in and around Toulon while French militia hindered Allied attempts to obtain supplies.

France was also largely immune to British amphibious attack and was able to suppress the only rebellion that occurred at home, that of the Protestants in the Cévennes mountains of southern France. As a consequence of these defensive strengths, French forces could take the offensive in the Low Countries, Germany, Italy and Spain. Their ability to campaign simultaneously in these areas testified to France's military, fiscal and administrative might.[45]

France's opponents were also effective. The British were willing to deploy their troops to the Danube in 1704, and, from his victory at Blenheim on, Marlborough refuted France's claims to military superiority. He combined tactical, operational and strategic skills. Bringing the British army to a peak of success, Marlborough used his cavalry as a massed shock force, handled the artillery well, and maintained continuous fire from his infantry. An expert in conducting mobile warfare, Marlborough was also skilful in holding the anti-French coalition together.[46]

Through Britain's subsidies to its allies, the coalition was able to draw on the strength of its far-flung and growing trading and financial system. Austria, the Dutch, Savoy-Piedmont, Portugal, and German principalities such as Hanover and Prussia, were crucial to the anti-French effort, providing forces, soaking up French attacks, and maintaining a united front for a decade. At the same time, there were serious difficulties, in part due to shortages in resources. For example, a lack of pay led to large-scale desertion in the Portuguese army in 1705, so that it achieved little.[47] Moreover, the range of allies entailed clashing commitments that caused problems over where best to allocate resources, both the choices and the processes involved.[48] There were also serious disputes between allies linked to competing territorial and strategic interests.[49]

As in East and South Asia, the campaigning demonstrated the importance of moving swiftly, not least in order to take the initiative from opponents, but such movements depended on a sound grasp of logistics. Prince Eugene, the leading Austrian general, outmanoeuvred and defeated larger French forces in northern Italy, culminating in victory at Turin in 1706, relieving the city, the capital of Savoy-Piedmont, from a French siege; and Marshal Berwick, the French commander in Spain, outmanoeuvred and defeated the Allied forces in Spain, notably at Almanza (1707).

Sieges were significant, as fortified positions anchored political power, contained supplies, controlled communication routes, and asserted progress in the war, which helped ensure an operational-level similarity between the War of the Spanish Succession and the Maratha/Mughal struggle in India. Marlborough's hard-won capture of Lille in 1708 showed that the French defence system could be breached, while Berwick's capture of Barcelona in 1714 marked the end of the Allied struggle in mainland Spain. Sieges had become more formidable undertakings because of advances in fortification technique associated in particular with Vauban, who developed the use of bastions, layering in depth, indirect fire and defensive artillery.

Although formidable defences were encountered elsewhere in the world, Vauban's advances were not matched there. In part, this was due to the specificity of particular military environments, notably the type of artillery against which protection was necessary, but the nature of the political challenge was also significant. There was no need in China to match the Western style of fortifications, notably because neither foreign opponents nor domestic rebels were strong in artillery. High walls, which were vulnerable to artillery, remained more important in China than in the West. In India, the standard locations for fortresses were mountains or hills, and the terrain provided a degree of protection not generally seen in Western Europe.

Conclusions

The practical and theoretical advances of Vauban and his opponents would have been of little value without the ability and determination of Western governments to spend massive amounts on such fortresses, even though it was a period of limited economic and population growth. Resources also emerge as a key element in the expansion of China under the Kangxi emperor. More generally, they were significant at the tactical, operational and strategic level, and in translating victory into a new political order. Troops, equipment and money were all important.

Yet, far more than resources were involved in explaining the success and failure of specific states, campaigns and generals. Each result takes on meaning in particular circumstances, but, in looking for commonalities, it is notable that taking the offensive was significant. It did not invariably bring success, as was spectacularly displayed with Charles XII's failure at Poltava, while Aurangzeb's campaigning against the Marathas indicated the strategic and political limitations of individual successes in the field. The French advance into Bavaria in 1704 met with defeat at Blenheim, and an advance into Belgium was defeated at Ramillies in 1706.

Nevertheless, a frequent theme, joining the Kangxi emperor to Eugene and Marlborough, was the determination to take the offensive and force the pace of events. This determination was frequently linked with decisiveness, both in battles and sieges, and in military and political goals and outcomes. This decisiveness contrasts with views that the warfare of this period was indecisive, part of a wider failure of method and purpose that was only overcome with the developments of the revolutionary period towards the close of the century. As this book shows, that account, in many respects the standard account, is not only Western-centric in content and Whiggish and teleological in approach. It is also deeply flawed.

3 1720–1740

The 1720s and 1730s tend to be overshadowed in military history, in part because of the fame of military leaders earlier in the century, notably Marlborough, Eugene, Charles XII and Peter the Great, but these decades again display the themes outlined in the introduction. The standard Western-centric focus ensures that the period only appears of consequence at the close, when the outbreak of war with Spain, the War of Jenkins' Ear (1739–48), began a period (1739–63) in which, having defeated France on land and sea in 1758–60, Britain ultimately became the strongest power in North America. Attention is also devoted to the outbreak of the War of the Austrian Succession in 1740, when Frederick the Great (II) of Prussia successfully invaded the Austrian province of Silesia. In contrast to both wars, the campaigning of the earlier years in the period 1720–40 is overshadowed. Moreover, the War of the Polish Succession (1733–5) and the Balkan conflicts of 1735–9 with the Turks seem far less consequential than the earlier conflicts in Europe of 1700–18, which also receive more attention.

The remainder of the world in the 1720s and 1730s is commonly ignored, but, insofar as any interest is shown, there appears nothing to match the drama of the earlier campaigning of Aurangzeb or the Kangxi emperor in South and East Asia respectively. This chapter sets out to show that this account is insufficient as a description of events around the world, and inadequate as a presentation of those in Persia, Europe, India and China. Again, by taking a period of two decades, important developments are not neglected in favour of what might appear, sometimes mistakenly, to be more significant long-term trends.

Persia

Persia is a major centre of civilisation that does not attract proportionate attention from military historians. It always shows up in order to be conquered by Alexander the Great of Macedon in 331 BCE, but, thereafter, is presented essentially as an 'other' with which more interesting empires, Rome, Byzantium, the Ottomans and the Mughals, competed. This approach is wrong, but so, even more, is the general neglect of Persia.

Any such neglect is particularly inappropriate for the 1720s and 1730s, for this period indicated both the vulnerability of sedentary empires to attacks from less settled regions, as well as the volatility of much of South Asian military history. Having lasted over two centuries and survived major wars with the Turkish empire, the Safavid (Persian) empire was overthrown from the east by the Ghalzai (Ghalji) Afghans in 1721–2. The Safavid attempt to impose Shi'ite orthodoxy on Sunni Muslims had led to widespread opposition, for example in Kurdistan, and, in particular, in the eastern, Afghan, regions of the empire where Sunnis were the majority. This opposition was especially pronounced among the Ghalzai tribe, who rebelled in 1704 and, more successfully, in 1709, in response to a harsh Georgian Governor of Kandahar, the major city of the region. The Safavid army sent to suppress the rebellion mounted an unsuccessful siege of Kandahar in 1711, and was heavily defeated as it retreated.

This defeat was followed by a rebellion of the Abdalis of western Afghanistan, a powerful confederation of tribes, and the Safavid failure to suppress them testified to the respective fighting quality of the two sides. Strong in cavalry, Persia was weak in infantry and also found it difficult to mobilise a large force for operations, especially rapidly. A shortage of funds was a serious problem. The lack of Safavid warmaking since the 1639 Peace of Zuhab with the Turks ensured an absence of fighting spirit, readiness and experience, while the Safavids were also weak in the vital political dimension that was crucial in the handling of 'barbarian' opponents. Shah Husain (r. 1694–1722), a poor leader, indolent, mild and pleasure-seeking, who suffered from divided counsels, failed, himself, to exploit divisions among the Afghans. There was no equivalent to the strategy of 'divide and rule' traditionally used by 'settled' societies against semi-nomadic, pastoral opponents.[1]

Moreover, the success of the Afghans encouraged rebellions elsewhere in the Safavid dominions, notably in Azerbaijan, Baluchistan, Khurasan, Kurdistan, Bahrain and Shirvan. Thus, the Afghans were not alone as tribes rebelling in the frontier provinces. The Turkmen did the same to the east of the Caspian, and the Lezghis from Daghestan in the Caucasus, while Kurds and Arabs posed problems in the western provinces. Sunni opposition played a significant role in these rebellions, which became, individually and cumulatively, more serious. For example, Lezghi pressure in Shirvan increased from 1709, rising greatly from 1718. The attempt to use neighbouring Georgia against the Lezghis initially failed, because Vakhtang VI of Georgia, who was supposed to provide troops, complained about a failure to pay for support, although, in 1719–20, Georgian support materialised and was important. However, in 1721, the Lezghi occupied the major town in the region, Shamakhi, slaughtering many of the Shi'ite population. To the east, serious Uzbek pressure from Bukhara on the frontier region of Khurasan in north-east Persia led to the loss of many people seized in raids as slaves.

In 1716, the Abdalis captured Herat, the major city in western Afghanistan. In 1719, the Ghalzai leader, Mahmud, advanced west to Kirman in eastern Persia, taking the city, whose defenders had fled, and looting it savagely, before returning to Afghanistan. In 1721, in contrast, Mahmud's advance became more than a raid. He besieged Kirman, failing to take the citadel, but accepting money to leave. The Ghalzais then advanced to the centre of Persia. On 8 March 1722, at Gulnabad, twenty kilometres east of Isfahan, the capital, they fought a far larger Persian army, much of which was tribal cavalry, but the Persians were poorly commanded and the Persian artillery made no real contribution to the battle. Superior Afghan fighting quality and command skills led to a Persian collapse. Afghan weaponry included *zanbüraks*, camel-mounted swivel guns, which were also to be effective against the Marathas at the battle of Third Panipat in 1761.

At Gulnabad, the Persian army suffered from serious rivalries and its units fought as if separate. Some of the individual units fought well, but there was no real co-ordination, circumstances also true of the Turkish army in its major defeats at Vienna (1683) and Kartal (Kagul to the Russians, 1770), as well as of the Marathas at Third Panipat. Military cohesion was a repeated feature in success or failure, underlining the central linkage between organisational practice and political culture. That many individual units were recruited from specific regions, could also contribute to a lack of co-operation.

The Ghalzais then blockaded Isfahan, defeating attempts at relief but lacking the numbers to storm the city and the artillery to breach its walls. Famine in the city caused by the seven-month siege led to its surrender on 23 October, the Shah abdicating in favour of Mahmud, the Ghalzai leader.[2] It is surprising that this campaign does not attract more attention for it was not only the sole violent end of the rule of a major dynasty during the entire century prior to the overthrow of the Toungoo in Burma in 1752 and the Bourbons in France in 1792, but also, like the last, provided the touch-paper for a wide-ranging struggle for international pre-eminence, one that rapidly drew in Russia and Turkey and that lasted until the negotiation of Turkish–Persian peace in 1746. The overthrow of the Bourbons occurred as a result of a radical rising in Paris, whereas that of the Safavids was the product of campaigning and battle.

The revolutionaries who overthrew Louis XVI in 1792 proved incapable of ending disorder. Similarly, the paranoid and violent Mahmud was unable to bring stability to Persia and died, probably murdered, in 1725. His successor, his cousin Ashraf (r. 1725–9), had Shah Husain beheaded in 1726, but the latter's third son, Tahmasp, opposed him, and Tahmasp's supporter Nadir Kuli (1688–1747), a Turcoman tribesman, defeated Ashraf at Mehmandust and Murchakhur in 1729, leading to the capture of Isfahan and the end of the Afghan Hotaki dynasty. The divided Afghans were driven from Persia, and Nadir secured the throne for Tahmasp. Opposition to the unpopular Afghans greatly helped Nadir just as the Zunghar invaders of Tibet in 1717 suffered from the opposition they fostered.

Meanwhile, chaos in Persia had led to it becoming the fulcrum of Russo-Turkish competition, which serves to illustrate the extent to which conflict in one area could spread because of wider questions of relative strength and cascading consequences. As such, bilateral measures of military power offer only limited guidance to developments. In 1722, Peter the Great of Russia advanced into the region to see what he could gain and to block the Turks from eastward expansion to the Caspian Sea, a possible gain that threatened to challenge the Russian position further north. The towns of Darbent and Resht were occupied by the Russians in 1722 and Baku followed in 1723.

The Russian advance was preceded by careful planning: naval and cartographical missions explored and mapped the coastline, and an army officer examined the roads.[3] Yet, aspects of the campaign were mismanaged: logistics were poor, especially the supply of food and ammunition. Whereas more facets of warfare were becoming professionalised, the key element of long-distance combat, logistics, remained poorly organised and arbitrary in part. Reforms were easier to envisage than to implement.

In September 1723, Tahmasp was persuaded to yield the provinces along the southern and western shores of the Caspian, in return for a Russian promise to aid him in pacifying Persia and defeating the Afghans. However, aside from the implausible nature of this promise, Russian gains were in a traditional area of Turkish interest and the Turks, in turn, advanced to benefit from Persian weakness, overrunning western Persia, and taking the major cities, Kirmanshah and Hamadan. The Turks did not accept the Afghans as rulers of Persia. The Turks also moved into the Caucasus, capturing the cities of Tblisi and Yerevan, the capitals of modern Georgia and Armenia respectively.

In June 1724, by the Treaty of Constantinople, the Turks accepted Peter's proposal for a partition, the result of which provided an indication of the complexities of alliance politics. Peter recognised Turkish occupation of

Georgia and a number of Persian provinces, which the Turks had had to renounce as part of their Treaty of Zuhab with Persia in 1639, while the Turks accepted the Russian gains from their 1723 treaty with Persia, which, as yet, Tahmasp had not ratified. Russia and Turkey agreed to support the restoration of the Safavids, but on the understanding that, if Tahmasp refused to accept the terms, they could seize their allocated territories. Tahmasp's failure to agree to those allocated to the Turks, led them to attack Persia in 1724–6. Tabriz, the major city in north-west Persia, was captured in July 1725.

Initial Turkish successes, which worried the Russians, were followed, after continued instability in Persia, by a Persian military and political revival. This revival affected both Russia and Turkey. By the Treaty of Rescht of 1729, the Russians promised to withdraw from some of their conquests, only to be threatened with the loss of the rest unless they provided assistance against the Turks. The crisis in Western power politics in 1729–31 may also have played a role as Russia was allied to Austria from 1726 and thereby involved in disputes in Germany in addition to its own concerns in the Baltic. In 1729, a dispute between Hanover and Prussia over forcible recruiting by the latter threatened to lead to a war that would have brought in Austria and Russia on Prussia's side, and Britain, France and the Dutch on that of Hanover. Unwilling to fight the Persians, and disillusioned by the cost of retaining their unhealthy Caspian provinces, where large numbers of troops died of disease, the Russians signed another Treaty of Resht in 1732 by which they agreed to evacuate most of Peter's gains.

The Persians were therefore able to focus on their major opponent, the Turks. Indeed, the contrast between the challenges posed to Persia by Turkey and (less seriously) Russia offers an instructive corrective to the tendency to focus on Western powers. Nadir defeated the Turks at Nahavand near Hamadan in 1730, one of the decisive battles of the century for it ensured that western Persia would remain outside the Turkish orbit and that the Turkish government would lack the prestige and spoils of success. This region had been in dispute for centuries, but, thereafter, there was to be no sustained Turkish attempt to conquer it.

Military reputation was important to rulership. In contrast to Nadir, who trained his troops with great energy, the alcoholic Tahmasp was a poor commander and was heavily defeated by the Turks at Kurijan in 1731. This defeat, and Tahmasp's willingness to accept a humiliating treaty with the Turks, paved the way for Nadir's successful pressure on Tahmasp in 1732 to abdicate in favour of his infant son, Abbas III. In turn, the Turkish sultan, Ahmed III, had been overthrown in 1730 in part because of discontent with his mismanagement of the war with Persia.

Nadir was an able general, making good use both of cavalry attacks and of musketeers, while, like John, Duke of Marlborough, he was effective at using his reserves. Cavalry charges against opponents' flanks were a characteristic tactic for Nadir. His skilful planning of logistics was also important. Nadir's successes over the Turks included defeating Topal Osman Pasha near Kirkuk in 1733 and Abdullah Köprülü at Baghavand in 1735, and capturing Tabriz on 12 August 1730.

In 1736, with the deposing of Abbas III, Nadir took total power when he made himself Shah on 8 March. However, his other commitments prevented Nadir from exploiting his victories over the Turks and invading the heartland of their empire, although in Constantinople it was feared that he would do so. Instead, Nadir had to turn east to deal with opposition: in 1730 in Afghanistan and in 1733 on the Persian Gulf coast. In the classic pattern of the successful war-leader, Nadir's victory over the Abdalis in Afghanistan in 1730 was followed by many joining his army, a process also seen in his career before 1729 and after the fall of Kandahar in 1738. More generally, however, within the Persian empire, Nadir faced rebellious tribes, hostile provincial governors, and Safavid pretenders. At the same time, his successes ensured that Persia would not collapse, nor be partitioned between Russia, Turkey and the Afghans as had seemed possible in the 1720s.

The large-scale warfare between Turkey and Persia had a key impact on conflict within the West, a point that needs to be borne in mind given the tendency to see Westerners as the essential drivers of world developments. The Turkish commitment in Persia made plans by Western diplomats to turn the Turks against Russia and/or Austria impracticable. The French sought to engage Turkish attention in the cause of Louis XV's father-in-law, Stanislaus Lesczczynski (earlier the protégé of Charles XII as king), as the next king of Poland. However, Persian affairs prevented any Turkish commitment, either before the outbreak of the War of the Polish Succession in 1733 or during the war itself, which was begun by a successful Russian invasion of Poland. A Turkish complaint in April 1733 about apparent Russian intentions towards Poland was forwarded to St Petersburg by Ivan Nepluiev, the experienced Russian envoy, with the assurance that the Turks were in no position to act. When, in August 1733, the Grand Vizier reminded Nepluiev of Peter the Great's promise not to intervene militarily in Poland, Nepluiev reported that Turkey's willingness to act would depend on whether it could secure peace with Persia.[4]

Encouraged by Russian military supplies, Nadir rejected Turkish peace proposals, while the Russians, by the Treaty of Gence of March 1735, returned Baku and Darbent to Persia and recognised Persian suzerainty over the Daghestan region of the eastern Caucasus. The Russians thought it necessary to help the Persians in order to prevent them settling with the Turks and either uniting against Russia or allowing the Turks to re-establish themselves on the Caspian. The alignment between Nadir and Russia suited both and was similar to that by which Russia and the Manchu rulers of China settled differences, thus isolating the Zunghars. However, Nadir was not to fight on against the Turks as the Russians hoped.

Russian policy in 1735 demonstrated, again, the need to respond to non-Western moves. The Turks replied to the Treaty of Gence by ordering their subject allies, the Crimean Tatars, to assert the Turkish claim to Daghestan, a move that would take them through Kabardia, an area to the north of the Caucasus claimed by Russia, and thus provide Russia with one of the major pretexts for declaring war on Turkey. A lack of Russian preparation ensured that the attempt to block this move by seizing the fortress of Azov, the leading Turkish base in this region, failed in 1735, the year in which war was declared by Russia. In 1736, the Russians seized Azov and attacked the Crimea, but these moves did not determine the course of the war between Nadir and the Turks.

Instead, the Russian attacks were insufficient to persuade Nadir to continue his war with the Turks or to refuse a peace with them unless it included the Russians, the course he had originally wished for. The Turks refused to yield the latter point, but their willingness to offer Nadir terms that reflected the Persian military advantage led to the Treaty, in practice Truce, of Erzerum of September 1736. The Russians, therefore, found that the favourable position they had enjoyed in 1724–35, under which they had benefited from the conflict between Turkey and Persia while not having to commit themselves heavily, had faded. More generally, the strategic dimension posed by competing geopolitical commitments requires emphasis in the literature,[5] as does the leadership requirements it entailed.

Meanwhile, Nadir turned east in 1736–9, marching through, and thus enforcing control over, the region of Seistan in eastern Persia in 1736, a key achievement in re-assembling the Safavid empire, before attacking the Afghans and invading India. On 24 March 1738, Kandahar, long a city in contention between Safavids and Mughals, and the independent centre of resistance by the Ghalzai Afghans to Safavid rule since the revolt of 1709, fell after a nine-month Persian siege, after which much of the city was destroyed. The siege, which greatly weakened the Ghalzais, was bitterly contested for a long time, but Nadir's eventual success owed much to help from within the city. Its capture was followed by those of Ghazni, Kabul, which had a strong Mughal garrison, Jalalabad and, after outflanking the Mughal units in the Khyber Pass, Peshawar in what is now Pakistan. The shelter provided to Afghan fugitives was the excuse given for the invasion of the Mughal empire. Advancing further, Nadir's crossing of the River Indus threatened northern India.

In 1739, Nadir annexed Kashmir, captured the city of Lahore in the Punjab region, and defeated the larger army of the poorly-prepared Mughal emperor, Muhammad Shah (r. 1719–48), at Karnal, 75 miles north of Delhi, on 24 February. The loss of effective imperial control over much of the Mughal empire since the death of Aurangzeb in 1707, combined with the takeover of imperial power at the centre by nobles, helped to ensure a weak and divided response to the Persian invasion, and, in particular, some key Mughal figures refused to fight at Karnal. The Mughal army was larger than Nadir's, but was less well trained and seriously divided. The Mughals were also outclassed in firepower, not least by Nadir's *zanbüraks* (camel-mounted swivel guns); while the use of burning oil led the Mughal elephants to flee.[6]

Nadir then sacked Delhi, which had fallen without resistance on 20 March, seizing the Peacock Throne and a vast treasure that he intended to use to finance subsequent wars. Rioting in the city was met by the slaughter of thousands of civilians. To buy Nadir off, the Mughals ceded Sind (the region round Karachi) and all territories west of the River Indus to Nadir.[7]

In 1740, having returned from India, Nadir pressed on to conquer the Central Asian khanates of Bukhara and Khiva, both in modern Uzbekistan. In 1737, he had already conquered the area of Balkh in northern Afghanistan from Bukhara. Indicating a continued dependence of European conflicts on non-Western politics, Nadir's truce with Turkey was maintained sufficiently long to enable the Turks to devote the bulk of their resources in the late 1730s to resisting Russia and Austria.

Nadir's operations were in part designed to gain spoils in order to reward his army and also to transfer the burden of its support from Persia. Moreover, his imperial model was not the Safavid one, but a more far-flung ambition similar to that of Timur (1336–1405, later called Tamerlane), a Turkic figure who, based in Samarkand, had campaigned widely, capturing Delhi, Baghdad, Damascus and Ankara, and creating a wide-ranging empire. As such there was a parallel between Nadir Shah and the situation in China where Manchu interests, ambitions and commitments were more far-flung than those of the previous Ming dynasty. However, China offered the Manchu a bureaucratic strength and institutional continuity that neither Timur nor Nadir enjoyed, and their achievements therefore proved ephemeral.

Like Timur and Napoleon, Nadir was a bold practitioner of warfare. He put the emphasis on mobility and employed reconnaissance adroitly to identify weaknesses among his opponents. Nadir used mounted musketeers, but it was their mobility, rather than their firepower, that was crucial, although his *zanbūraks* made an impact on the Indian cavalry. Nadir's cavalry was deployed as a shock force and appears to have been more effective than the Turkish cavalry. His infantry had heavy-calibre firearms that lacked bayonets, which made them vulnerable to cavalry.

Nadir preferred battles to sieges because the latter posed a logistical challenge, and it would be difficult to maintain the cohesion and morale of a besieging army composed in large part of tribal levies. In this respect, the Persian military differed from its Turkish and, even more, Chinese counterparts. Nadir's lack of adequate siege artillery left risky, wasteful assaults or lengthy blockades as the only alternatives when attacking fortified positions. Blockade meant delay and demanded patience, which did not suit his personality. At any rate, by 1740, Nadir had expanded Persian power further than any of the Safavids, defeating the Turks in battle more consistently than they ever managed, gaining an entry into India the Safavids had not enjoyed, and subjugating Central Asian cities like Khiva, Bukhara and Samarkand, with their historical resonances of Genghis Khan and Timur, that the Safavids had never reached.[8]

An important recent study of Nadir's army has suggested that it was possibly the most powerful single force in the world, not only because of its size but also due to the development, for Persia, of a new-style army, well-equipped with firearms, ably trained and commanded, and based on more effective governmental policies. Comparison with Peter the Great is possible, but, because Nadir had less time than Peter, he was unable to match his achievements. Moreover, the domestic challenges Nadir faced were far greater, and the basis of state authority was weaker than in Russia. In addition, Nadir's pressure for money helped cause instability and his subsequent downfall;[9] although, far from this being a clear-cut instance of non-Western personal monarchy contrasting with more successful bureaucratic Western processes, Peter's death was followed by serious instability in Russia in 1725–30. This thesis about Nadir's army serves as a reminder that military progress should be regarded neither as clear-cut nor as a monopoly of Western states. A ready contrast between Nadir and Peter is provided by the latter's determination to Westernise his forces, but being Westernised was not necessarily a marker of force effectiveness as Peter also discovered in 1711. Warfare in Persia was different, rather than somehow less developed. Moreover, there was a common theme in the preference for offensive warfare.

India

The major Mughal defeat at Karnal in 1739 contrasted greatly with Mughal success in holding back Safavid advances in Afghanistan in the seventeenth century and led to a serious loss of prestige. Nadir's campaign was a crippling blow for Mughal power, but this power was already under pressure from a weakening of authority and from Maratha advances. The former undid the earlier fruits of Mughal expansion. Asaf Jah, the Nizam of Hyderabad, returned from Delhi to the Deccan in 1724 and then used help from the Marathas to defeat Muhariz Khan, Mughal military commander in the Deccan, at Shakarkhera in 1724. This victory enabled the Nizam to take control of Hyderabad in 1725, and he became independent, which sundered one of the major achievements of the Mughals, the control of Hindustan over the Deccan. Founder of the dynasty of Nizams of Hyderabad, Asaf Jah went on to annex the region of Berar, although he was defeated by the Marathas, for example in 1728.

Moreover, greatly weakening the Mughals, the Nawab of Bengal in eastern India became independent in 1733. That year, Bengal also annexed neighbouring Bihar. The emergence of these and other successor states enhanced political rivalry, increasing the demand for soldiers in India as well as the competitive search for greater military effectiveness.

So also did the challenge from the Marathas, who made important gains from the 1730s onwards. The Mughals fielded large forces against them, especially in 1735; but the more mobile Marathas, with their raiding light cavalry (they also had infantry), generally refused to engage in a major battle. Instead, they concentrated on outmanoeuvring their opponent and cutting off their grain supplies and reinforcements, as in 1728, and again in 1735 when they forced the surrounded Mughal emperor, Muhammad Shah, to buy them off with a cash tribute.

The Marathas made major territorial gains in a number of directions. The Mughals were increasingly pushed back into the Delhi area, with the Marathas in effective control to the south and west of Agra. The Marathas also made gains further south, notably Malwa, from the Nizam of Hyderabad in the Treaty of Bhopal in 1737. The hostility between the Nizam and the Mughals greatly helped the Marathas. In 1740, moreover, some 50,000 Marathas invaded the Carnatic in south-east India, defeating and killing the Nawab of the Carnatic at the battle of Damalcherry, and then pressing on to capture Arcot, the capital. Alongside Nadir's victory at Karnal in 1739, this campaign demonstrated the effectiveness of cavalry and the extent to which control of cities followed on from victory in battle.

Maratha military activity and prominence led other parts of India to accept Maratha claims to levy taxes, as the Mughal Governor of Gujarat did in 1725, and also to ally with the Marathas, as did the rajas of Bundelkhand in 1737. Moreover, the Marathas played a significant role in disputes between the Rajput clans.

The Westerners were also placed under major pressure. The Portuguese, who had failed in their 1722 campaign against the strongholds of the Maratha naval leader, Kanhoji Angria, were hard hit in 1737–40 when they were involved in a disastrous war with the Marathas. The Portuguese bases proved vulnerable: Salsette was taken in 1737, Bassein fell on 12 May 1739 after a siege, Goa was nearly lost the same year, and Chaul was taken in 1740. The Marathas benefited in this conflict from the support of disaffected peasantry who provided an infantry to complement Maratha cavalry, an infantry that proved crucial to successful sieges. Like Persia, India in 1720–40 scarcely conforms to any model of the rise of sedentary empires, the dominance of gunpowder weaponry, and the growing prominence of the West.

China and Central Asia

The Kangxi emperor (r. 1662–1722) had made the defeat of the Zunghars a personal crusade and, seeking victory rather than the transient possession of territory, had pushed hard those generals who were more hesitant about campaigning on the steppe. These themes were to be resumed under the Qianlong emperor (r. 1736–96).[10] However, the importance of personality is illustrated by the role of the intervening Yongzheng emperor (r. 1723–35), who put less of a consistent effort into campaigning against the Zunghars. Moreover, unlike his father, the Kangxi emperor (but like the Qianlong emperor), the Yongzheng emperor did not campaign in person. Nevertheless, he took a role in planning war with the Zunghars and, to that end, established a Military Finance Section under the Ministry of Revenue, in 1729. The war was launched that year, the Emperor arguing that it was necessary for stability in Tibet and Khalka (eastern) Mongolia.

The Emperor, however, did not persist after the defeat at Hoton Nor in 1731 when the Chinese force that had advanced into Xinjiang was lured into a trap and nearly destroyed with the loss of many thousands of troops. Another army that marched on Urumchi, also in Xinjiang, avoided destruction, but retreated. The death in 1730 of Yinxiang, the Emperor's brother, who had been in charge of planning the war, had brought a temporary halt to it in 1730 and also lessened the commitment to the conflict. After the defeat of 1731, the Zunghars invaded the country of the pro-Chinese Khalka Mongols, seeking to conquer them, but the latter mounted a successful resistance, holding the crossing points of rivers and defeating the Zunghars at Erdene in west-central Mongolia in 1732. A small-scale success for the Chinese in renewed campaigning in 1732–3, with defeats of the Zunghars, and the Chinese advancing as far as the Irtysh river, permitted the negotiation of a face-saving truce in 1735, and it became a peace in 1739. Costly for the Chinese in money, troops and prestige, the campaigning was not resumed. The distances involved posed a major burden, as did the difficulty of fixing the Zunghars in battle, while there was also concern that continued conflict might lead to a Khalka revolt.[11] The advance to the Irtysh, however, demonstrated the growing pressure on the steppe peoples as the Russians had already established bases on the river further north.

Had the Yongzheng emperor ruled as long as his aggressive predecessor or successor, the Zunghars might have expanded once more and become a powerful Central Asian empire. Indeed, they expanded to the north and west, advancing into central Kazakhstan in 1723 and overrunning Turkestan in Central Asia in 1724–5. The cities of Sairam and Tashkent were captured by the Zunghars, and dominion was gained over the cities of Kashgar and Yarkand. Turfan was put under great pressure in the early 1730s and, as the Chinese could not provide security, the population left in 1733–4.[12] Moreover, the Zunghars displayed interest in developing weaponry. Johan Renat, a Swedish artillery officer in their service in 1716–33, was employed in making guns and mortars, and in teaching the smelting of iron and the manufacture of bullets.

In 1733, the Zunghar leader, Galdan Tsering (r. 1727–45), showed great interest in Russian weaponry when he met a Russian envoy. None, however, was provided because, by the Treaty of Kiakhta in 1728, Russia and China confirmed their frontier agreement of 1689, and thus deprived the Zunghars of the possibility of Russian support. Indeed, in 1731, the Kazaks turned to the Russians for military assistance. The Kazak Younger Horde became a Russian vassal, followed by the Middle Horde in 1740. The absence of unity among the steppe peoples is a key qualification of the tendency to treat the military history of inner-Asia in terms of a dichotomous rivalry of steppe peoples and bureaucratic states.

The attempt by Lobzang Danjin to unite the Khoshot Mongls and restore their control over Tibet in 1723 led the Yongzheng emperor to dispatch an army to Tibet under Nian Gengyao. In 1724, Lobzang was rapidly defeated as a result of a risky surprise attack before the grass began sprouting, and he fled to the Zunghars. The respective significance of Chinese intervention and the struggle within Tibet is unclear. Rebellion there in 1727 led to a civil war in which the pro-Chinese faction, supported in 1728 by Chinese forces advancing from three directions (Qinghai, Sichuan and Yunnan), triumphed, while, at the end of 1728, the Dalai Lama was made to leave Lhasa to stop his presence in the capital being a motive for rebellions. The Chinese chose to rely on the Panchen Lama and on Pholhane, a noble they referred to as Prince of Tibet.[13]

However, the reign of Yongzheng was not characterised by major Chinese military initiatives elsewhere. Indeed, Yongzheng was not willing to devote significant resources to preserving the position in Turfan, which was under Zunghar pressure. This throws light on the difficulties of assessment, for Yongzheng was also a great reformer and a very tough emperor. His financial reforms[14] laid the basis for Qianlong's military success, and it is unclear whether, without Yongzheng, this success would have been won.

At the same time, the government faced a degree of opposition within China, with tribal risings a response to the state's pressure for the integration and control of minorities, a pressure that continued the longstanding use of force in Chinese expansion.[15] In 1726, the Miao of the Guiyang prefecture in the province of Guizhou were pacified, with native chiefs forcibly removed and replaced by Chinese civil administrators, but government policies, which were pushed hard by the Emperor from 1726 to 1728, continued to arouse opposition. Guizhou in southern China was a centre of conflict, while it was also significant in neighbouring Yunnan. Ortai, a Manchu who was the Governor-General of Yunnan and Guizhou, was particularly associated with the move from a reliance on local chieftains toward an emphasis on regular bureaucratic processes. This move led to resistance by the tribal population of south-west China in the mid-1730s, notably the Guizhou rebellion in western Guizhou which was met in 1735–6 by large-scale slaughter in a campaign commanded by Zhang Guangsi, a protégé of Ortai. In 1740, there was a major rebellion by Miao people in the region of eastern Guizhou and western Hunan. Millenarian fantasies about a new order similar to those that were to be seen among Native Americans in the 1760s played a role, but, in the end, the rebellion was suppressed.

Further west, the Russians had greater success but against a weaker rival. The Russian achievement east of the Caspian Sea was a case of logistics, alliances and consolidation, rather than of battle. Thanks in part to the Russian use of native allies, the Bashkirs were suppressed to the north-east of the Caspian in the 1720s and 1730s. Russian control was anchored by a new line of forts from the River Volga to the new fort of Orenburg on the River Ural, built from 1733. Other lines of forts consolidated Russia's advancing frontiers, closing the way for nomadic invasions, and both providing security and preparing the ground for subsequent advances, especially by sealing off regions from hostile reinforcement. The Usinskaya Line based at Troitsk (1743) was constructed along the River Uy to protect the developing agricultural zone to the east of the Urals.[16] The strength of Russia's southern frontiers, and the related steady pressure of Russian power in a part of the world traditionally characterised by the advances of steppe peoples, were both impressive.

Africa

The tension between settled societies and attacking pastoralists was also seen in Africa, notably with Berber incursions on the plains of Morocco, and Tuareg raids out of the Sahara Desert against Timbuktu on the River Niger, the latter part of a pattern of desert pressure on more settled regions still seen with Tuareg attacks in Mali and Niger in 2012. Timbuktu was raided in 1729, its trade routes were attacked in 1736 and 1737, and in 1737 the Tuareg were victorious in battle. Further south in West Africa, the state of Dahomey was subjected to invasions by the cavalry of Oyo in a series of conflicts between 1726 and 1748. Although the cavalry could be held off by musketeers sheltering behind field fortifications, their mobility enabled them to pillage Dahomey and force it to surrender and pay tribute. Asante, which sought to expand further west, could not defeat the cavalry of the savannah and became reliant on winning allies who had their own cavalry.

The provision of Western arms became more significant in coastal areas. Dahomey in part owed its rise under Agaja (r. *c.* 1716–40) to an effective use of Western firearms combined with standards of training and discipline that impressed Western observers. Weaponry alone was not enough, but it was important. In Madagascar, firearms played a major role in the powerful kingdoms of Menabe and Boina. In 1719, the crew of a Dutch ship recorded their surprise at the skilful use of muskets by the 4,000–5,000-strong army of Menabe, and, three years later, another Dutch commentator was impressed by that of Boina. By mid-century, Boina had at least thirty large cannon, and its army was estimated as 15,000 strong in 1741.

Plentiful firearms were obtained from Western traders in return for slaves. Major John Corneille noted of the Madagascans in 1754, 'most of them have a gun, powder horn and shot bag, and the rest have spears'. He also wrote that the religious figures claimed that they could provide invulnerability to shot and arrows.[17] The issue of invulnerability to shot was a cultural factor into the 1890s when France conquered Madagascar. The availability of firearms probably played a role in the consolidation of powerful kingdoms in Madagascar and elsewhere, but there were also significant political and economic dimensions. Moreover, Western intervention was significant in Africa largely in terms of how it affected existing balances of power.[18]

The spread of firearms in African warfare should not only be considered with reference to the standard assumptions of Western technological superiority and technological determinism. Instead, fighting in parts of Africa, and indeed elsewhere, notably parts of South-East Asia and South America, was perhaps less sensitive to technological change. Close-quarter fighting, especially ambushes, in bush and jungle cover tended to nullify improved range and accuracy, which was why Africans could still fight effectively with late seventeenth- and eighteenth-century firearms in the later nineteenth century.

The Americas

European advances that owed much to a quest for resources helped lead to conflicts with Native Americans. In the Portuguese colony of Brazil, the discovery of goldfields in the interior in the region of Minas Gerais led to a major movement of people into the interior, from both Portuguese Brazil and Portugal, and a significant advance of the frontier of settlement. The consequences of exploitation worried the Native Americans. A convoy of gold seekers in canoes was destroyed by the Paiaguá on the River Paraguay in 1725 and another was mauled the following year. The Paiaguá fired their bows more rapidly than the Portuguese their muskets, and they also made masterly use of their canoes, not least by leaping into the water and tipping them up to protect themselves from musket fire. In 1730, the annual Portuguese flotilla carrying gold was ambushed and mostly destroyed on the way back from Cuiabá, the major settlement in the region of Mato Grosso in south-west Brazil. Punitive expeditions achieved little in 1730 and 1731, but, in 1734, the combination of surprise attack and firepower devastated the Paiaguá. Although the Paiaguá mounted successful attacks in 1735 and 1736, their casualties led to a slackening of activity, and they were also affected by disease and by the attacks from the Guaicurú people.[19]

In the Yucatán, in modern Mexico, where the Itza Mayas had been overcome in 1697, there was a major revolt in 1746, and the thick forests limited Spanish control. The Spaniards were helped by the rapid decline of the Itza under the pressures of Spanish seizures of food and terrible epidemics, probably influenza and, later, smallpox. The Spaniards were able to impose a measure of control thanks to moving the population into towns, and to the impact of proselytisation by Christian missions. Those who evaded control lived in isolated forest areas, but were no longer able to challenge Spanish dominance.[20]

Native resistance greatly restricted European activity in North America. Guerrilla warfare by the Abenaki in Dummer's War (1722–7) kept British settlers out of Vermont. On the Mississippi, upstream from New Orleans, the Natchez initially accepted French trade and expansion, and the French were able to establish a fortified trading base at Fort Rosalie (Natchez) in 1716. However, in 1729, a French land fraud led to a Natchez attack in which Fort Rosalie was destroyed and more than 200 settlers killed. Nevertheless, the Natchez did not receive the support of other tribes, and in 1731 were crushed by the French and the Choctaw in a campaign of systematic extermination. The French began a practice of burning prisoners alive.[21] The uprising showed the weakness of the colony of Louisiana, as it had been necessary to call in troops from France, but also the strength of an imperial system that could do so.

The war with the Natchez led to a spread of French commitments. Having been driven back by the Natchez in an attempt to reach the Arkansas country in 1731, the French established a garrison at Arkansas Post in 1732 in order to keep an eye on the Chickasaw. Demonstrating the interweaving of Native with European rivalries, the remnants of the Natchez had taken refuge with the Chickasaw, who were both rivals of the pro-French Choctaw and, partly as a result, traded with the British and looked to their assistance. Chickasaw independence concerned the French, who, in 1736, launched attacks from Canada and Louisiana. Both were ambushed and defeated, and French captives were burnt to death. However, in 1739, a larger French force was sent and the intimidated Chickasaw agreed to a truce.[22]

Further west, the Spanish expedition against the Apache in 1732 was hindered by the lack of fixed points to attack. Moreover, punitive expeditions were, at best, of limited and short-term value. These expeditions were dependent anyway on Native support. Much activity was defensive, with the expansion of the presidial system in the province of Sonora designed to protect northern Mexico from raiding both by Apache and by Hokan-speaking nomads from the desert coast of the Gulf of California.[23]

The colonial powers, however, were more concerned by their relations with each other. Worried about the new British colony of Georgia, where the fortifications of the main base, Savannah, were designed to resist Spanish attack, Spain improved the fortifications of its major position in neighbouring Florida, St Augustine, which successfully resisted a British siege in 1740. This siege saw British forces supported by Native allies. Meanwhile, Britain and France used trade and the supply of weapons in a competition for influence over Natives between the Appalachians and the Great Lakes.

In 1741, a larger-scale British attack on a more significant position, Cartagena (in modern Colombia), also failed. This was a testimony not only to British operational deficiencies but also to the revival in Spanish military strength from the 1710s.[24]

Europe

The primacy of politics in strategy was amply demonstrated in the War of the Polish Succession (1733–5). The war started when Russia successfully invaded Poland in order to prevent Stanislaus Lesczczynski becoming king. This step was taken because of Russian concern that a hostile Poland might seek to revise territorial losses to Russia in the seventeenth century and might co-operate with Sweden and Turkey in opposing Russia. Intervention led to Russia's protégé, the Elector of Saxony, becoming king. France was able to do little to affect the struggle in Poland, and a small French expeditionary force that sought to relieve besieged Gdansk in 1734 was defeated. Instead, allied to Spain and Sardinia (Savoy-Piedmont), France attacked Russia's ally Austria, which had not intervened in Poland. However, France signed a neutrality agreement for the Austrian Netherlands (Belgium) and decided not to exploit a successful advance down the Moselle Valley in 1734 because it did not wish to bring neutral powers, especially Britain and the Dutch, into the war on the Austrian side.

The variety of warfare was displayed during the conflict. Decisive campaigns, such as the Franco-Sardinian invasion of Austrian-ruled Milan in 1733, the Russian invasion of Poland the same year, and the Spanish invasion of southern Italy in 1734, all of which were successful, contrasted with those in which only limited advances were made, such as the campaigns in the Rhineland in 1733, 1734 and 1735, and near the major fortress of Mantua in 1735, in all of which Austria and France competed.

Decisive battles, such as the Spanish defeat of the Austrians at Bitonto in 1734, which left Spain supreme in southern Italy, contrasted with others where there were no sweeping triumphs or results, such as the engagements between France and Austria later in 1734 at Parma and Guastalla in northern Italy. Battles proved more important than sieges in Poland and Italy, although sieges could be central to campaigns, notably those by the French in the Rhineland in 1733 and 1734, at Kehl and Philippsburg respectively, and in northern Italy in 1735. In the last case, the Austrian ability to hold Mantua denied the French the appearance of success.

Fighting the Turks

The problems of establishing a hierarchy of military proficiency are amply demonstrated in the case of Austria as she suffered more at the hands of the Turks than of France in the 1730s, without that meaning therefore that Turkey was somehow more militarily advanced than France. Deprived of Persian assistance against the Turks, Russia devoted great attention to ensuring that Austria, their ally since 1726, entered the war with the Turks. However, the Austrians urged restraint, and Russia fought the 1736 campaign alone. Azov was besieged and captured on 19 June by the Don Army under Lacy, while the earthworks that barred the isthmus of Perekop at the entrance to the Crimea were stormed by the Dnieper Army. After a bombardment, General Burkhard Münnich, the German-born head of the Russian War Ministry, ordered a night attack on 20–1 May, in columns, against the western section of the lines. The Russians then invaded the Crimea, occupying the towns and burning down the palace of the khans; but, repeating the methods used in the 1680s, the Crimean Tatars avoided battle and the Russians retreated, greatly debilitated by disease (especially the plague) and heat. Russian control, however, was retained over the newly-captured fortress of Kinburn, further west at the mouth of the Dnieper river.

Fearing that neutrality would lead to the loss of their only major ally, Austria promised to enter the war, but Venice and Augustus III of Saxony-Poland refused to help revive the Holy Alliance of the 1680s and 1690s, while, to the concern of the Austrians, Russian ambitions had expanded to include the bringing of Moldavia and Wallachia (modern eastern and southern Romania) under Russian protection. Although Münnich took the major fortress of Ochakov on the River Bug on 2 August 1737, logistical problems, disease and Tatar scorched-earth practices hindered both this campaign and the 1738 attempt to invade Moldavia and Wallachia. Time and manpower were lost. Plague hit Münnich's army hard, and the Turks were able to recapture Ochakov and Kinburn. However, Lacy invaded the Crimea, defeating the Tatars in June 1738 and devastating the region. His army included Kalmyks from Central Asia, an instance of the willingness of steppe peoples to fight in the armies of major states.

In 1739, the Russians were far more successful and had a far more victorious campaign than the Austrians. Under Münnich, their main field army crossed the River Dniester, defeated the Turks at Stavuchankh, took the major fortress of Chotin and seized Jassy (Iasi), the capital of Moldavia. This success prefigured those of Russian armies under Rumiantsev against the Turks in 1770 and 1774.

However, the Austrians had followed their unsatisfactory campaign of 1737, in which they were beaten at Banja Luka, and their unsuccessful one of 1738, with a disastrous one in 1739. A failure of nerve among the commanders (similar to what would affect the Chinese in Burma in 1769) after the battle of Groczka on 22 July, when the Turks had fought well, left the Turks able to besiege Belgrade and denied it relief. The Austrians suffered from the lack of a good commander and from the losses in troops, horses, cannon and territories in the War of the Polish Succession (1733–5). Moreover, despite the armistice in 1735, the peace ending the War of the Polish Succession followed only in 1738, and Austria had to retain forces to protect the relevant frontiers, notably because Philip V of Spain wanted to fight on. Overawed by the apparent strength of the besieging army, the weak Austrian negotiator accepted peace, ceding Belgrade, northern Serbia, and Little (Western) Wallachia. Signed on 18 September, the Peace of Belgrade ignored the continuing resistance of the city.

Against Münnich's advice, Russia, now isolated and concerned that France, which had sent a naval squadron into the Baltic in 1738, would persuade Sweden to attack, accepted peace with Turkey at the end of 1739. However, unresolved articles, including the titles by which the Sultan and Tsar would be addressed, as well as the exchange of slaves, border demarcation and the status of Azov, were not resolved until May 1741, and the treaty was not ratified until that September. Russia returned most of its conquests, but gained Azov, which was to remain unfortified, and some of the steppe. However, Russia still lacked a coastline on the Black Sea and was not allowed to have a fleet on the Black Sea or the Sea of Azov.

Conclusions

It is not immediately clear why military history should discuss, for 1733, the French capture of the fortress of Kehl, the sole gain of their Rhineland advance that year (which anyway would be returned in the peace), rather than the major battle the same year at Buleleng, thanks to which Gusti Agung Alěnogkajěng maintained his hegemony on the island of Bali in modern Indonesia. More generally, the conflicts of the 1720s and 1730s indicated the continued importance of the struggle between empires and their allegedly less 'developed' opponents, specifically the conflict with steppe peoples; and also suggested that the West was far from setting the agenda. Austria's defeat by Turkey excited Western attention, but the Russian failure in Persia was also indicative of the degree to which the West was scarcely in control. Earlier, short-term Russian success in Persia had owed more to Persian weakness in the 1720s, in the face of Afghan invasion followed by Ottoman attack, than to Russian capability, and, subsequently, the Russians felt unable to maintain their position.

The diffusion of Western weaponry and techniques, however, indicated a direction of influence to at least part of the non-Western world, and this diffusion was true of Turkey as well as Madagascar. Renegade Westerners played a major role in encouraging Turkish interest in emulation. Ibraham Müteferrika, a Hungarian renegade who founded a Turkish printing press, argued in his publications of the 1730s, including his *Usul ul-Hikam fi Nizam al-Umam* (1731), for major changes in Turkish military organisation, better training and discipline, geometric troop formations, volley fire, and improved co-operation between infantry and cavalry, in emulation of the military reforms of Peter the Great. Also in the 1730s, a French noble, Comte Claude-Alexandre de Bonneval, sought to develop a modern artillery service and corps of bombardiers in Turkey, only to be thwarted by *janissary* and political opposition.

It would, however, be mistaken to argue that Turkish success against Austria in 1739 was due to the borrowing of Western techniques. Instead, although significant in the long term, these techniques were not inherently superior, especially in the short term. There was also Islamic opposition to the importing and copying of Western ideas and technology, although this opposition was not a simple case of religious 'backwardness'. Furthermore, more general questions of warmaking, including sound strategy, appropriate operational methods, and the successful application of resources, remained more significant than this borrowing, or even the respective quality of combatants' weaponry as a whole.

4 1740–1760

The Seven Years' War (1756–63), known in the USA as the French and Indian War (1754–63), dominates conventional accounts, with the central narratives being 'the miracle of Prussia' – Frederick the Great's ability to fight off a stronger coalition, and the conquest by his ally Britain of French Canada, which centred on Québec.[1] These achievements were important, but the presentation of the conflict as the first world war, while capturing the range of the fighting, both underplays earlier instances of wide-ranging warfare between European maritime powers, notably Spain and the Dutch in the seventeenth century, and also fails to deal with the autonomy and importance of major wars across much of Central and South Asia in the mid-eighteenth century. These conflicts were not linked to this supposed first world war.

As the theme of empires is indeed significant, the major focus, for this period, could be on the establishment of imperial power in continental hinterlands, notably the Chinese in Xinjiang as well as the British in North America. Simultaneously, there was imperial weakness, especially the end of Nadir Shah's empire in Persia and the growing collapse of Mughal rule in India. In comparison, the short-term significance of Prussian success is less apparent.

The end of the Zunghars

The personal determination of the Qianlong emperor (r. 1736–96) was crucial to the defeat of the Zunghars. Greatly concerned about his image, he wanted to surpass the achievement of his grandfather, the Kangxi emperor, by ending the frontier problem. The Qianlong emperor also brought the Manchu military system to its apogee. The Manchu conquest of Ming China in the mid-seventeenth century had infused the Chinese military with a new dynamic and a greater ability to operate successfully in the steppe. Cavalry played a larger role in an army that, in effect, was a Manchu–Chinese hybrid. The Ming, in contrast, lacked adequate cavalry because there was a shortage of cavalry horses in China and they were unable to obtain them in sufficient numbers from the steppe.

The crucial factor in Chinese military capability was not weaponry but the ability to deliver considerable power at a great distance. This situation matched that within the Western world where organisational developments, range and capability were more important than military technology, and in terms of both absolute and relative power. Western weaponry was better than that of China. Chinese soldiers were frequently armed with muskets, but these were poor matchlocks. The Chinese had not made the transition to flintlocks, while their gunpowder was low-grade. Partly as a result, the Chinese continued to use bows, notably as mounted archers, as well as swords, spears, pikes, halberds and spears. They had cannon, but not field artillery. Given the role of China in developing gunpowder, this situation might appear surprising, but the Chinese had not felt a need comparable to that of Western powers to focus on firearms.

Before fighting the Zunghars anew, the Chinese intervened in Tibet where Pholhane, who had died in 1747, was succeeded by his unstable second son, Gyurme Namgyal. He was soon distrusted both by the Qianlong emperor and by his local agents, the *ambans*, not least because Gyurme Namgyal reportedly sought Zunghar support, thus reviving the geopolitical anxiety seen earlier in the century. The *ambans* killed him, only for a popular rising to lead to their death. In response, the Emperor sent an army to Lhasa where the ringleaders of the rising were executed. Rather than appointing new *ambans*, the Emperor had the Dalai Lama become head of the Tibetan government. Tibet was left as autonomous although with a reinforced Chinese garrison.[2] This outcome proved reasonably stable.

No such compromise solution was offered further north. Combined with serious divisions and smallpox among the Zunghars, Chinese military capability led to total victory over them in the 1750s, a result that had certainly not seemed inevitable, or even likely, in the early 1740s. The nature and calibre of the political leadership proved a key element in the eventual military outcome. The death of Galdan Tsering, the Zunghar leader, in 1745 had been followed by a political breakdown linked to a lack of effective leadership. His son, Dorji Namgyal (r. 1745–50), was deposed and blinded in a rebellion by leading Zunghars, while his successor, Darja (r. 1750–3), faced a revolt by his troops and was killed as a result. A new, energetic leader, Dawaci (r. 1753–5), who had been defeated by Darja in 1751, then drove out his own former ally, Amursana, a Khoit prince who had helped him gain power. The relatively loose nature of the Zunghar confederation ensured that these rivalries were far more serious than the differences on the Chinese side. Civil wars destroyed Zunghar unity, just as they were also to weaken the Marathas, in the latter case also to the benefit of an outside power, Britain.

The defeated Amursana turned to the Chinese in 1754, and the government was divided about whether to use the opportunity in order to destroy the Zunghars, which was Qianlong's choice, or whether to be more cautious, which was the view of most courtiers. As in the 1690s, the view of the Emperor prevailed. Despite the differing scale of the states, Prussia under Frederick the Great and China under the Qianlong emperor were very much personal monarchies when it came to the decision for war, although unlike the Kangxi emperor and Frederick, the Qianlong emperor did not command in the field.

In the event, a major offensive was prepared for 1755, one that was greater in scale than those in the 1690s. Two advances, each with 25,000 troops, were launched in March 1755, the Northern Route army advancing into Xinjiang from the north-east via Outer Mongolia, and the West Route army from Gansu, further south, which moved forward via Hami. Dawaci, a drunkard, was defeated and captured at the Ili river in a night attack on 2 July 1755, an unexpectedly quick success.

However, Amursana, who had initially helped the Chinese, rebelled in August 1755, as he felt that their new arrangements left him little scope. Pan-ti, the Manchu marshal who had commanded the invasion in 1755, was surrounded by Amursana's forces later that year and committed suicide; a response to failure and an alternative to surrender, both of which were humiliations. In 1756, moreover, some of the Khalka Mongols launched a supporting rebellion.

The situation was saved by Zhaohui who held on in the oasis of Urumchi over the winter of 1756–7 until reinforcements from the garrison-town of Barkol could arrive. In 1757, the Chinese forces advanced anew and Amursana fled into Russia, dying there of smallpox in September. The Russians had refused to provide help to Amursana, just as they had earlier turned down Dawaci. There was a mass slaughter of Zunghars that year as well as devastating smallpox. The fragile nature of their Zunghar confederation had contributed to its failure, as Chinese success led to defections by subordinate tribes: there was no longer confidence in the ability of the confederation to produce spoils or tribute. Instead, many tribes switched to being tributaries of the Manchu.[3]

China had solved the logistical problems central in managing steppe warfare[4], which was considered the supreme strategic threat by all Chinese dynasties. In the 1750s, the Chinese established two chains of magazine posts along the main roads on which they advanced. Supplies were transported for thousands of miles, and the Mongolian homelands controlled by their eastern Mongol allies provided the horses and fodder. These improvements in logistics – due partly to a desire to keep the troops from alienating the populace and partly to the latter's very lack of food – ensured that the Chinese armies did not disintegrate as Napoleon's did in 1812 when he encountered serious problems in invading Russia despite advancing over a shorter distance. Comparisons are difficult, not least because Napoleon faced greater resistance than the Manchu armies had done in 1755, but the contrast in the supply situation was very important.

In order to wage war with the Zunghars, there was a massive transfer of resources from eastern to western China. As with other instances of Chinese warmaking, this capacity reflected both administrative capability and the extensive resources of well-developed mercantile networks. Alongside the capability of the government system, however, it was also affected by limitations, including the leakage of tax revenue to officials and the extent of illegal tax farming.[5] This situation, nevertheless, also helped in drawing on non-governmental resources. More generally, for both financial and organisational reasons, the extent of commercialisation and market integration in the Chinese economy was important.[6] Economic strength and logistical capability had foci and links in the stability and range of entrepreneurial networks, and in the relative effectiveness of state finances,[7] conspicuously in comparison with all other major Asian states. The significance of financial networks can also be seen with attempts in the West to hinder those of Western opponents.[8]

The application to military purposes of the great demographic and agricultural expansion of China during the century was also seen, at a smaller scale, in Western warmaking. More specifically, just as the expansion of arable farming in Ukraine and Hungary served as a basis for enhancing and sustaining Russian and Austrian operations against the Turks (without, however, guaranteeing success), so the Chinese benefited from the extension of arable farming in Gansu.[9]

Having conquered Xinjiang, the Chinese pressed on to advance into eastern Turkestan. This had rebelled against the Zunghars in 1753–4, in part as a Muslim rejection of their rule, only to be captured in 1755 by the Afaqi Makhdumzadas led by the Great and the Little Khojas. In 1758, the Chinese under Chao Huei invaded. Success was initially limited as the towns of Kashgar and Yarkand held out, but, in 1759, reinforcements helped lead to their fall. The Khojas took refuge in the region of Badakhshan in northeast Afghanistan, but the ruler yielded to Chinese pressure and executed them. Subsequently, the Chinese encountered renewed problems in eastern Turkestan. A Muslim rising in 1765 was to be suppressed and tens of thousands of people were then deported.[10]

The establishment in the new conquests, especially the Ili valley south of Lake Balkhash, of a large number of colonists, many enforced, led to a marked increase in agricultural production there, supporting the Chinese military presence. Moreover, there was a change in the type of agriculture and society, with the Chinese shifting the focus from animal husbandry to cultivation.[11]

Less prominent was the struggle to suppress the Tibetan minority of western Sichuan, who were known as the Gyalrong or Golden Stream tribes and have also been called Jinchuan. They referred to themselves as the people of Kham and were a Tibetan community. The First Jinchuan War broke out in 1747 as the Emperor sought to bring an essentially autonomous people under administrative control. Religious animosity played a role, as the Golden Stream followed the indigenous, animist, Tibetan Bon religion and Tibetan Buddhism's Red Hat sect, resisting the Yellow Hat sect which the Emperor supported. In part, the conflict therefore involved a struggle between different types of prestige, magic and providential support, an element that was more generally true in East Asia as leaders were sacral figures.[12] Similarly, as Caliph, the Turkish Sultan was a sacral figure, while Nadir Shah's religious ambitions played a role in his conflict with the Turks and helped encourage opposition to him in Persia.

Success in the difficult mountainous terrain of Sichuan, where the Golden Stream had strong, well-sited stone fortresses, proved limited for the Chinese. It proved very costly and time-consuming to take the towers, but bypassing them led to a vulnerability to attacks on Chinese supply lines. In 1747, Andreas Ly, a Chinese Catholic priest in Sichuan, noted the report that the war was 'being fought with tremendous difficulty because of the mountainous terrain of that region', while on 2 February 1748, he wrote:

> I heard of a terrible massacre of many in the Chinese army sent against the barbarians, in which very many officers and men were killed by the barbarians. While the campaign lasted, some were cut to pieces by the barbarians, or maimed by cold and hunger; others dashed themselves to pieces off the cliffs, unable to bear the onslaught of the enemy; a great many officers of the ravaged army hanged themselves because of the destruction of the army. Troops have been summoned from various provinces and new soldiers enrolled that they might take the place of the dead; the Chinese people openly groan over the increased burden.[13]

The failure of the first major Chinese campaign, the expensive campaign of 1748, resulted in the disgrace of Necin, the chief grand councillor since 1737. He was put on trial and sentenced to death. Necin's replacement, another Manchu, Fuheng, was ordered by Qianlong to bring the costly war to a close. Over 200,000 troops were deployed and over seven million taels of silver were spent, mostly on hiring military labourers to transport supplies.[14]

Yue Zhongqi, a general with local knowledge, was able to persuade the Golden Stream leader, a former subordinate, to settle the conflict, which ended inconclusively in 1749. Qianlong had ordered that Necin be executed in front of the forces involved in the war, but, as the conflict ended before that could happen, Necin was instructed to commit suicide. The credit for ending the war was given to Fuheng who soon became chief grand councillor.[15] The Chinese were to have to campaign anew in Sichuan in the 1770s (see p. 110).

South-West Asia

The Persian-based empire of Nadir Shah collapsed before that of the Zunghars, although for different reasons. Having returned from India, Nadir was the Napoleon of Southern Asia, a usurper who had risen from humble beginnings to be a force able to press on neighbouring empires and thus to affect wider currents of power. On a small-scale map of the world, his achievements may not seem so great, but he campaigned over a vast area, from Delhi to Baghdad, Khiva to Muscat, Daghestan to Kashmir. Having dealt with his north-eastern frontier in 1740, Nadir campaigned against the rebellious Lezges in Daghestan in the eastern Caucasus mountains in 1741 with less success because they relied on guerrilla operations rather than battle. Nadir also had supply problems. Usually he planned logistics carefully to avoid his men running short, but on this occasion the Russians, seeing him dangerously close to their own outposts south of Astrakhan on the lower Volga, withheld much-needed supplies of food and clothing, and prevented others from carrying them across the Caspian Sea. In the event, the rebellion was not quelled.

War resumed in 1742 to deal with a renewed threat from the Turks. Nadir had bold religious and political ambitions, notably a wish to resolve the schism within Islam and to integrate Shi'ism into Sunn'ism. In 1743, Nadir invaded Turkish-held Iraq, allegedly with a main army of about 200,000 troops, capturing the city of Kirkuk, but being repelled from Mosul and Baghdad, the major Turkish bases. Despite the establishment of a major siege train, siegecraft was a capability in which Nadir's army was deficient, and storming attempts on Mosul failed. Alongside the use of troops from the *janissary* garrison at Aleppo in northern Syria, the sultan relied on local forces under the control of Husayn al-Jalili Pasha, and the latter's network of alliances produced the necessary resources.[16]

However, in 1744, Nadir put down the widespread rebellions that the heavy forced contributions for his warfare had provoked. Nadir then focused anew on the Turks, defeating them at Baghavard near Yerevan in

1745, by using his reserves to attack the Turkish flank. The Turks retreated to their fortified camp where the troops mutinied, killing their commander, before retreating. Nadir also overran Turkish-ruled Armenia that year, a success that challenged the Turkish position in eastern Anatolia. This Persian success led the Turks to new talks, just as the Persian challenge had helped lead in 1745 to the renewal of the Turkish treaty with Austria. The irrelevance of an account of developments in this period focused on Western expansion emerges clearly.

The debilitating Turkish–Persian struggle ended in 1746 when the 1639 Treaty of Zuhab was essentially revived, with Nadir recognised as ruler of Persia. Yet, like Napoleon, Nadir's continual wars and heavy taxation (which was enforced with torture and slaughter) placed a terrible burden on his subjects and encouraged repeated opposition.[17] Nadir's brutal repression of successive rebellions, notably by mass executions, did not end the opposition.

Again like that of Napoleon, Nadir's empire proved ephemeral. His attempt to fuse Turkic tribal groups with the Persians created tensions, and, if the Manchu success in a comparable task indicated that it was not impossible, the Kangxi emperor had faced the serious Revolt of the Three Feudatories in the 1670s. The empire split apart after Nadir was assassinated in June 1747 by Persian officers both concerned about his favour towards Afghans and Uzbeks and linked to his rebellious nephew, Ali Qoli.

Nadir's Afsharid dynasty continued, although much weakened. Ali Qoli seized power as Adel Shah and then dispatched troops to Nadir's strongpoint at Kalat-e Naderi in Khurasan (north-eastern Persia) where all bar one of Nadir's sons and grandsons were slaughtered, a process of dynastic consolidation taken further by cutting open the bellies of pregnant members of the harem. Adel Shah was swiftly deposed by his brother Ebrahim, but the latter lost control of most of Persia. Instead, it was soon dominated by two tribes, the Zand under Karim Khan and the Bakhtiari under Ali Mardan Khan. Karim Khan proved the more adroit, killing Ali Mardan Khan in 1754.

The divisions in the empire resulted in sustained conflict, with battles, such as at Chamchamal in 1754 and Urmiya in 1757, in which betrayal was as important as military tactics. The eastern part of the empire, most of modern Afghanistan, was taken over by Ahmad Khan Abdali, formerly a cavalry commander under Nadir Shah, and a Pashtun tribal chief who founded the Durrani dynasty. Ahmad Khan Abdali, who assumed the title Ahmad Shah, had a client buffer state in Khurasan, based in Mashhad, that was ruled, for most of the second half of the century, by Nadir's surviving grandson, Shahrokh. Another tribal commander under Nadir, Erekle from Georgia, returned there and founded an independent kingdom.

Despite the problems of Persia, there was no resumption of Turkish expansion. This reflected not only the Persian resilience against the Turks seen from the 1720s to 1746, but also the problems of campaigning so far east. Baghdad was 1,334 miles from Constantinople, compared with Belgrade's 587,[18] and there was no sea and river route to Iraq comparable to the Black Sea and the Danube and Dniester rivers to ease campaigning and logistics. Moreover, the recent campaigning had imposed a serious financial burden on the Turkish state, while the 1730 _janissary_ revolt that led to the overthrow of Ahmed III reflected strains linked to the war. There were also the longstanding problems for the Sunni Turks caused by Shi'ite heterodoxy in Anatolia, as well as the preference for fighting Christians as opposed to fellow Muslims even if the latter were heretics. Russian expansionism also posed a challenge to the Turks that the divided Persians no longer did.

Meanwhile, the Turks were to be challenged, notably in their prestige as guardians of the Muslim holy cities, as a result of the developments in Arabia. In 1745, Muhammad bin Saud (r. 1725–65), the ruler of Dar'iya in the remote Arabian area of Nejd, gave shelter and promised protection to the fundamentalist Sheikh Muhammad bin Abdul-Wahhab. Their compact led to the establishment of a theocratic state in Nejd that showed deep intolerance of Shi'a and Sufi Muslims, and great capacity for expansion. The context was different, but there were similarities with Afghan expansion. In the case of Arabia, religion was to the fore, as the compact provided the Al-Sauds with a sanction that gave the status of a _jihad_ to their campaigning. In turn, the Sheikh gained new followers.

The Turks were also challenged by tribal opponents elsewhere. Rebellions of Arab and Kurdish tribes in Iraq in the 1730s and 1740s threatened Basra, the major Turkish base in southern Iraq, in 1741, and, as part of a programme of response, in 1753 the Turks attacked the Yezidis of Sinjar whose raids were affecting the caravan routes between Iraq and Syria. There was also an Arab revolt against Persian rule in 1741. These episodes can be seen as instances of a more general tribal breakout in 1720–60, especially by Afghan, Persian, Turcomen and Arab tribes, in which neighbouring states were invaded and the importance of tribal cavalry in the wider region increased.[19]

The military challenges facing the Turks in the 1750s, however, did not match those encountered in the 1730s and early 1740s, notably because there was no resumption of conflict with Persia, Russia and Austria. Moreover, it seems likely that the Turks' major success over Austria in 1739 encouraged a sense that military reform was not required. Nor were military supply networks maintained at a level adequate to permit an easy resumption of wartime activity.[20]

At the same time, there was an important development in policy, with an emphasis on maintaining peace. In particular, there was no attempt to intervene against Austria and Russia in the Seven Years' War (1756–63) as Frederick the Great would have liked, because such intervention would have lessened the pressure on Prussia. As a result, the pacific Koca Mehmed Ragib Pasha, *Reis* (Foreign Minister) and Grand Vizier for much of the period 1741–63, was a significant figure in the military history of the period. In 1764–5, moreover, Turkey refused to respond forcibly to Russian intervention in Poland as France would have liked.

India

Ahmad Khan Abdali, the founder of the Durrani empire based in Afghanistan (r. 1747–73), where its capital was at Kandahar, benefited from the role of the interior of Asia in providing effective cavalry horses as well as from his training in war under Nadir Shah.[21] Moreover, the Durranis used cavalry armed with flintlocks, joining gunpowder firepower to the fluid tactics associated with Central Asian horse archers.[22] These tactics and weapons were to be emulated by Indian rulers, notably in northern India. The death of Nadir Shah was followed by the Afghans breaking away from Persia, and the tribal chiefs chose Ahmad Khan as ruler. The chief of the Sadozai clan of the Abdali tribe, he had led the Afghan forces in Nadir's army. He assumed the title Ahmad Shah, and then moved against the Persian garrisons in Afghanistan. The Governor of Kabul, where there was a considerable garrison, attempted to defy him, but, lacking allies, he abandoned his attempt and Kabul, followed by Ghazni and Peshawar, fell without significant opposition. The promise to treat the Persians the same as the Afghans proved effective.

Aggressive warfare became a major theme of the new reign. In order to ensure support and stability, Ahmad Shah sought to gain plunder for the Afghans and to find them occupation. As his expeditions produced much loot, they were seldom opposed by the Afghans. Moreover, these benefits helped the position of the tribal chiefs who provided Ahmad Shah with contingents for his army.

Repeating the Mughal axis of advance in the early sixteenth century, Ahmad Shah repeatedly and successfully attacked north-west India, a far more fertile and prosperous region than Afghanistan or its other neighbours. He first invaded the Punjab in 1748, leading 30,000 cavalry across the Indus river in a quest for plunder and food. The Mughal governor offered only weak resistance and his army retreated in disorder. This led the Mughal Crown Prince, also Ahmad Shah, to advance with a powerful army, accompanied by Wazir Qumaruddin. Seriously ill, the Emperor, Muhammad Shah, remained in Delhi.

Near the village of Manupur on 11 March 1748, the Afghan Ahmad Shah, with 12,000 troops, was opposed by about 60,000 men in the Mughal army as well as a much more powerful artillery. The initial Afghan cavalry attack lost heavily to the fire of the Mughal cannon, although the use of about 200 swivel guns helped the Afghans overcome the Rajputs on the Mughal left. Firepower was more generally significant in the battle with a force of about 1,700 musketeers in the Mughal army under Safdar Jang, Nawab of Oudh, helping to weaken the Afghans before a general Mughal advance drove them back. Ahmad Shah, however, retreated successfully, returning to Kandahar where he suppressed a rebellion, executing the leaders.

When the Afghans under Ahmad Shah invaded anew in 1749, Muhammad Shah was dead and his inexperienced successor, Ahmad (r. 1748–54), proved ineffective. The Afghans captured Lahore anew in 1749. After indecisive skirmishing in 1750, the Mughal emperor promised the Afghan leader fourteen lakhs of rupees, a sum equivalent to the annual surplus of the four districts that Muhammad had assigned to Nadir Shah in 1739, in return for an end to hostilities. Thus, the Afghans had won the position gained by the latter, a prestigious as well as a practical achievement.

Like Nadir Shah, Ahmad Shah of Afghanistan had commitments on a number of fronts. In 1750, he turned west against Nadir's grandson, Shahrokh. The city of Herat was successfully besieged and, at Turbat-i-Shaykh-Jan, Khurusan cavalry under Mir Alam of Seistan was defeated by the Afghans. Ahmad Shah then besieged and took Mashhad, followed by Nishapur in 1751, before allowing Shahrokh to regain control of Khurusan in return for money and an acceptance of subordination.

The following year, Ahmad sent an army north into northern Afghanistan where it secured the submission of the regions of Balkh and Badakhshan. Meanwhile, as the Mughals had not paid the money agreed in 1750, Ahmad invaded the Punjab anew in December 1751. He outmanoeuvred the Mughal army north of Lahore, advancing to threaten the city so that the army fell back to protect it. After a four-month siege, Lahore, receiving no reinforcements, surrendered. The Emperor then ceded Punjab and Multan. Ahmad also gained control of Kashmir in 1752.

These were Afghan gains from the Mughal world at least as important as the British gains elsewhere in India, and arguably far more important because they were closer to the traditional centres of Mughal power. This power had already been gravely weakened. In response to Nadir Shah's victory at Karnal in 1739, an attempt had been made by the Mughals to raise a new imperial central army, but, in 1743, this was abandoned due to financial problems, and by 1748 the empire was totally bankrupt.[23] The collapse of Mughal power was followed by the creation of a new political and social order in which the rulers of successor states across India were matched by other important individuals, including large landholders, service gentry and prominent members of mercantile groups. In combination, these provided the patronage and protection that kept both society and the economy functioning.[24] In turn, these rulers and other individuals sought protection in the midst of the instability of the period.

In particular, Maratha expansion continued to put pressure on other Indian rulers. In the Carnatic (south-east India), the Maratha invasion of 1740 had been taken further in 1741 with the capture of the fortress of Trichinopoly and an advance further south into Madura. The Mughals were in no position to stop this, and, instead, the Nizam marched south from Hyderabad in 1743, capturing both Arcot and Trichinopoly, appointing a new Nawab, and pressing on to drive the Marathas from Madura.

Rivalry between the British and French came in the 1740s to play a role in the complex regional power politics of the competing Indian powers in the Carnatic. On 1 August 1749, the Nawab of the Carnatic, Anwar-ud-dīn, was defeated and killed at Ambur by a challenger, Chanda Sahib, who was supported by Joseph-François Dupleix, Governor of the main French base at Pondicherry. The French provided 400 Europeans and 2,000 native troops they had trained to support the 12,000 men of Chanda Sahib. The following year, the Nizam, Nāsir 'Alī, died in the Carnatic while fighting in support of Anwar-ud-dīn. The new Nizam, Nāsir Jang, rewarded Dupleix for military assistance by granting him extensive territories.

However, despite French support, Chanda Sahib was unable to subdue Muhammad 'Ali, the son of Anwar-ud-dīn and the claimant to the Carnatic, who was backed by the British, Mysore and the Marathas, none of which wished to see the Nizam too strong. In 1751, Robert Clive of the English East India Company surprised and captured the Carnatic capital, Arcot, and then held off a siege by Chanda Sahib, after which, in June 1752, the British drove, first, the French, and then, Chanda Sahib to surrender. Both Chanda Sahib and the French suffered from an inability to finance their armies, and this problem, which was symptomatic of Indian powers as a whole, ensured that much campaigning became an attempt to collect tribute.[25]

The Maratha role in the Carnatic was modest after 1743, but, elsewhere, there was significant expansion. In 1743, Raghūjī Bhonsle, a Maratha leader, established himself at Nagpur in central India, from where he expanded east with repeated raids from 1745, being ceded the revenues of part of the region of Orissa in 1751 by Alivardi Khan, Nawab of Bengal, who had fought him repeatedly in the 1740s. Moreover, the Nizam and Dupleix had attacked the Marathas, but found it difficult to obtain any lasting victory, while the lengthy campaign exhausted the Nizam's finances. In 1752, by the Treaty of Bhalki, the Nizam ceded the territories of West Berar, Khandesh and Baglana to the Marathas, following in 1760, after heavy defeat at Ugdir on 2–3 February, by ceding Bijapur. At the scale of Europe, these were substantial territories.

In western India, having taken a share in Gujarat in 1752, the Marathas ended Mughal authority there in 1757. The previous year, with French support, the Marathas had defeated the Nawab of Savanur (east of Goa) and annexed most of his territory. Maratha pressure also led to cessions further north, including Ajmer in 1756 from Bijay Singh of Marwar, whose forces were defeated in 1754 and 1755, and the Lower Doab in 1758 by the Mughals. In 1754, a Maratha army had occupied Delhi and taken a role in the coup that led to the overthrow of the Mughal emperor, Ahmad Shah, by his chief minister, Imad-ul-Mulk. The latter manipulated the new Emperor he created, Ālamgir II.

The Marathas were pressing north at the same time as the Afghans were moving south-east into northern India. The death in 1753 of the governor of the Punjab (who Ahmad Shah of Afghanistan had left in position) was followed by chaos there, and the Mughals sought to regain control, occupying part of the Punjab. Ahmad Shah of Afghanistan responded in December 1756, crossed the Indus, and seized Lahore, the major city in the Punjab. Mughal requests for help played a role in Maratha moves. At Narela on 16 January 1757 near Delhi, however, a larger Afghan force defeated the Marathas. The Afghans occupied the defenceless Delhi, which was extensively pillaged, deposed the Emperor, Ālamgir II, and stormed the cities of Brindaban, Mathura and Agra. Indeed the Nawab of Bengal, who was to be defeated later that year by Robert Clive at Plassey, felt it necessary to divide his forces to meet a possible Afghan attack.[26]

However, the mass-slaughter of the inhabitants of the stormed cities contributed to an outbreak of cholera that led the Afghans to return home. Ahmad Shah had his son Timur Mirza marry Ālamgir II's daughter, with Punjab and Sind granted as her dowry. Ahmad returned to Afghanistan leaving his son to govern his lands east of the Indus.

In response to Afghan gains, the Marathas in 1758 invaded Punjab where the Sikhs were already in successful rebellion against Afghan rule. The Marathas captured the cities of Lahore, Multan, Attock and Peshawar from Timur Mirza. Ahmad Shah was engaged in tackling a rebellion by Nasir Khan, the ruler of Baluchistan to the south of Afghanistan, a rebellion that was particularly serious because Baluchi cavalry had played a major role in Ahmad Shah's army, notably in the 1750 campaign against Khurusan and the successive invasions of India. Having defeated the Baluchis in 1758, Ahmad Shah besieged their capital, Kalat, but five storming attempts failed. As a result, Ahmad Shah had to negotiate. Alongside a matrimonial alliance with Ahmad Shah, Nasir Khan agreed to acknowledge his overlordship and to provide troops for his army.

Thus strengthened, Ahmad Shah crossed the Indus in August 1759 in order to drive the Marathas back. Lahore was evacuated by the Marathas, but Ahmad Shah pressed on, defeating their forces in late 1759 and early 1760: Dattaji Sindhia was defeated north of Delhi at Thaneswar on 24 December, while Mulhar Rao Holkar was also beaten. This success helped consolidate Ahmad Shah's position in his empire, leading the Amir of Sind to end his rebellion.[27] Meanwhile, in 1759, seeking to consolidate his position and also to weaken the Afghans, Imad-ul-Mulk had the unsuccessful Ālamgir II killed.

The Marathas launched a renewed response to the Afghans in 1760, but the Marathas were without allies, in part because they were seen as a more serious threat than the Afghans by other Indian princes and in part because Ahmad Shah was a more skilful negotiator. Both the Rohillas, enemies of the Marathas and well-armed exponents of volley fire, and the Nawab of Oudh joined the Afghans. In the meantime, there was a longer-term change in the nature of Maratha fighting. Their armies had also grown larger and more professional, but this increased the cost of their operations and reduced their mobility.

British expansion took place in this context. The British and French East India Companies were part of a process of advancing interests and statebuilding in the violent shadow of Mughal decline, through taking over the carrying trade, as well as being directly linked to some of the problems affecting Indian overseas commerce, notably the decline of the major Mughal port of Surat.[28] Intertwined with Indian politics, for example collecting rents due to local rulers and helping subdue recalcitrant companies,[29] the East India Companies were also linked to international interests. Thus, in Bengal from 1757, as earlier in the Carnatic, the British backed their nominee to the Nawabship of Bengal. Victory over the Nawab, Surajah Dowla, at Plassey on 23 June 1757, in many respects, was a British intervention in a struggle for dominance between the Nawab and a key general, Mir Jafar. Major John Corneille wrote of the battle 'the plain seemed covered with their army'. He also noted that Clive's cannon were more effective than the 'large unwieldy pieces' of his opponent.[30] Mir Jafar's desertion, to Clive, was the key event in the battle as it ensured that the Nawab was unable to use his superior numbers. Plassey was not a victory for superior Western tactics or firepower, although Clive's forces were better at protecting their powder during the rainstorm that occurred.

This victory was followed by a major British commitment to Bengal, at the same time that Mir Jafar succeeded the Nawab, who was captured and killed soon after Plassey, therefore making the battle more consequential than as a military engagement. In some respects, the British role was not too different from that of the Marathas intervening east of Delhi from 1751 in support of the state of Oudh against its rival, the Rohilla kingdom.

The British also played a role in south-west India, where Martanda Varma, Rajah of Travancore (r. 1729–58), was supported by the British East India Company in building up an army, defeating local opponents, both aristocrats and opposing rulers. His policies led to conflict with the Dutch, rival traders to the British, and Martanda Varma defeated their forces at Colachen in 1741.

Westerners operated in a region in which the demographic situation was very adverse (unlike in the contact zone in North America), and without any levelling up from disease as there had been for the Spaniards in Mexico against the Aztecs in the early sixteenth century. As a result, hiring local manpower was crucial and, although long used in India by the Portuguese, became more significant from the 1740s.[31] At the same time, the British and French focused on particular military tools and skills, notably flintlock rifles, bayonets, prepared cartridges, cast-iron cannon, and the appropriate tactics. Western-equipped and trained infantry with their lighter muskets could move forward on the battlefield, whereas the muskets of the army of Nadir Shah of Persia were too heavy and therefore useful essentially for firing from a static position.

Improving fortifications was also a Western forte. Indian rulers had made little effort to strengthen them by means of adding bastions and reducing the height of high stone walls, which were vulnerable to cannon, but, concerned to lessen their exposure to attack by each other, Western powers introduced new techniques in India. John Corneille noted in 1754 that when Fort St David in the Carnatic was acquired by the East India Company, it was 'an irregular square fortified according to the Moorish manner, with round towers at the angles', whereas the Company had 'modernised the fortifications with a good bastion at each angle, a hornwork before the gateway, two half-moons in the ditch … and a well-mined glacis'. They were fortifying Madras with 'several excellent good bastions, and a broad, deep, wet ditch', and at Trichinopoly had replaced a reliance on high battlements and round towers by adding bastions.[32]

The specific environmental context of military operations was also relevant to the effectiveness of particular weapons and tactics. British-trained infantry proved more effective in operations on the Carnatic coast, near their base at Madras, and in the marshy Lower Ganges valley, near their base at Calcutta, than they were to be in conflict against the Marathas and Mysore in regions that favoured light cavalry. The latter deficiency was serious as it was necessary to operate beyond the security of coastal bases if the British were to have a chance of supporting, and thus retaining, Indian allies.

Tensions in India were drawn into the broader struggle between Britain and France. Due to local politics, the strength of the British navy, and British battlefield victories, the French were unable to exploit Indian opposition to the British to lasting success. Chandernagore, the French base in Bengal, fell in March 1757 to a bombardment by British warships, and Thomas-Arthur de Lally, the new French commander, arrived in Pondicherry in the Carnatic, the main French base in India, in April 1758 too late to reverse that result. Moreover, Lally's alienation of local rulers harmed the French war effort, and his defeat by the British at Wandiwash, between Madras and Pondicherry, on 22 January 1760 ruined French chances and left their surviving bases vulnerable to attack. By cutting French communications, the British navy ensured that the French were short of money, which made it difficult to sustain operations. Pondicherry surrendered on 16 January 1761, the same month in which the Jacobite John Law of Lauriston, co-operating with the Mughal Emperor, Shah Alam II, son and successor of Ālamgir II, was beaten by the British at Hilsa.

South-East Asia

The Western impact on South-East Asia was far more limited than that in India. Instead, the military and political history of the region was set by developments within the major states. Key in mid-century was the improvement in Burma's fortunes under 'Alaungpaya, which indicated that the causes of revival and success rested primarily not, as is often assumed, on the adoption or adaptation of Western technology and/or organisa-tion, but rather on indigenous causes. Successful leadership was crucial, as seen with such rulers as Rudra Singh, who led the Ahom people in the Brahmaputra valley in 1696–1714, and Gharib Newaz (r. 1714–54), who revi-talised the state of Manipur in north-eastern India in the 1720s and 1730s, mounting raids on Burma from 1724.

'Alaungpaya's Burmese army followed an organisational pattern that was common to many states. A permanent professional force under the central government was supplemented during a war by conscript levies. However, Burmese warmaking was different from that in the West. First, as with the Turkish *janissaries*, the permanent force was hereditary in membership. In Burma, it was also hereditary in leadership and was supported by the provision of state land. Soldiers were obliged to grow their own food, a crucial restraint on their operational independence.

Secondly, the weaponry and tactics were very different. As in Nepal, Sri Lanka and Kerala in south-west India, all forested regions, tactics in Burma involved extensive use of ambushes, ruses and temporary fortifications, especially stockades. Pitched battles were generally avoided. Most fighting was with bludgeon, spear, sword and bow, although firearms also played an important role, notably from the 1750s. The Manipuris commented that their Burmese opponents first employed firearms in 1755. Thereafter, firearms were used by the permanent Burmese force and by some of the levies. The Burmese artillery, however, was less impressive.[33] Thus, there is a parallel with the relative weakness of many Asian powers in artillery, notably the Zunghars and Afghans.

Although they were fighting in a different way from the Afghans and Marathas, Burmese successes also indicated that it was not necessary to use Western-style arms in order to prevail. In the 1740s, a rebellion by the Mons of the region of Pegu in southern Burma had thrown off the rule of the Toungoo (Burmese) dynasty, before going on to conquer its heartland further north around Ava in 1752. The city, in the Irrawaddy valley near Mandalay in central Burma, was stormed, sacked and burnt down that year. Toungoo requests for assistance from China had been unsuccessful.

However, Aung Zeya, a dynamic local leader from north of Ava, who was one of a number of rebels against the Toungoo, established a new dynasty, the Konbaung, in 1752. Calling himself 'Alaungpaya (r. 1752–60), meaning the great lord who will be a Buddha one day, a name rich in religious meaning, he drove the Mons from Ava in December 1753. In response, the Mons sent a large force against Ava in 1754, but its attacks failed and the army fell back.

'Alaungpaya was determined to entrench the new dynasty, expand his territories, and strengthen control over the tribes. In 1756–7, he pressed on to conquer the region of Pegu in hard fighting. 'Alaungpaya benefited from cannon and muskets he had seized in 1756 from stranded French warships. In May 1757, the city of Pegu (north-east of Rangoon) was besieged and then stormed, with a mass slaughter of the population. The city walls were then razed, an outcome that was symbolic as well as practical. Next, 'Alaungpaya successfully invaded the kingdom of Manipur to the north-west of Burma in support of a pretender to the throne. The Manipuris were defeated, the empty capital captured, and 'Alaungpaya returned to Burma, leaving garrisons in new stockaded positions, a characteristic feature of warfare in the region. Prisoners were marched back to provide labour, those who refused to march being slaughtered.

In 1759, 'Alaungpaya invaded the region of Tenasserim to the south of Burma. A search not only for prestige but also for subjects, notably the Mons who had fled, led to a focus on attacking Siam. Disease and the strength of its fortifications, however, thwarted the Burmese siege of the Siamese capital, Ayuthia, in 1760. 'Alaungpaya was wounded by an exploding cannon while commanding the siege and died on the retreat.

East Indies

The Western presence was stronger in the East Indies (mostly now covered by modern Indonesia) than in South-East Asia, but it was still secondary to local powers. In part, this was because the prime Western colonial power in the East Indies was the Dutch East India Company, which lacked the success of its British counterpart. The Dutch had been the most dynamic Western power in the Indian Ocean in the seventeenth century, but the situation was different in the eighteenth. Problems in the Dutch empire interacted with weaknesses at home, while there were also the consequences of the Dutch being superseded as the leading Western naval and colonial power by Britain.

The island of Java was the centre of Dutch political and military power and economic activity, but, although the British did not operate there, the Dutch encountered many difficulties from local powers. Indeed, Dutch effectiveness greatly depended on local allies, for the Dutch forces found it difficult to operate successfully away from the coastal areas, not least (but not only) because of the absence, in this context, of the naval support the Dutch could offer. In 1741, the Dutch were hard-pressed and their coastal headquarters at Sěmarang were besieged by an estimated 23,500 Javanese and local Chinese, supported by thirty cannon, but their position was saved by an agreement with Cakraningrat IV of Madura, whose forces proved crucial to Dutch operations in the interior. But when Pakubuwana II of Mataram reached terms with the Dutch in 1743, a dissatisfied Cakraningrat began a war with them.

As with the British in India, Dutch interventions in the persistent civil wars in the kingdom of Mataram were affected by the always-shifting balance of military and political advantage, and any unexpected pressure could lead to crisis. As a consequence, in the Third Javanese War of Succession (1746–57), the Dutch suffered defeats in 1750 and 1755, while, in the kingdom of Banten in west Java, a rebellion in 1750 led to the defeat of Dutch forces. Linked to these problems, the profits of the Dutch East India Company fell in the 1730s, 1740s and 1750s, ending the earlier programme of long-term expansion.

Dutch attempts to defend, let alone expand, their power elsewhere in the East Indies also faced difficulties, in part because they lacked the strength and position they had in Java. On the island of Sulawesi, a Dutch attempt in 1739–40 to crush the dynamic Arung Singkang, ruler of Wajo, had only limited success: disease and bad weather greatly hindered the Dutch. In India, the Dutch were defeated by Travancore, a relatively minor power, in 1741. In 1759, a Dutch force sent from Java was beaten by the British at Biderra when it unsuccessfully intervened in Bengal.

Russian expansion

In a very different context, Russian expansion in Asia was more successful than that of the Dutch, the contrast underlining the great variations that affected Western expansion, notably in location, strength, and opponents. As also earlier for Russia, fortifications were important, with new lines of Russian forts added as settlement advanced southwards. The Ishim Line was replaced by Petropavlovsk (west of Omsk, 1752) and its Presnogor'kovskaya Line (1755), in modern northern Kazakhstan. By the second half of the century, a chain of forts, over 4,000 kilometres in length, extended from the Caspian to Kuznetsk in the foothills of the Altay mountains. These forts were more effective than the Spanish *presidios* (bases) in North America, not least because the Russians, whose centres of power and population were far closer, devoted more military resources to the task. Five regular infantry regiments alone were added to the Irtysh Line in 1745, when Russia was not at war with any other power, and therefore could strengthen the frontier.

Africa

Among the conflicts that can be noted in this period are those in northeastern Africa where, as for example in Southern and South-East Asia, the fate of polities was very much bound up with the success of particular war-leaders. A good example occurred in Tigrai (Tigré), an area of northern Ethiopia and southern Eritrea that benefited from lying athwart the route from the Turkish Red Sea base of Massawa into Ethiopia. As a result of this location, the ruler, or Ras, had access to a supply of Turkish muskets which proved a major military and political asset. Mika'el Suhul (d. 1780), Ras of Tigrai, played a key role in Ethiopian politics. In 1745, he aroused the anger of the Negus (Emperor), Iyasu II (r. 1730–55), who invaded Tigrai in order to end Mika'el's resistance. A second invasion, in 1746, was successful, and the isolated Mika'el surrendered, only to be restored.

To the west, in modern Sudan, the supply of horses and iron was similarly important, the iron being made into armour and swords. Two states, the Funj kingdom of Sinnar in northern Sudan, and the rising state of Darfur in western Sudan, competed over the area of Kordofan, where warrior-rulers gained tribute by using their cavalry both to intimidate subjects and to defend them from foreign rulers. In 1745 and 1755, Sinnar campaigned against Kordofan. Abu Likaylik, who served in the 1745 campaign, was the commander in 1755. Having built up a power base, he invaded Kordofan from Sinnar and deposed the Sultan.[34] Haidar Ali was to follow a similar trajectory in Mysore in southern India in 1761.

The Americas

In South America, the struggle between expanding numbers of Europeans and Natives continued, but, as elsewhere, Native allies were crucial for the Europeans. Thus, in Brazil, the Portuguese were unable to defeat the Caiapó, whose tribesmen ambushed Portuguese convoys and attacked their settlements. However, the Bororo, under the leadership of a Portuguese woodsman, António Pires de Campos, pressed the Caiapó hard in a bitter war between 1745 and 1751. In contrast, when the Europeans could use their firepower, they proved more effective. At Caibaté in 1756, a joint Portuguese–Spanish army employed muskets and cannon to smash a Native force resisting their advance on Jesuit mission colonies in Brazil and Paraguay. Allegedly, 1,400 Natives were killed compared with three Europeans. The use of cannon fire led another Native force to retreat.

In North America, the Spanish presence on their northern borders proved vulnerable to Native opposition, including the rebellion of the Pima in Arizona in 1751, and the attack seven years later on the position at San Sabá, eighty miles north-west of modern Austin, Texas. About 2,000 Comanche and their allies, armed with at least 1,000 French muskets, attacked the mission, killing all but one of the missionaries, beheading the effigy of St Francis, a totemic act of religious violence and control, and obliging the soldiers to leave the nearby *presidio* (base).

The French proved particularly active in the interior of North America, establishing forts as bases from which they hoped to increase their influence over Native trade routes. This process and influence led them into conflict with hostile Natives and exacerbated rivalry with the British who sought allies among these Natives and constructed forts of their own. The destruction of villages and crops by the French forced the Chickasaw to accept terms in 1752, but the British colonists competing in the Ohio Valley region proved a different task. The defeat of a force of Virginia militia under

George Washington at Fort Necessity in July 1754, led, instead, to counter-measures backed by the strength of the British empire.

British regular troops were dispatched to North America in 1755, at a time when there was no comparable British commitment elsewhere. An advancing force of them was defeated close to modern Pittsburg in 1755 by the well-aimed fire of a smaller French and Native American force using forest cover, but in 1758–60 the deployment of massive British strength in North America transformed the situation. As with the Chinese in Xinjiang, the campaigns were an impressive triumph of resources and planning, and one that indicated the accumulated skill of the British army in North America.[35] As a complement in imperial expansion, the British also benefited from a growing sophistication of naval strength, notably an ably-managed amphibious capability.[36] The fate of Canada was finally settled in 1760, with a three-pronged advance successfully converging on Montreal where the French surrendered.

The close similarity of weaponry and methods of fighting between the combatants ensured that these battles were different from those between the British and Natives. The French defeat outside Québec in 1759 was similar to an engagement between the British and French in Europe. The major difference was the size of the armies. James Wolfe climbed the riverside cliffs to the Plains of Abraham outside Québec with fewer than 4,500 men, while the casualties on 13 September were about 650 on each side. Decisive battles in Europe involved much larger numbers, for example 89,000 troops (Austrian and Prussian) in total at Leuthen in 1757 and 62,000 (French and Prussian) at Rossbach the same year.

The relatively small forces deployed in North America, and notably in the interior, put a great premium on leadership, an ability to understand and exploit terrain, morale, unit cohesion and firepower. The British were generally adept at all of these, but so too were their opponents and sometimes more so. The French were helped by the difficulties of the British task, not least among them the complications of amphibious operations, as at Louisbourg in 1758,[37] the problems of operating in the interior of North America, the need to allocate limited resources across a number of operations, logistical issues, and the resourcefulness of the leading French commanders: Montcalm in Canada and Lally in India. Thus, in 1757, Montcalm's understanding of warfare in the interior of North America combined with his effective use of French troops and Native allies.

Nevertheless, at Louisbourg in 1758, and indeed on a number of other occasions, the British translated their superiority in ships and troops into success thanks to skill in combined operations as well as a bold ability to seize the tempo of operations. Moreover, outside Québec in 1759, it was

British firepower that was superior, halting the advancing French columns, and thus preparing the way for a successful bayonet charge. At the same time, this success followed a frustrating two months in which the natural strength of the position, French fortifications and the skilful nature of Montcalm's dispositions, had thwarted the British. The balance between success and failure was close, which, yet again, raises questions about the clarity with which relative proficiency is sometimes discussed. After the victory outside Québec, in which both Montcalm and Wolfe were killed, the French garrison in Québec surrendered. In turn, having been defeated outside the city by advancing French forces, the British found themselves besieged the following year, but their garrison was relieved when the thawing of the St Lawrence river at the end of the winter permitted the arrival of British warships and reinforcements.

Viewed from Europe, this was a two-sided conflict, but, on the ground, the shifting support and fears of Native groups were also important. The French position was weakened when Pennsylvania authorities promised the Native Americans that they would not claim land west of the Appalachians. The consequent shift of Native support obliged the French to give up the Ohio region.[38]

Europe

There were major conflicts at the beginning and close of the period, and they placed a significant burden on states and societies. The War of the Austrian Succession (1740–8) began with a sweeping triumph: Frederick the Great of Prussia's conquest of Austrian-ruled Silesia, a valuable, industrially-advanced territory in what is now south-west Poland. This invasion led to the battle of Mollwitz in 1741 in which the Prussian cavalry was ridden down by the more numerous Austrians, causing Frederick to flee. However, the well-trained and more numerous Prussian infantry prevailed over their slower-firing opponents, the decisive clash in the battle. As a reminder of the difficulty of judging success, it is hard to ascribe the Prussian success to any superiority in weaponry or generalship. Instead, their more numerous infantry and the fact that many of the Austrians were raw recruits were each important, reflecting hurried Austrian measures to restore force levels after their recent defeats in the 1737–9 war against the Turks.

Had the opportunity then arisen for Austria to mobilise its greater strength and concentrate on Frederick, he would have been hard-pressed, but, as ever, the political context was crucial. In 1741, once weakened by Prussia, Maria Theresa of Austria was also attacked by France, Bavaria and Saxony, while her system of alliances collapsed. Indeed, Frederick made it clear that, as long as he was sure of Russia, he was not worried by attack from elsewhere.[39]

At war with Sweden, Russia did not come to Austria's assistance while Britain, which had fought France alongside Austria in 1689–97 and 1702–13, was already at war with Spain, the War of Jenkins' Ear (1739–48), and did not enter the new war until the pace of operations against Spain had eased.

The Austrians took hard knocks in 1741, as opposing forces (French, Bavarian and Saxon) advanced to near Vienna and captured Prague. Strategy, however, was overthrown by politics as Prussia and Saxony then abandoned their allies in 1742. Moreover, ignoring the maxim that *ancien régime* warfare, allegedly inherently limited and indecisive, avoided winter campaigns, the Austrians struck back in the early months of 1742, over-running Bavaria. Similarly, as examples of winter campaigns, northern Italy saw a remarkable level of activity in the winters of 1703–4, 1733–4 and 1745–6, including sieges, stormings, and the relief of besieged cities. The war broadened out with British entry into conflict with France in 1743 (troops moved to Belgium in 1742, war was declared in 1744), while Frederick attacked the Austrians anew in 1745, fighting them until 1746. British pressure helped ensure that Charles Emmanuel III of Sardinia, ruler of Savoy-Piedmont, fought alongside Austria, as he had done in 1703–13, and not with France and Spain against Austria as he had done in 1733–5.

Aside from the combination of effective Prussian commanders, flexible tactics and fighting quality, Frederick's forces also benefited from their new attack in oblique order, so as to be able to concentrate overwhelming strength against a portion of the linear formation of the opposing army. Frederick devised a series of methods for strengthening one end of his line and attacking with it, while minimising the exposure of the weaker end. This formation depended on the speedy execution of complex manoeuvres for which well-drilled and well-disciplined troops were essential, and benefited from the greater mobility provided by the move from matchlocks and pikes to flintlocks and bayonets. Such attacks helped to bring victory at Hohenfriedberg and Soor in 1745 and, initially, Leuthen in 1757. Marshal de Saxe, the leading French commander, claimed in 1749 that the Prussian army was only trained to attack. By retaining the tactical, operational and strategic initiative, it was able to do so.

As with most tactical innovations, the oblique order was not without precedents, and Frederick's success with it rested not so much in *invention* as in transformation. The idea of the oblique battle order was already found in the works of both Classical (Vegetius) and modern (Montecuccoli, Folard, Feuquières) military theoreticians, and had been employed by Alexander the Great of Macedon in winning a sweeping victory over Darius of Persia at the battle of Issus in 333 BCE. Even elements of the Highland Charge of Gaelic warfare, especially the 'cluster' or 'wedge' designed to hit at a particular point in the enemy's line, as well as the practice in the War of the Spanish Succession of strengthening an army's wing to envelop that of the enemy, were both important precedents.

Saxe himself emulated Marlborough in his preference for bold manoeuvres, his emphasis on gaining and retaining the initiative, his ability to control large numbers effectively in battle, and his stress on morale. Combined with the well-honed nature of the French army, these skills helped give the French a series of successes in 1745–8 that contrasted with their failures against Marlborough in the 1700s. Again comparisons, for example of Marlborough's attacking success over the French at Ramillies in 1706 with the defensive victory of the French under Saxe against British attack at Fontenoy in 1745, raise questions about how best to assess relative capability, as well as how far it is appropriate to argue for fundamental causes of success (and failure), and how far, instead, the stress should be on short-term factors, such as individual command skills. Saxe's emphasis, in his *Rêveries*, on charging with bayonets rather than relying on firepower, reflected a willingness to challenge received wisdom. In practice, he was very ready to use firepower.

Further south, in the last major conflict in Italy prior to the outbreak of the French Revolutionary War in 1792, Franco-Spanish forces were defeated by the Austrians and Sardinians at Piacenza in 1746, ending a quarter-millennium of French efforts to dominate northern Italy. The swiftly-changing course of the conflict in Italy indicated the volatile character of war in this period. Moreover, the Genoese revolt against Austrian control in December 1746, a successful popular rising in the city that was followed by a failed Austrian attempt to retake it, prefigured much that was to be associated with the revolutionary warfare of the close of the century.[40]

The Genoese revolt also indicated the variety of warfare in Europe in this period. This variety had been demonstrated earlier that year with the decisive defeat at Culloden by the British army over the Jacobite force of Scottish Highlanders led by Charles Edward Stuart, 'Bonnie Prince Charlie'. Had the rebellion been successful, it would have ended Britain's ability to support Austria and Sardinia against France, notably with subsidies; the profits of oceanic trade being used to influence Continental power-politics.

The Jacobites relied on an infantry charge, an instance of the Gaelic preference for the frontal assault,[41] but at Culloden they were heavily outnumbered which permitted the British army defence in depth. Any gaps in the British front line could be filled. William, Duke of Cumberland's artillery, firing canister shot, and his infantry, so thinned the numbers of the advancing clansmen that those who reached the British line were driven back by bayonet.[42] As another instance of variety, the war saw extensive mountain fighting in the Alps, with Spanish and French attempts in 1743, 1744 and 1747 to fight their way into Piedmont.

The end of the War of the Austrian Succession, negotiated with the Peace of Aix-la-Chapelle in 1748, left many issues unresolved, especially Austrian anger over the loss of Silesia to Frederick the Great. Tension over this issue led to the outbreak of the Seven Years' War in 1756, as Frederick, correctly fearing Austro-Russian plans, launched a pre-emptive strike against Austria's ally Saxony, which was located between Prussian Brandenburg and Austrian Bohemia.

Thus began a conflict in which Austria, France, Russia, Saxony and Sweden opposed Frederick, who was allied only to Britain and a small number of German princes. Frederick's survival owed much to impressive victories, especially at Rossbach (1757) over the French, and Leuthen (1757) and Torgau (1760) over the Austrians, but also to the failure of his opponents to combine their strategies. After their defeat at Rossbach, while on the march, by a surprise Prussian attack, the French concentrated on operations against Frederick's allies (British, Hanoverian, Hessian and Brunswicker forces) in Westphalia and Hesse in western Germany, rather than on sending troops east into Saxony to help fight Frederick himself in concert with the Austrians. More significantly, the directions and pace of Austrian and Russian advances on Prussia were not adequately co-ordinated, and there was a serious failure to co-operate when Frederick was hard-pressed, not least in 1759 after the Russian victory at Kunersdorf. There was no equivalent to the partnership of Marlborough and Eugene that had played a major role in defeating the French in the War of the Spanish Succession, especially in the Blenheim campaign of 1704. The major British victory in Germany, at Minden in 1759, was obtained as part of an Anglo-German army, but without Prussian participation.

Nevertheless, the pressure on Prussia from Austria and Russia was very strong, and they had no alternative military commitments. Turkey did not intervene against them, while Austria and Russia did not go to war with Britain, the government of which ignored Frederick's urging them to send a fleet into the Baltic in order to threaten Russia. Frederick repeatedly was put under great stress. The summer and autumn of 1757 was a period of particular difficulty for Frederick, with a Russian invasion of East Prussia, a Swedish invasion of Pomerania, the French conquest of Hanover, the raising of the siege of Prague and the end of the Prussian invasion of Bohemia after the Austrian victory at Kolin, and the Austrian capture of Berlin and most of Silesia.

Frederick saved the situation that year at Rossbach and Leuthen. Whereas the first was an easy triumph, the latter was a hard, drawn-out battle as the initial Prussian attack did not bring victory. With the help of reinforcements, a new Austrian position was created and had to be overcome. As a result, the battle's second phase centred on repeated Prussian attacks on the new Austrian line. It was a hard-fought victory by a well-honed army. Prussian firepower, Frederick's skilful exploitation of the terrain, the fighting quality of the Prussian cavalry, and the ability of the Prussian commanders to take initiatives were all significant. In 1758, the Russians captured East Prussia, which they were to hold for the remainder of the war, but Frederick's close-run success at Zorndorf blocked their invasion of the central region of Brandenburg.[43]

The pressure on Frederick reflected recent improvements in the Austrian and Russian armies, notably the development of their artillery since the War of the Austrian Succession. Moreover, the Austrians, whose performance in the war was far better than is usually argued,[44] also increased their battlefield flexibility, making successful use of dispersed columns in 1758–9, while developing effective counter-tactics to the oblique attack, notably the retention of reserves that could be moved to meet the attack. The French had done the same at the battle of Malplaquet in 1709, learning to respond to Marlborough's tactics, and thus making this last victory very costly. Frederick was in grave difficulties at the close of the period, although he had not suffered the fate of the Zunghars, while he was also doing far better than the Mughal emperor, whose relevance was limited in his lands, which were greatly under Afghan and Maratha pressure.

The Seven Years' War saw all the combatant powers forced to change their tactics. As each sought to avoid the mistakes of the previous year's campaigning season, warfare was shaped by the contending armies' fluid dynamics as well as by their operational and strategic goals. For example, in 1757 Frederick moved from cold steel to firepower, while he subsequently employed artillery as a key to open deadlocked battlefronts. At Burkersdorf against the Austrians (1762), Frederick made use of howitzers with their arching trajectory and explosive shells. Frederick's artillery-based tactics were not simply a response both to the enhanced capability of his artillery and to the decline in his reserves, but also to the Austrian Field Marshal Leopold Joseph von Daun's defensive use of hilly positions. The defensive potential of the North Bohemian and Moravian hills had revealed the defects of the Prussian tactics and, in particular, of the oblique order. Instead, at Burkersdorf and Freiberg in 1762, the Prussians used dispersed columns successfully in attack.

Like the Burmese and Americans vis-à-vis China and Britain in the 1760s and 1770s respectively, Frederick, however, was unable to strike at the centres of Russian, Austrian, Swedish or French power. He was saved by the death of his most implacable foe, Tsarina Elizabeth, in January 1762. She was succeeded by her nephew, Peter III, who treated Frederick as a hero, and, once Peter has signed a peace restoring the Russian conquests, the Austrians were left exposed and made peace with Frederick at Hubertusberg in 1763 on the basis of a return to pre-war boundaries. This political dimension was more significant than Frederick's change of his tactics in the last years of the war, not least by putting more emphasis on artillery. Looked at differently, Frederick's success in holding off his opponents provided an opportunity for power politics to work to his benefit.

Conclusions

The failure of the Highland Charge at Culloden in 1746 might seem to mark a European equivalent to the defeat of less 'developed' forces elsewhere, notably the Zunghars by the Chinese. It is certainly attractive as well as instructive to draw parallels between events in different parts of the world. However, aside from the problems entailed in such a process, as parallels are often tenuous, there is also the difficulty of assessing individual episodes. Culloden may appear to demonstrate the failure of such warmaking by less 'developed' forces, but, rather than drawing such a conclusion, it is necessary to emphasise that the victorious Duke of Cumberland had the advantages of a larger army, superior firepower, an excellent site and a foolish opponent. Moreover, earlier in the rebellion, the Jacobites had won the two battles that occurred, Prestonpans (1745) and Falkirk (1746), suggesting that there was no inherent advantage for the use of firepower against the Highland Charge.

Nevertheless, drawing on an effective military machine,[45] the government forces were able to recover from their defeats, deploying and concentrating fresh units, while the Jacobite cause was destroyed by Culloden. There was no recovery for them. This contrast in resilience is instructive. There were of course instances in which disease, terrain and fighting characteristics helped ensure that the less 'developed' side could fight on, as with tribes in Amazonia under Portuguese pressure. However, in general, there was a relationship between the strength and sustainability of the forces of major states and success. As in the case of the Chinese against the Zunghars, 'Alaungpaya against Manipur, and the British in North America, ably-led forces supported by well-deployed and plentiful resources had a major advantage. This basis for comparison between Western and Asian states and forces is as helpful as the emphasis, instead, on a 'small and accelerating divergence' between Asian and European societies that has been identified as beginning in the sixteenth century.[46]

The 1740s and 1750s are certainly important in this matrix of developments, because they saw the establishment of effective Western military power in India, which greatly accentuated the existing contrast between South and East Asia, the two most populous areas in the world, and, in turn, looked toward what was to be a still more significant divergence between the two. China was not to be under Western military pressure until the late 1830s, and did not become a Western colony. At the same time, as this chapter indicates, the 1740s and 1750s could also be discussed for Southern Asia with reference to the rise of the Afghan empire and the struggle between Afghans and Marathas, each a dynamic power and neither focused on Western military methods. Moreover, by 1760, China was not only the largest empire in the world by both size and population, but also, in its recent expansion, the proven recipient of heavenly grace.[47] Readers are asked to consider these points and to assess the situation without assuming that it had been foreclosed by a Western military revolution or was helping define what can be presented as such a revolution.

5 1760–1780

The focus of attention in this section will be on India, notably the fate of the Marathas, defeated by the Afghans under Ahmad Shah at Third Panipat near Delhi (1761), possibly the largest battle in the century, but, in turn, able, in a relatively minor clash, to defeat the British at Wadgaon in western India in 1779. It is also pertinent to consider the rise of Haidar Ali of Mysore in southern India and what this rise indicated about the potential variations in military development, not least compared with the British success in establishing a powerful position in Bengal. Other developments in Eurasia were not on the scale of India, but successful Russian expansion against the Turks contrasted with failed and costly Chinese campaigning in Burma. In turn, Burma proved successful in Siam.

The New World saw the rise of problems within empires, with resistance to the British in North America and to Spain in Latin America. It is constructive to compare Native opposition to the spread of imperial power, for example Pontiac's War, with rebellions within areas of imperial control, notably in New Orleans in 1766 and the Andean chain in the late 1770s and early 1780s, both against Spain, and, in the Thirteen Colonies, against Britain from 1775.

India

The Afghan attacks on north India culminated at the Third Battle of Panipat, north of Delhi on 14 January 1761, probably the largest land battle of the century, and certainly one that should not be overlooked in comparison with more famous battles that receive attention, notably Plassey in India (1757) and Rossbach in Germany (1757), victories by Robert Clive and Frederick the Great respectively. In response to the Afghan presence in northern India, a Maratha army sent by the *Peshwā* had marched north in March 1760, reaching Delhi in July, and driving out the Afghan garrison there. Inconclusive negotiations then took place while campaigning stopped in the monsoon season, a demonstration of the importance of environmental factors.

The Marathas under Sadashiv Rao Bhau, an indifferent commander who was running short of food and money, then marched north in October against Kunjpara, a fortified position 93 miles north of Delhi, held by an Afghan garrison, that was important because it controlled a ford across the Yumuna river and also held a large quantity of Afghan supplies. As in Europe, notably in the wars between the Russians and the Turks, but also, in the cases of Kehl (1733) and Philippsburg (1734) with the Austro-French struggle in the Rhineland, crossing places over rivers were of key operational importance. After a bombardment by the effective Maratha cannon, Kunjpara was stormed on 17 October, but Ahmad Shah then outmanoeuvred the Marathas by fording the river between them and Delhi, and thus cutting their communications.

The capacity for manoeuvre was a key tactical and operational skill that was particularly important due to the vulnerability of supply links. Cavalry-based armies tended to be most adroit at manoeuvring and it, repeatedly, gave them an advantage over the more infantry-based forces of settled states. Moreover, the cavalry of the latter tended to be heavy, and therefore slower, whereas that of the steppe or semi-nomadic peoples, such as the Afghans, was light.

The Marathas failed to drive Ahmad Shah back, and, instead, retreated north (away from Delhi and their homeland) to Panipat, where Bhau dug in from 29 October in a strong position which he protected with his numerous cannon. Rather than risking all by assaulting this position, Ahmad Shah waited the situation out. Blockaded and without allies, the Marathas lost the mobility that was so important to their tactical and operational effectiveness. Their food ran low and the Marathas came out of their positions to attack the Afghans. The faces of the Marathas were anointed with saffron, a sign that they had come out to conquer or die.

Like nearby Karnal in 1739, Third Panipat reflected the continued role of cavalry and helps to explain why the military challenge that many Indian rulers were seeking to resist was not that of British infantry. The Afghan forces consisted largely of heavy cavalry equipped with body armour and muskets; although their Rohilla allies provided an important contingent of infantry armed with flintlock muskets. Their Maratha opponents, outnumbered by about 45,000 to 60,000, included the traditional mobile light cavalry, armed with swords, shields, battleaxes, daggers and lances, as well as the 8,000-strong trained flintlock-equipped *gardi* infantry of one commander, Ibrahim Khan. The Marathas, however, had little experience in integrating the different capabilities of their various units, in particular the need to combine the offensive characteristics of their light cavalry with the more stationary tactics required by the artillery and infantry, who needed the cavalry to defend their flanks from opposing cavalry.

The battle began at dawn after a fierce discharge of artillery and rockets in which the Maratha gunners, probably deceived by the light, fired too high. Nevertheless, the Marathas pushed back the Afghans, who were initially only able to hold their own on their left flank. But, while the Maratha infantry under Ibrahim advanced in disciplined order on the Maratha left, driving back the opposing Rohilla infantry, they were only a small part of the army, and there was no co-ordination with their undisciplined cavalry. The Maratha cavalry advances were checked, and the slow-moving cannon, many of which were dug in, failed to keep up. Thus, the absence of a satisfactory command structure, and Bhau's weaknesses as a commander, exacerbated problems of control caused by the composite nature of the Maratha army. Unlike the Maratha cannon, which were stronger in heavy cannon, the Afghans were superior in the more mobile camel-mounted light cannon.

While the Rohillas on the Maratha right were hard-pressed, in the centre the Maratha advance drove back their opponents. In the afternoon, however, Ahmad Shah committed his 5,000-strong cavalry reserve and Afghan attacks were launched simultaneously all along the line. The Marathas lacked reserves and were exhausted. Their men and horses had had little food for weeks, and none since dawn. Nevertheless, they fought hard until resistance collapsed. Nearly all Ibrahim's unit died fighting. In the face of the Afghan cavalry attacks, which were supported by *zanbüraks* and by Persian musketeers, the Maratha centre disintegrated and there was a general rout, with the death of many of the Maratha commanders, including Bhau. The Afghans pursued the fleeing Marathas all night, killing many. The following morning, the camp was stormed and many more Marathas were killed. The prisoners were all beheaded. Allegedly, at least 30,000 Maratha soldiers were killed.[1]

A number of factors were responsible for the Afghan victory including the more coherent state of the Afghan army and Maratha divisions between the core units in the *Peshwā*'s forces and the large number of light cavalry under Maratha *sirdars*, in effect autonomous commanders, particularly Jankoji Sindhia and Malharao Holkar. The latter proved much less ready to engage with the fire from the Rohilla allies of the Afghans. The Afghans benefited not only from superior firepower, but also from the strength of their cavalry, which was heavier than the Maratha cavalry.

However, the battle had seriously weakened the Afghans and they proved unable to consolidate their success, not least because they fell out with their Indian allies. Having sacked Delhi on 22 March, Ahmad Shah returned home to Kandahar. Sated with plunder, his men wanted to go back to Afghanistan. As a result, Ahmad Shah was unable to exploit his victory at Panipat. Instead, in 1762 he reached an agreement with the Marathas and the Mughal emperor, Alam II. However, like many of the agreements reached by the East India Company, this proved to be a precarious settlement.

Indeed, Ahmad Shah's Rohilla allies were subjugated by the Marathas. In addition, the Punjab, which the Afghans had annexed in 1752, frequently rebelled, leading them to mount repeated punitive invasions, including three by Ahmad Shah. His opponents there were the Sikhs, a military confederacy, who proved increasingly effective from 1762. In February 1762, Ahmad Shah recaptured Lahore, defeated the Sikhs, and razed their temple at Amritsar to the ground as well as attacking other Sikh sacred sites. However, this destruction encouraged Sikh animosity, and opposition increased. After Ahmad Shah left the Punjab in December 1762, the Sikhs overran it. In 1764, Ahmad Shah advanced anew to take Lahore, but was forced to return to Afghanistan in order to tackle a rebellion. The Sikhs then captured Lahore, where they defiled and destroyed the mosques. Ahmad Shah's last invasion of the Punjab occurred in 1767, but, although he retook Lahore, he failed to end Sikh opposition and ended up by leaving them the central Punjab while he retained Peshawar, the gateway to Afghanistan.

The Afghans continued to rule Kashmir, where a revolt by the governor was suppressed in 1762. Moreover, Sind, which had rebelled when the Marathas occupied the Punjab, had submitted after Panipat. The Durrani dynasty of Ahmad Shah faced mounting problems, including increasing opposition in northern Afghanistan, which they had conquered in 1750–1. However, it did not collapse as Safavid Persia had done in the 1720s. In 1768, Ahmad Shah thwarted an Uzbek attempt by the Emir of Bukhara to regain Balkh. A border on the Amu Darya (Oxus) river was agreed. Moreover, a major rising in Khurasan was crushed, with a victory outside Mashhad followed by the successful siege of the city.

Nevertheless, as a result of their problems, the Afghans were unable to develop their potential of the 1750s and to maintain a wide-ranging presence in northern India. Moreover, divisions within the Afghan élite proved significant. Ahmad Shah died in 1773 and was succeeded by his second son, Timur Shah (r. 1773–93), the son of his favourite wife, who both faced opposition from within his own family and lacked the personal prestige, authority and aggressive expansionist drive of his father. The family divisions reflected the absence of a system of primogeniture and all the problems that the succession therefore gave rise to. In some respects, this was an instance of meritocratic monarchy in the sense of the fittest gaining power, but the disruption produced was a serious hindrance to international strength, as well as providing opportunities for foreign meddling. In 1773, Timur Shah faced opposition from his elder half-brother, Sulayman Mirza, who also claimed the throne; but Timur advanced on Kandahar from where Suleyman fled to India, while his father-in-law, Ahmad Shah's vizier, Shah Wali Khan, was executed. The capital was then transferred to Kabul in 1775–6 by Timur in an effort to lessen the power of the Pushtun tribal chiefs.

The Afghan failure to sustain Ahmad Shah's successes provided opportunities for other powers, notably the Marathas and the British. Panipat greatly hurt the Marathas and weakened the authority of the *Peshwā*, by then the leading member of the confederacy. His heir and cousin both died and the battle ended the prospect of an imperial *Peshwāship*.

However, underlining the difficulties of providing a simple guide to the consequences of individual battles, the Marathas were able to regain much of their position, even though they did not again mount a large raid on Lahore as they had done in 1758. A revival was brought about by Madhav Rao I, who became *Peshwā* in 1761. Maratha strength was shown in 1770 when the Jats were defeated at Bharatpur.[2] Also in 1772, and again demonstrating Maratha power in northern India, Madhav Rao and Mahadji Shinde (Sindhia), one of the Maratha leaders, restored the Mughal emperor, Alam II, to his throne in Delhi, but under Maratha protection. After the death of Madhav Rao I in 1772, however, there were serious succession disputes.

The Marathas faced rivals, including Oudh in northern India, the Nizam of Hyderabad in the centre, and Mysore in the south. In 1761, the Nizam advanced on the Maratha capital of Pune (Poona), only to be defeated at Koregaon when his army was outmanoeuvred and attacked from front and rear by the more mobile Marathas. He was defeated anew at Urali (1762) and Rakshasbhuvan (1763), and surrendered territories as the price of peace. Mysore was under Maratha pressure in mid-century, which helped ensure that a Mysore general, Haidar Ali, became a central figure there. In 1761, he took over the rule of Mysore, before expanding its territories, which led to conflict with both the Marathas and Britain. Haidar was defeated by the Marathas in 1764 and at Chinkurali in 1771, but maintained control of Mysore.

Religion played a role in local conflict. When Haidar Ali successfully invaded the vulnerable and fragmented Malabar coast in 1766, he allied with a local Muslim ruler, Ali, Rajah of Cannanore, and they displayed a harsh attitude to local sensitivities. Initially successful, Haidar Ali, like the Afghans in northern India, notably in the Punjab, returned home to Mysore only to face rebellions on the Malabar coast against his garrisons and allies, which, in turn, were countered by fresh action, including massacres.

Force was a key aspect of politics across India. In the Himalayas, the ruling Malla dynasty in Nepal was overthrown in 1769 by Prithvinarayn Shah, who was from the ruling house of the Gurkhas, a people from west Nepal.

The British, primarily the East India Company but also the British government, had found that victories in India in the 1750s drew them into further commitments, in both north and south-east India. Support for Mir Jafar, their candidate as Nawab of Bengal, led to conflict with larger invading Mughal forces under Ali Gauhar in 1760, and at Patia on 9 February the Mughals were victorious over a seriously divided force. However, on 22 February, the disciplined conduct and close-range volley firepower of the East India Company's *sepoys* (Indian troops fighting in the Western manner) led to victory at Sirpur. In 1763, at Gheria, the Company's forces defeated the new Nawab, Mir Kasim, who had resisted the Company's financial demands. In 1764, Company firepower proved decisive over Indian cavalry at the battles of Patna and, in particular, Buxar, defeating the now former Nawab as well as his allies, the Mughal emperor, Alam II, and Shuja-ud-daulah, the Mughal *Subadar* of Oudh. Victory at Buxar was exploited in February 1765 with the capture of Oudh's leading fortresses.

Contemporary Indian historians focused not on British military superiority, but on the factionalism and moral decline of the ruling Indian families. The British were certainly greatly helped by the ability to win local allies, but it was also necessary to sustain forces and to defeat opponents. Rather as the Portuguese had benefited in the sixteenth century from the diversion of Chinese interest from the Indian Ocean in the mid-fifteenth, in part in response to Mongol success, so the British profited from the impact on the Mughals of Ahmad Shah's invasion in 1759.

The Treaty of Allahabad of 1765 saw the British forcibly accepted into the Indian government structure, with Alam II conferring on the East India Company the profitable right to collect revenue and conduct civil justice, the *diwan*, in Bengal and Bihar. Shuja-ud-daulah was restored to Oudh, but had to pay heavily and to accept the Company's position in neighbouring Bengal and Bihar, a position which was to provide a solid source of revenue and manpower and to be the basis of British imperial power in Asia.

In 1773, after the advance of Company troops, Oudh came under Company protection from the Marathas. The following year, the Company helped Oudh occupy neighbouring Rohilkhand, defeating the Rohillas at Lahykira (Miranpur Katra) on 23 April 1774. The firepower of the East India Company forces and the Westernised infantry of their Oudh allies saw off the attack of the Rohilla infantry and cavalry, and the pursuit by the Oudh cavalry prevented the Rohilla forces from regrouping. Maratha influence was ended. In 1775, Company troops suppressed a mutiny amongst those of Oudh against its new ruler. At the same time, it is important to note that the latter operation entailed heavy casualties for the Company forces.

Relations with Mysore in southern India proved more problematic. In a difficult war in 1767–9, the Company's forces used their firepower in late 1767 to beat off attacks by Haidar Ali and the Nizam, Company *sepoys* notably holding the fort of Ambur, before moving onto the initiative and driving the Nizam to terms in February 1768. When Mysore was invaded in 1768, the British were able to use their artillery to reduce opposing forts, but the resources and determination to sustain an invasion were absent. Instead, in 1769, Haidar Ali and his light cavalry ravaged the Carnatic, advanced as far as Madras (Chennai), and dictated peace. The smaller Company army could not respond successfully to the numerous and mobile Mysore cavalry.

The British were more successful against weaker opponents. Fortified positions provided targets that were more vulnerable than the Mysore cavalry. In south-east India, Vellore was successfully besieged in 1762 and stormed in 1771, and Tanjore successfully besieged in 1775. Madura fell in 1764 as the result of another successful siege. It had been under the control of Yusuf Khan, an outstanding *sepoy* officer in the Madras army in the 1750s and 1760s, who had become an agent for the Nawab of the Carnatic in Madura before breaking away. As the sponsor of the Nawab, the East India Company had to suppress Yusuf Khan. Indicating one of the disadvantages of the mobility of British forces and the interdependence of its commitments, John Call, the Chief-Engineer on the Coromandel Coast, blamed Yusuf Khan's defiance on the dispatch of much of the Madras army on the successful expedition against Spanish-held Manila in the Philippines in 1762. In 1763, Call described the difficulties of campaigning against Madura:

> We should not be the least uneasy about the certainty of defeating him were it not for the difficulty of penetrating through the woods to get at him. … The narrow roads are at all times difficult to an army, but retrenched and secured as they are at present we are well assured it is impracticable to penetrate by any route but that of marching by the sea side. … Another grand obstacle is the want of water … as well as rice … in spite of all we should have marched against him and could have drawn together a body of 600 Europeans … but such was our weakened state that we could not send half that number into the field.[3]

The campaign demonstrated the increased military commitments that stemmed from the spread of British political interests. In the event, Yusuf Khan was betrayed to the British by one of his French officers and hanged.

Nevertheless, the failure to defeat Haidar Ali of Mysore, like the earlier blows in the initial stages of Pontiac's War in North America (see p. 121), indicate the mistake of reading too much from Britain's success in India and North America in the latter stages of the Seven Years' War (1756–63). Conflict on land with non-Western opponents, who not only fought in a different fashion, but were also products of contrasting socio-political systems, proved more difficult than war with other Western powers.

This weakness was demonstrated anew when, after an unsatisfactory conflict in 1774–6, Britain went to war anew with the Marathas in 1778. Bombay, the weakest of the East India Company's three Presidencies (the others were Calcutta and Madras), was drawn into struggles between the Maratha leaders, supporting Raghunathrao, the pretender to the office of *Peshwā*; but its intervention proved ineffective. In late 1778, a slow-moving army of 3,200 infantry, with 12,000 bullocks pulling guns and supplies, advanced from Bombay into the difficult terrain of the Western Ghats (mountains) towards the Maratha capital Pune (Poona). However, the army was not up to the task and failed to master the crucial equations of mobility, logistics and terrain. In 1770, indeed, a member of the Bombay Council had opposed hostilities with the Marathas on the grounds that the British could do nothing to prevent their cavalry raids.[4] Under pressure, in early 1779, the expedition's leadership disagreed over whether to press on, only to lose the initiative as they were rapidly surrounded by a far larger Maratha cavalry army. Defensive firepower held off Maratha attack, but, with falling morale and failing ammunition supplies, the British signed a convention at Wadgaon that provided for the withdrawal of the army to Bombay and the surrender of territories acquired by the Bombay government since 1773.

This convention, which was swiftly repudiated, rarely features in the annals of British military history, but there are instructive parallels with Peter the Great's advance to the Pruth in 1711 (see p. 30) and with Burgoyne's ultimately disastrous advance to the Hudson valley in 1777 in the War of American Independence. A well-trained force could only achieve so much, especially if on difficult terrain, in the face of considerably more numerous opponents, and if reconnaissance was inadequate. In India, moreover, unlike America, the British suffered from the greater mobility enjoyed by their opponents thanks to the role and superiority of their light cavalry.[5] At the same time, much of the blame for the British failure in 1779 can be put on logistics and on the command structure.

The British also faced problems in southern India, where Haidar Ali's opposition, including his co-operation with the French during the War of American Independence, seriously threatened their position. The British capture on 19 March 1779 of the French coastal base of Mahé, which Haidar saw as under his protection and through which he acquired French arms, angered Haidar. So also did the British refusal to provide help against the Marathas as they were obliged to do under the treaty of 1769. Anglo-Maratha hostilities in western India gave him an opportunity to attack.

In July 1780, with an army 80,000 strong, largely cavalry, Haidar Ali invaded the Carnatic, meeting an inadequate and confused British response that reflected serious command failings as well as the availability of only 26,000 troops. On 10 September, a force under Colonel William Baillie was attacked by the entire Mysore army at Parambakam. Baillie drew up his men in a defensive position, only to find that badly disrupted when his numerous camp followers fled. Baillie was heavily outnumbered and, in the end, the square of his troops, under fire from more numerous cannon (about 50 to 10), was fought down by repeated attacks by Mysore cavalry and infantry. The British fell back on Madras.

The British situation deteriorated as Haidar pressed on to make gains in the Carnatic, notably Arcot where the defences were breached in October 1780, in part thanks to the help of the French officers in Haidar's army.[6] Furthermore, his capture of magazines of supplies in the Nawab's hands, as well as the devastation spread by his cavalry, created serious supply problems for the British army, which were exacerbated by its size. Thus, the maintenance and protection of its supplies became the major operational objective of the army,[7] which helped accentuate its vulnerability.

However, the Calcutta presidency was not put under comparable pressure, and, as a result, the considerable resources of Bengal could be deployed to help resist Maratha and Mysore pressure, a situation that was to continue until both were eventually subjugated. Moreover, in 1781, Company forces in southern India defeated Haidar at Porto Novo, Sholinghur and Polilur, all difficult battles.

The British were not alone in encountering serious problems. In 1761–6, the Dutch faced a difficult war in Sri Lanka that also indicated the limitations of the Western military. Far from the conflict beginning with an act of Western aggression, it was launched by Kirti Sri, the ruler of the interior kingdom of Kandy which had, the previous century, defeated Portuguese forces. The Dutch had conquered the Portuguese positions in the mid-seventeenth century, but were not to have comparable success against Kandy. Exploiting discontent in the militarily weak Dutch coastal possessions, Kirti Sri attacked and overran much of the coast. As elsewhere, however, where Western power was assaulted, for example in North America during Pontiac's War (1763–4), it proved far harder for the indigenous forces to capture fortified positions, especially well-fortified ones, and the Dutch-held town of Negombo successfully resisted attack in 1761.

Furthermore, Western empires benefited from their ability to deploy troops and money from elsewhere in their imperial systems. The Dutch sent reinforcements, many from the East Indies, and by the end of 1763 they had regained the coastal regions. Similarly, the British were able to move resources between Bengal and the Carnatic, although Bombay was relatively isolated from both.

In 1764, the Dutch set out to conquer the interior of Sri Lanka. Six columns were sent against the capital, Kandy, but they were as unsuccessful as the earlier Portuguese expeditions into the interior in 1594, 1630 and 1638. There had been no improvement in Western offensive military capability since then, and the usual problems of operating in the tropics, especially disease, difficult terrain and an absence of maps, were exacerbated by effective Kandyan resistance. Taking advantage of the jungle terrain, Kandyan sharpshooters harassed the Dutch, inflicting heavy casualties.

However, learning from past mistakes was an important characteristic of successful operations. Lubert Jan, Baron Van Eyck, the Dutch Governor, had new maps drawn by Jacques Louis Guyard while his forces operated. In January 1765, the Dutch launched a new campaign, replacing swords and bayonets with less cumbersome machetes, providing troops with a more practical uniform, and moving more rapidly, a key issue in such operations, as the British showed when they moved slowly against the Marathas in 1778–9. Speed helped in gaining the initiative, and also lessened the impact of disease.

To begin with, the Dutch triumphed, capturing the deserted capital to which they were guided by their new maps;[8] but the Kandyans refused to engage in battle, always a sensible response to Western firepower. This refusal meant that Dutch energies were dissipated in seeking (and failing) to control a country rendered intractable by disease and enemy raiders. Peace was made in 1766. Kandy would not be conquered until the British, on their second attempt, overran it in 1815.

South-East Asia

Dutch failure in Sri Lanka was part of a more general lack of Western expansion which contrasted with the successes that were to be obtained a century later. There was no Western military pressure on China, Japan or Siam (Thailand) in the eighteenth century, which represented a total failure to follow up the bold plans of conquest foolishly advanced in the sixteenth century. The general pattern was of limited activity, in part due to the frequency of war in Europe in the eighteenth century, and of few results. Spain had scant success in subduing and Christianising the southern Philippines. British and French attempts to establish a presence in southern Burma failed in the 1750s; and the Persian Gulf remained largely closed to

Western power. The Dutch adopted a hesitant role in the Malay world, not least because of concern over the contrast between their weak defences in their main base, Malacca, and the military strength of the expanding Bugis who were based in south Sulawesi. Far from there being a tide of Western advance, there were no important Dutch operations in the Malay world, after a punitive expedition against Siak in Sumatra in 1761, until 1784.

In contrast, there were major conflicts further north. In 1764, Burma launched a pincer campaign against the Siamese capital, Ayuthia. This operation led first to the occupation of lands to the north, especially Chiang Mai and Laos, although the Burmese force in southern Siam was defeated by P'Ya Tashin at the battle of P'etchaburi. Despite the latter, the war continued, and in 1767 Burmese advances led to the storming of Ayuthia and the capture of the Siamese king. The campaign had persisted through two rainy seasons, the soldiers growing their own rice so that the army did not fade away.

This success contrasted with Chinese failure against Burma. War began in 1765 over what had hitherto been the buffer zone of the Shan states, and reflected Chinese concern about Burmese expansion into Laos and Siam and over Burmese attempts to make their authority effective over the Shan princes. These attempts reflected a determination on the part of Hsinbyushi (r. 1763–76) to protect the prestige of the Burmese crown, but also a need to secure more servicemen. As such, Burmese policy was similar to the overlordship and expansionism seen with many African rulers. Burma benefited from the intense paddy cultivation in the Irrawaddy valley, which generated a huge amount of rice that enabled the Burmese monarchy to maintain a large number of infantry conscripts.

In 1766, the scope of operations widened from the Shan states to include a Chinese advance on the frontier of Burma proper. At first, the Qianlong emperor had thought that his border troops would settle the issue in just one campaign, but initial problems led him to send more troops, who failed in 1766–7, and then to dispatch, in 1767, élite Manchu banner units under Mingrui, an experienced Manchu general who had campaigned in the steppe lands. Mingrui decided on a knockout blow, an advance by two routes, on the Burmese capital, Ava in the Irrawaddy valley near modern Mandalay. In some respects, this plan represented another version of that successfully employed against the Zunghars in 1755. However, the Chinese had far less experience of fighting in Burma, about which they knew comparatively little.

Mingrui's invasion started in mid-November 1767. The winter season was considered the best season to fight in Burma as the chance of disease was less acute then. Mingrui was able to advance deep into Burma, to near Ava, but the supporting invasion failed and the Burmese cut Mingrui's communications. Isolated in early 1768, and with his troops gravely weakened by disease, Mingrui eventually tried to retreat to China, but Burmese guerrilla attacks took a heavy toll, and most of the army died, the badly-injured Mingrui committing suicide at the end of March 1768. Like the Kandyan forces, the Burmese relied on guerrilla attacks, which avoided providing the Chinese with a target and also profited greatly from the terrain and forest cover.

Qianlong's prestige was greatly involved in success in war. The new commander, Fuheng, was Mingrui's uncle, an official closely associated with bellicose positions, and linked by marriage to the imperial family. In April 1768, Fuheng was appointed military commissioner in charge of operations against Burma. He was backed up by Manchu generals experienced in the frontier wars in eastern Turkestan. Qianlong rejected the suggestion from two of his generals that it would be better to negotiate peace, dismissed the generals, and sent more troops to the frontier. In March 1769, Fuheng was given a chief commander's seal, which further committed Chinese prestige. Fuheng planned an invasion, by three routes, designed to subjugate and annex Burma.

Warnings about disease being stronger in the autumn were ignored, and the invasion was launched in October 1769, being greatly hit by disease including malaria. Similarly, the British were to be affected by yellow fever in the American South in the War of Independence. Not advancing as far as Mingrui had done in the winter of 1767–8, the main Chinese force only reached the upper Irrawaddy valley, moving to the well-fortified town of Kaungton which the Chinese besieged, fighting heavily at the same time with Burmese forces there. The attacks failed, while thousands of Chinese troops died of disease. Concerned about repeating Mingrui's failure, the Chinese generals began negotiations, although the process is unclear, which is unsurprising given the honour and prestige at stake. At any rate, the Chinese felt forced to accept terms. This outcome repeated Peter the Great's surrender at the River Pruth in 1711, and prefigured those of the British at Saratoga in 1777 and Wadgaon in 1779.

Successive Chinese commanders against Burma committed suicide or otherwise died, a sure indication of failure. However, Burma's focus on war in Siam and Laos led to the negotiation of a peace that salvaged Chinese prestige, although the ban that the Chinese imposed on trade with Burma reflected their uneasiness about the settlement. Indeed, the war was followed by a stalemate in relations.

Chinese preparations for a renewed confrontation with Burma reflected Qianlong's anger with the outcome but were superseded by a resumption of the conflict with the Gyalrong tribes of western Sichuan. Serious disputes between the local chieftains interacted with issues of Chinese authority, leading to the outbreak of the Second Jinchuan War in 1770. Troops and commanders were moved from Yunnan, resulting in the abandonment of preparations for a new war with Burma.

As in the first war (see pp. 75–6), the Chinese were hindered by the numerous stone towers of their opponents, which were now strengthened against Chinese cannon by the use of logs and packed earth. Capturing the towers took major efforts and the Chinese armies found themselves bogged down, while their supply lines were threatened. From late 1774, the situation changed as over 200,000 Chinese troops were committed, while natives were also used by the Chinese government. Chinese operational and tactical effectiveness improved. A Chinese switch to mobile columns permitted the harassing of opposing supply lines. In addition, there was a methodical attack on the towers. In this, the Chinese used cannon forged under the direction of a Portuguese missionary. Lasting until 1776, the expensive and difficult war led to the subjugation of the area. As increasing numbers of Jinchuan commanders surrendered, opposition fractured.

The opportunity was also taken to enforce the authority of Yellow Sect Buddhism at the expense of the traditional Bon belief.[9] Moreover, military colonies staffed with Chinese troops were established in the area. However, the high wartime expenditure, more than sixty million taels, compared with nearly twenty million for the First Jinchuan War, caused the Qianlong emperor considerable concern.[10]

Less seriously, the government also faced opposition on the island of Hainan off south China where the Li people of the highlands used force from 1766 in what was to be a longstanding attempt to drive out settlers. This opposition was similar to that encountered in south-west China. The Wang Lun sectarian rebellion in Shandong in eastern China in 1774 was another expensive commitment, although the rebellion, in a more central and sensitive province, was swiftly suppressed. Confronting local uprisings was part of the pattern of Chinese military activity.[11]

The difficulties of campaigning in Burma led Qianlong to reject the idea of another invasion in 1782 in order to take advantage of political divisions there. The development of a more pragmatic stance was linked to the abandonment of expansionism. China did not seek to advance further west nor to attack Russia or Japan.

The Chinese failure in Burma, repeated against Vietnam in northern Vietnam in 1788–9, is a reminder of the dangers of adopting any notion of a scale of military achievement or of advancing a Western-centric interpretation of military history. The Chinese were less successful along their southern frontiers than they were in Central Asia, in part because the area was not of prime strategic interest to China, although the Qianlong emperor showed a degree of commitment with a series of formal southern tours between 1751 and 1765, two more following in 1780 and 1784.[12] Often the generals sent to the southern frontiers were less competent than those who went to Central Asia, while the Qianlong emperor, who distorted the record of the campaigning, argued that he had failed in Burma because he had sent insufficient troops. Moreover, the unfamiliar heavily-forested environment was very difficult for large-scale military operations, and notably for Chinese logistics, and for the Manchu cavalry, who reported a high death-rate among their horses. Tropical diseases also affected the Chinese troops.[13]

However, rather than focusing solely on reasons for Chinese failure, it is necessary to note those leading to Burmese success. The skill of the Burmese generals, especially Maha Si-tu and Maha Thiha Thura, the latter the victor at Kaungton, was important as they outmanoeuvred the Chinese forces. Maha Thiha Thura sought a compromise peace as he did not regard a continuing war with China as appropriate. Colleagues had wanted to fight on in order to destroy the Chinese army at Kaungton and the angry king, Hsinbyushi, sentenced Maha Thiha Thura to imprisonment. The Burmese also benefited from trade with the West, which brought them Western firearms. They used these, as well as land mines, alongside traditional weapons, as well as using elephants. The Chinese lacked equivalent firearms and employed their traditional weapons including bows and fire weapons.[14]

The Chinese campaigns weakened the Burmese hold on their eastern conquests, and also helped lead to the undoing of Hsinbyushi's success against Siam in 1767. However, there was no comparison at all for the Chinese with Qianlong's successes the previous decade in Central Asia. Moreover, the Burmese showed their effectiveness by also operating in other directions, sending major expeditions against the kingdom of Manipur to the north-west in 1764 and 1775. Burma controlled resources sufficient to deploy large forces, dispatching 55,000 troops against Manipur in 1764, which was larger than the field armies of the British East India Company at this stage.

The Burmese position was challenged not only by the Chinese, but also by a Siamese revival under Phya Tashin. Having raised a new army in south-eastern Siam, Tashin recaptured the central area around Ayuthia. However, he was unsuccessful when he attacked Chiang Mai in northern Siam. Tashin also defeated two other claimants to the Siamese throne, reunited Siam, and re-established government control in the country. He moved the capital to Thonburi near Bangkok. Between 1770 and 1773, Tashin turned east and, after some difficulty, installed a client ruler in Cambodia. In 1775, he finally drove the Burmese from Chiang Mai.

By driving the Burmese out of Siam and the Lao principalities, Tashin ended the Burmese encirclement of 1764–7 and produced fresh manpower and resources for the Siamese army. A Burmese attempt to repeat the encirclement strategy in 1773 collapsed in the face of rebellions, but a new invasion was launched in 1775–6. The struggle also greatly affected the neighbouring Lao principalities. In 1776, these principalities were evacuated by the Burmese and, in 1778, Tashin invaded, capturing Vientiane, the major city, and forcing the region to recognise Siamese suzerainty. This was one of the most bitter conflicts of the century. There was no other war on this scale in this period.

South-West Asia

Warfare involving Persia was not on the scale of Nadir Shah's years. His grandson only held onto Khurasan in north-east Persia, which, after a major rising was crushed, remained a client state under the Durranis in Afghanistan. Instead, the Zand tribe under Karim Khan established itself in Persia from 1750, initially dominating the south-west and subsequently gaining control over most of Persia. With his capital at Shiraz, Karim Khan was able to bring a certain amount of order until his death in 1779. He fought the Turks in 1774–9, in part in a struggle over controlling trade routes and the related ports. Basra, the major port for (Turkish-ruled) Iraq, was blockaded into surrendering in 1776 after a 13-month siege.[15]

Nevertheless, there was nothing in this conflict on the scale of the wars of the 1720s–40s, not least nothing to match the Persian advances of those years, nor indeed the Turkish attacks on Persia in the 1720s. The 1746 treaty between the two powers had seen an acceptance of relations as being those of states rather than religious opponents. The Turks, moreover, were exhausted after their disastrous war with Russia in 1768–74, a war that in part arose because their earlier peace with Persia gave them an opportunity to concentrate on other opponents.

Russo-Turkish War

The international context helps explain the Turkish willingness to fight in 1768. Concerned about Russian intervention in Poland, and encouraged by the French government, which was anti-Russian, the Turks responded to the violation of their territory by Russian forces pursuing Polish opponents. When the Turks declared war, the Russians were unprepared for conflict, but they swiftly moved onto the offensive, and successfully so. Russian forces overran the Crimea, Moldavia and Wallachia. The Russians proved less successful in the Caucasus where they failed in 1769 when they besieged Poti, on the coast of modern Georgia north of Batumi.

Count Peter Rumiantsev, who was given the title of Field Marshal and sole command after his victory at Kartal (Kagul to the Russians) in 1770, proved particularly successful at the head of Russian armies in 1770 and 1774, although his offensive in 1773 was less so. A skilful innovator, he abandoned traditional linear tactics and, instead, organised his infantry into columns that could advance rapidly and independently, and could re-form into hollow divisional squares while affording mutual support in concerted attacks. The columns relied on firepower to repel Turkish assaults and included mobile light artillery, which became more numerous during the century. A major role was also played by bayonet charges: the use of firepower was followed by hand-to-hand fighting. In this way, the mobility of Turkish cavalry, which so threatened forces deployed in a linear fashion by turning their flanks, had been overcome.

These Russian tactics prefigured those of the forces of Revolutionary France, serving as a warning against the misleading tendency to see the latter as the leader in military development, and also challenging the mistaken linkage between political radicalism and such development, a linkage that underplays the crucial role of military professionalism. The Russian tactical and operational measures seen in the 1768–74 war had been anticipated to a degree in Münnich's 1739 campaign (see p. 68), and, as then, they greatly affected the fate of campaigns.[16]

Russian advantages were amplified by the flaws of the Turkish army. The weaknesses of its supply system, which had been neglected in the region from 1740, were exacerbated by the Russian capture of Turkish bases, and there was to be a serious shortage of food, which hit morale. Moreover, there were problems with the availability and quality of gunpowder.[17] Supply difficulties contributed to the loss of major Turkish bases, notably Chotin in 1769. A cumulative process was at work, as Turkish operations traditionally relied heavily on supplies from the dependent territories of Moldavia and Wallachia, notably grain from the latter. Their conquest by the Russians made it harder for the Turks to retain other territories, while also providing the Russians with additional supply possibilities and thus lessening the need for cumbersome supply trains.[18]

Furthermore, in addition to serious issues of command capability, the Turks were faced with major problems of indiscipline that were compounded by failure, a process that was also frequently seen in India. The Crimean Tatars, a key source of cavalry for the Turks and, traditionally, a major force north of the Black Sea, proved unreliable as troops (readily fleeing from the battlefield of Kartal in 1770) and also, eventually, as allies, with the Russian ability to win the alliance of the Khan dividing the Tatars. In addition, contrasting with the more uniform nature of Western armies, including the large Russian army, there were major divisions within the main Turkish force between the *janissaries* and the provincial forces, in large part resting on the contempt by the hereditary military, the *janissaries*, for what they saw as upstarts. The Turkish military was less well integrated than its Chinese counterpart. These factors affected the motivation and cohesion of Turkish forces, contributing to Russian victories; although there was also considerable bravery on the part of individual Turkish commanders and units. The fierce defence of individual fortresses abundantly displayed this bravery, but battles revealed a serious lack of cohesion on the part of the Turks.[19]

Rumiantsev's tactics helped to bring success in battles such as Ryabaya Mogila, Larga and Kartal in 1770, and Kozludji in 1774. At Kartal, where the Russians were, as usual, heavily outnumbered, the Turks, although fighting bravely, suffered from fighting north of the Danube. Having been defeated, many Turks were killed re-crossing the river, as also happened with Prince Eugene's victory over the Turks at Zenta in Hungary in 1697. The fortress of Ismail fell soon after Kartal. Although there are issues with the accuracy of figures, Turkish casualties were far greater than those of the Russians: at Larga, 3,000 Turks to fewer than 100 Russians, at Kartal maybe 22,000 to between 900 and 1,500.

At Kozludji in 1774, the Russian square advanced and beat off a *janissary* attack supported by the artillery being developed by Baron François de Tott, a French-trained Hungarian noble. Rain spoiled the cartridges in the cloth pockets of the *janissaries*, whereas the Russians, who used leather pockets, were more fortunate. Russian firepower was supported by a cavalry attack that broke the Turkish will to fight; and twenty-five of Tott's cannon were captured.

The Russians overran the Crimea in 1771, while the Turkish fortress system on the Danube was breached in 1770 and 1774. Indeed, it was in order to defend these fortresses that Grand Vizier Halil Pasha had advanced north of the Danube in 1770. The 1774 campaign led the Turks to terms. Short of supplies, their army was demoralised and unable to take the initiative.

Success was more than a matter of battlefield skill and determination. The Russian army was also increasingly expert in the deployment of its forces. The adoption of more flexible means of supply helped to reduce the cumbersome baggage trains, although logistics remained a serious problem. The situation was eased in part due to a better ability to mobilise resources from near the zone of operations, a product of success in transforming Ukraine governmentally, politically, socially and, to a degree with Russian settlement, ethnically. Improvements permitted better operational planning, including greater use of river links to ease supply movements. Nevertheless, aware of the logistical difficulties faced by the need to supply the army, Rumiantsev grasped the need to take the initiative in order to produce results.

By the Treaty of Küçük Kaynarca (Kutchuk-Kainardji) of 21 July 1774, the Russians gained territory to the north of the Black Sea, including the coast as far as the River Dniester, as well as the right to fortify Azov and to sail through the Dardanelles. Russia acquired the right to protect those associated with a new Orthodox church in Constantinople, a provision that was to be extended to wide-ranging demands to protect Orthodox Christians living under Turkish rule. Russia also obtained the independence of the khanate of the Crimea from Turkey, a move that was assumed, correctly, to be a preliminary to Russian annexation. Such an annexation was necessary if Russia was to be a major Black Sea power.

This conflict, the most successful for Russia against the Turks so far, marked an important shift in the military balance as well as in the politics of Eastern Europe. The Eastern Question, the fate of the Turkish empire, moved up the international agenda. Moreover, Russian success in the Crimea represented a major stage in the closing off of the prospect of action by steppe peoples against more settled societies. The struggle was not simply one of the West versus the Rest, but also reflected and helped mould the character of the West. There was no comparable Western action against the Turks elsewhere, which separated the success of Russia, its politics and its army, from the other Western powers, notably Austria, which had no similar success.

In addition, although the Russian fleet was victorious in the Aegean in 1770 (see p. 172), there were no Western conquests at the expense of the Turks in the Mediterranean, either in that war or until Napoleon arrived in Egypt in 1798. Indeed, as a result of their reconquest of the Morea in 1715 and their conquest of Crete in 1669, the Turks held more territory in the eastern Mediterranean in 1780 than they had done in 1700 or 1600. The contrast between Western territorial expansion against the Turks by land and by sea was important to the geopolitics of Eastern Europe and to power relationships within the West.

Africa

At the same time in Africa, not only was there no real Western military pressure, but also the Turks, who had played a role in Ethiopia and on the Swahili Coast in the sixteenth century, were inactive. As a result, the politics of the Horn of Africa were separate from those of Eurasian and Western international competition, although they were linked, notably through trade in arms. In the 1760s, Mika'el (Michael) Suhul, formerly Ras of Tigrai and now of Gondar, built up an army 30,000 strong, and equipped 8,000 of them with muskets. The cost of supporting this army led to harsh exactions.[20] Mika'el was opposed to Muslim and Galla influences at the imperial court and posed as a Christian and national champion. He tried, without success, to persuade the Negus (Emperor) Iyoas (Yohannes or John) I (r. 1755–69) to attack the Funj kingdom of Sennar in modern North Sudan. Iyoas tried to have Mika'el assassinated. The latter defeated his master Iyoas in 1769 at Azezo, his musketeers wrecking the opposing cavalry. Iyoas was publicly hanged after the battle. Later in the year, Mika'el's musketeers overcame resistance at the battle of Fagitta.

A puppet emperor, Yohannes II, the elderly son of Iyasu I (Joshua) (who had been killed in 1706), was put on the throne. Mika'el planned to keep control of Yohannes by making him accompany him on campaign, but Yohannes wished, instead, to go to the imperial capital, which led Mika'el to have Yohannes poisoned.

However, in 1771, at Sabarkusa, a battle that lasted several days, Mika'el was defeated by rival provincial warlords, especially Wand Bewasen of Begemder, whose army made successful use of shock tactics. This result underlines the extent to which, although they were important in warfare in Ethiopia, firearms alone could not determine conflict, and also underlines the need to consider battles rather than looking at only one, whether supposedly decisive or not, in isolation.[21] As so often, methodology, historiography and conceptualisation are linked in military history. In this period, in what is now northern Nigeria, Babba Zaki was the first ruler of Kano to have a guard of musketeers, although he also had a large force of cavalry.

Ethiopia continued unstable. Under Yohannes II's son, Takla Hāymānot II (r. 1769–77), the emperor remained weak, while there was division and conflict between the leading Ethiopian chiefs, the rulers of Tigrai, Gondar, Gojām and Shoa, the last of which had become effectively independent in mid-century.

Europe

Just as against the Turks, so against the Prussians and Poles, Russian power proved formidable. Indeed, Russia was the most obvious counterpart to China in Eurasia. That did not mean that the Russians were always successful, but, despite his fame, Frederick the Great proved less adept at resisting them during the Seven Years' War than the Burmese were at holding off China. That instance, however, underlines the problems of comparisons as Prussia was geographically far more exposed to pressure than Burma and was fighting several powers at once.

Russian success across a range of warmaking was shown not only against the Turks and Prussians, but also in the conflict with Polish patriots from 1768 that culminated in the First Partition of Poland by Russia, Austria and Prussia in 1772. An attempt by the Russians to suppress Polish independence of action was assisted by the divisions amongst their opponents, but the campaigns were far from easy for Russia. The problems of controlling a vast territory were exacerbated by the mobility of the Polish light cavalry, while the decentralised nature of Polish politics ensured that it was not possible for the Russians to win the war by identifying and capturing a small number of targets.

There was an emphasis on mobility. Russian victories depended on the remorseless deployment of major resources, as in the successful three-month siege of Cracow in 1772, and on their willingness to force rapidly-moving engagements on the Poles by bold attacks. At Landskron in 1771, Russian cavalry and infantry stormed the Polish position. In the ensuing battle, the cavalry put the Polish infantry to flight while the Russian infantry held off the Polish cavalry. At Stalowicz the following year, a bold, surprise dawn advance into the village where the forces of Lithuania were based brought the Russians, under Suvorov, victory. More generally, the Russians' successful emphasis on speed, notably when under Suvorov, indicated that, far from it being simply formulaic, as might be suggested by volley training and linear formations, there was a dynamism and flexibility in Western warfare in this period. In his *Travels* (1772), Joseph Marshall, possibly a pseudonym, commented:

> If we judge from the present state of the Russian army, we may look for great success; for the first foundation of it, experience, is strong in most of the officers, and the men may also be called veterans. It is the same army that saw all the campaigns against the king of Prussia ... and that have since been in continual action in Poland. ... It consists of two hundred and fifty thousand old soldiers ... with a train of artillery as fine as any in the world, and, what is of yet greater consequence, well supplied with officers and engineers from all parts of Europe. ... The Russians are very sensible, that the losses they sustained, and their want of success in general, against the king of Prussia, was owing to their artillery being very badly served, and it has given them a great eagerness to remedy this fatal evil.[22]

In the 1770s, troops were also used to suppress opposition among the Cossacks. In 1772, a rising by Yaik Cossacks was suppressed by regulars supported by Kalmyks and Cossacks. In June, an attack by Cossack cavalry on a Russian square was beaten off, and the rebellion was suppressed, after which a garrison was stationed at Yaitsk.[23]

A far larger Cossack rising under Yemelyan Pugachev broke out in September 1773. In an instructive instance of the influence of governmental models, Pugachev established a College of War that was modelled on the Russian War Ministry and divided his troops into regiments. Their numbers were swelled with peasant runaways, especially from the harsh working conditions of the mines and metallurgical plants of the Urals. The fortress of Orenburg on the River Ural was besieged, Russian relief forces beaten off, and the rebellion spread, especially into the Urals. However, there was no real co-ordination of the rebel bands, and also a shortage of cannon and ammunition. The Urals' armaments industry was not organised to the benefit of the rebels, many of whom were armed only with spears, axes and sticks. While Pugachev remained unable to take Orenburg and Yaitsk, whose fortifications defied attack, Russian troops advanced from a number of directions in the winter of 1773–4, and, on 22 March, Pugachev was defeated at Tatishchev. Morale collapsed, Orenburg and Yaisk were relieved, and a new rebel force under Pugachev was dispersed.

Nevertheless, Pugachev raised a new army, captured the fort of Osa in June and, on 10 July, defeated a force of armed citizens outside the major city of Kazan on the Volga river east of Moscow, which was captured on 12 July, although the citadel held on. Pugachev won fresh support by promising freedom to the serfs of the Volga valley. A mutiny by the garrison of Saratov, a major city on the Volga, led to its fall to Pugachev, but the rebel movement lacked organisational structure. Moreover, Russian troops, which had been pulled back from the Turkish front, ensured that the rebels' military position deteriorated. Defeated in late August, Pugachev was betrayed in September and executed.

Russia's military strength was much feared in the West, not least because Russian forces had been deployed into Germany in 1716, 1735, 1748, and during the Seven Years' War, briefly capturing Berlin in 1760. As a consequence, Russia's neutrality in the War of the Bavarian Succession of 1778–9 fought by Austria and Prussia was both important to contemporaries and contributed to the misleading subsequent sense that those two were the key military powers and Prussia the most important. In practice, continuing the pattern of the last stage of the Seven Years' War, Frederick was no longer as successful as earlier. He advanced in Bohemia in 1778 and 1779, only to be blocked by the Austrians who preferred to rely on strong defensive positions rather than on the risks of battle, a choice that proved successful. The cost and stalemate of the conflict rapidly led to peace.

The War of the Bavarian Succession has not been the subject of much separate work in English. Usually it is covered as the last of Frederick the Great's wars and as representing the diminishing quality of Prussian warmaking. As such, it invites comparison with Napoleonic warmaking, which became less tactically, operationally, and strategically effective in his last years.

There was conflict elsewhere in Europe, notably in Corsica as the island's purchase from Genoa by France in 1768 led to a rebellion in 1768–70 that was suppressed in an effective display of counter-insurgency warfare.[24] Nevertheless, compared with the period 1740–62, that from 1763 to 1789, especially to 1776, was generally peaceful in Christian Europe. As a result, it is possible to argue that, freed from the pressure of conflict, there was a stagnation in military practice and development that contributed to the idea of an *ancien régime* style of warfare that was anachronistic and limited. The American War of Independence can then appear as a radical break. However, in Christian Europe, the 1760s–80s was also a period, notably, but not only, in France, of theoretical debate, institutional development, and preparation for war.

The Americas

Russia, Austria and Prussia were not to be involved in the major conflict in the Atlantic world. Beginning in obscure Massachusetts townships in 1775, a rebellion spread and widened out to become a trans-oceanic and naval war that was greater in scale than the comparable sections of the Seven Years' War. The origins of the conflict, however, did not lie in Franco-Spanish attempts to reverse the verdict of the last. Indeed, in 1770–1, they had pulled back from the brink when war with Britain had seemed in prospect over competing claims to the Falkland Isles, from which Spanish forces had expelled a British position in 1770 leading to a large-scale British naval mobilisation directed at Spain and her ally France. Instead, the War of American Independence not only began, as that in 1754 had done, with a North American quarrel, but also stemmed from initiatives taken by colonists. Their successful defiance of British rule, which, however, was very different from the politics of 1754, then provided the basis for eventual Franco-Spanish intervention against Britain.

Resistance to European rule took many forms in the Americas. The Portuguese continued to face opposition from unsubjugated Natives. By the 1780s, the Paiaguá had been largely wiped out, but the Muras of central Amazonia, adept with their bows and arrows, and effective owing to their mobility, harried Portuguese settlements and trade routes in the 1760s and

1770s, ambushing Portuguese canoes; although they could only check, not reverse, the tide of advance. The same was true of Native resistance to the Spaniards, whether in the Guajiro Peninsula in Colombia in the 1770s,[25] on the Mosquito Coast of Nicaragua, or by the Araucanians in Chile.

In contrast, rivalry between the European powers in South America was limited, other than longstanding rivalry between Portugal and Spain over the northern bank of the Plate estuary. The French meanwhile developed a base at Cayenne (French Guiana) on the northern coast of South America. As Portugal had long been pressed to accept the interest of France, a stronger power, in the region, this expansion to the north of Brazil did not lead to conflict.

In North America, the spreading use of firearms and horses helped put the Spaniards under pressure. Their expedition against the Apache in 1775 was unsuccessful, while that year the Ipai burnt the mission at San Diego; and by the end of the century many missions and *presidios* had been abandoned, although there had also been significant Spanish expansion north along the Californian coast. This expansion was helped by the local availability of Spanish naval power based on the Pacific coast of Mexico, an availability that testified to the global range of the major Western powers.

The Russians, meanwhile, having sailed across the North Pacific from Siberia, were extending their power along the Aleutian Islands. In 1761, effective resistance on the Fox Islands began, only to be overcome in 1766 by an amphibious force deploying cannon. Massacre and disease secured the Russian 'achievement'.

The British faced opposition by Native Caribs on the Caribbean island of St Vincent, and, more significantly, a large-scale slave rebellion in Jamaica in 1760, Tacky's Revolt. At the same time, not all the slaves in Jamaica rebelled, and the willingness of others to fight for their masters helped ensure success for the latter. As with the more general problem of assuming a misleading dichotomy between Western and non-Western forces, this instance of securing local support helped explain the success of Western power. However, it could also be necessary for the British to use regular troops in large numbers, as when faced with Maroons (escaped slaves) in Jamaica in the 1730s and with rebelling slaves in the West Indies in the 1790s, for example on Grenada.[26]

There were also serious problems in the North American interior. In 1759–61, the British deployed regulars, colonial forces, and allied Natives such as the Chickasaw, to force the Cherokee to terms. This remark, however, provides no indication of the difficulty of the struggle, its destructiveness, which included the killing of hostages and the torching of villages leaving lasting damage,[27] nor the extent to which, far from there being a total victory, this war was followed by a compromise peace. However, British strength was also revealed. It proved possible to move troops from elsewhere within an integrated military system. Once the French in Canada had been defeated, units could be moved south, both against the Cherokee and, in 1762, to help capture Havana from Spain as the result of a major deployment of strength. These operations showed the range of British campaigning in the Americas.

Like the conquest of Canada, the Cherokee War indicated the British ability to renew operations, notably with new forces, after initial setbacks. The latter were much in evidence in Pontiac's War (1763–4), a struggle that reflected Native opposition to the movement of colonists into their area of activity. In the initial stages of the war, there were successful attacks on a series of British forts, while the British felt obliged to abandon others, and their field forces were also ambushed. The British proved less effective at fighting in the woodlands of the frontier zone than their Native opponents, and the army's dependence on supply routes made it more vulnerable to ambush.

Owing, however, to the British conquest of the French bases in Canada in 1759–60, the Native Americans had no access to firearms other than those they had captured. The Anglo-French rivalry that had given a measure of opportunity to the Native Americans, providing, for example, French arms and ammunition to the Abenaki of Vermont for use against New England, had been ended. Furthermore, in 1763–4, helped by the end of war with France and Spain, large numbers of British troops were deployed in North America. The capacity of the regulars and colonists to respond to Native successes and to mount fresh efforts was indicative of the manpower resources they enjoyed and, crucially, could deploy and sustain; and the situation was stabilised anew. The combination of demographic and economic factors led Adam Smith to suggest, in *The Wealth of Nations* (1776), that, although the Natives in North America 'may plague them [European settlers] and hurt some of the back settlements, they could never injure the body of the people'.[28] Yet, it has also been argued that, had there been greater Native unity, this could have ensured that the Allegheny Mountains were a more effective barrier against white expansion westward.[29]

In an important indication of the political dimension, the stabilisa-tion of relations with the Native Americans in 1764 entailed the British accepting the limitations of the use of force. Instead, they turned back to diplomacy. Although the British authorities assured themselves that their terms were imposed, the settlement was in practice a compromise. The Natives returned all prisoners, but ceded no land. Indeed, Native resistance encouraged the British government to oppose colonial settlement west of the Alleghenies, which greatly helped to increase colonial anger with British control, contributing to the developing crisis in relations with the colonists.[30]

Indeed, British authorities encountered difficulties not only with some of the Natives, but also (less violently) with some colonists, notably in the Stamp Act Crisis of 1765–6, a hostile reaction against taxation that had been imposed by the government in London. The Seven Years' War had left the British government with an unprecedentedly high level of national debt and it looked to America to meet a portion of the burden. The Americans, however, no longer felt threatened by French bases in Canada and were therefore unwilling to see British troops as saviours. The Stamp Act of 1765 led to a crisis as Americans rejected Parliament's financial demands, and, thereafter, relations were riven by a fundamental division over constitutional issues.

However, in the 1760s, the British government did not face the opposition nor respond with the level of force that was to be seen in Massachusetts in 1774–5. Pontiac's War and the Stamp Act Crisis indicated the extent to which mid-century conflict produced both changes and strain in the Native and European societies in North America, strains that increased anxiety and tension over governmental policies.[31]

Conflict with Natives tested both regulars and colonials, and encouraged the development of experience with what was termed small war, as well as a process of brutalisation and fear through conflict in a challenging cultural context.[32] Nevertheless, in 1765, despite the enhanced capability represented by British experience of small war, most of North America was still under the control of Native Americans, and both the Cherokee War and Pontiac's War had indicated their resilience in regions reasonably close to centres of British settlement. In the South-East, moreover, the Creek Confederacy was a potent Native element.

Settler pressure continued but was resisted by the Natives. Thus, in 1774, 1,500 Virginia militia advanced against the Shawnee, who had attacked settlers in their territory and had ambushed a volunteer force that went to the settlers' assistance. The Shawnee were defeated at the Battle of Point Pleasant. At the same time, the Native American issue was much less prominent for the British in the early 1770s than it had been a decade earlier. In place of the extended network of forts, defended portages, and roads created by British troops then, there were, by the 1770s, few military posts in the interior. In part, this new distribution of troops reflected growing anxiety, instead, about the loyalty of the British colonists who were concentrated in coastal areas, notably in Boston.[33]

Rebellions by colonists were better able than opposition by Natives to strike the centres of imperial power in the colonies. Opposition to Spanish rule, after trade outside the Spanish imperial system or in non-Spanish ships was banned, led to a rebellion in New Orleans in 1768. Mindful of its ally's determination to restore authority, France rejected this attempt to return to its rule (Louisiana had been transferred from France as part of the Peace of Paris, the peace settlement after the Seven Years' War), and Spanish forces reimposed control.

Amid a number of rebellions in Spanish Latin America, including by the Mayans of Central America,[34] the rigorous collection of taxes led to a general insurrection, or Great Rebellion, in Peru in 1780–1 headed by José Gabriel Túpac Amaru, a descendant of the last Inca rulers. Millenarian beliefs played a role in the rebellion, beliefs that owed something to Jesuit proselytisation. This proselytisation had also been a factor in the Guarani War of 1754–5 as Native Americans resisted the transfer of authority over Jesuit *reducciones* (settlements) east of the Paraguay valley and to the north of the Plate estuary from Spain to a more intrusive Portugal. Like the White Lotus rising in China in the 1790s, the Great Rebellion showed the importance of popular religious convictions in encouraging a defiance of the conventional equations of military strength.

More than 100,000 people died in the subsequent conflict, but the uprising was suppressed. At Arequipa (in the Andes mountains of southern Peru) in 1780, superior Spanish firepower helped ensure the defeat of local rebels armed with lances, sticks, and the traditional Andean weapon, the sling. Helped by a profitable surge of sugar production in Mexico and by the reforming initiatives of Charles III (r. 1759–88), Spain proved more dynamic as a power than it had been in mid-century.[35] Moreover, alongside rebellions, it is important to emphasise the extent of Native co-operation with Spanish rule, and, indeed, this co-operation was also seen during the rebellions.[36]

The American War of Independence

The rebellion in thirteen British colonies in North America in 1775–83 thus emerges as distinctive because of its success. This was doubly true because other rebellions in the British world failed, notably the Jacobite risings of 1715–16 and 1745–6 in Scotland and northern England, and the Irish rising of 1798. The latter examples indicate the value of looking at the wider scale because the American case suggests that foreign intervention might be the key element in the New World as only the rebels in the British colonies attracted long-term, large-scale support. More specifically, French intervention was crucial to British defeat by an American–French force at Yorktown in Virginia in 1781, a defeat that led to a change of government in London the following year. In contrast, more modest French assistance, at a time when France was also heavily engaged with other European powers, did not help the Jacobites to victory in 1745–6 nor the Irish in 1798. Looked at differently, each case has to be judged on its individual merits and the possibilities of different outcomes in each of the rebellions has to be assessed. Fighting broke out near Boston in 1775 as a result of the determination of the government of Lord North to employ force, and the willingness of sufficient Americans to do likewise. An ill-advised attempt to seize illegal arms dumps led to clashes at Lexington and Concord, and the British were soon blockaded by land in Boston. Their attempt to drive off the Americans led to very heavy losses at the battle of Bunker Hill. The British were driven from the thirteen colonies from New Hampshire to Georgia in 1775.

The fact that Britain's most important colonies in the western hemisphere, those in the West Indies, did not rebel, despite the sensitivity of their élites on questions of constitutional principle, suggests, however, that there was no inevitable crisis in the British imperial system, but rather that factors particular to the American colonies were crucial. Similarly, there was no rebellion in Ireland.

The Declaration of Independence, issued on 4 July 1776, was intended to encourage international backing, notably from France, by making it less likely that the conflict would end in a reconciliation within the British empire. The conflict ceased to be a rebellion and, instead, became the first instance of a European settler colony seeking independence, which was a radical step. This outcome made foreign support more worthwhile, both to foreign powers and to the American Patriots.[37]

Conversely, it became necessary for the British to secure military results that achieved the political outcome of an end to a drive for independence, an outcome that was likely to require both a negotiated settlement and acquiescence in the return to loyalty and in subsequently maintaining obedience. This outcome rested on very different politics from those of the conquest of New France (Canada) during the Seven Years' War, a step secured by the governor's surrender in 1760 and the subsequent Anglo-French peace negotiations in Paris in 1762–3. The demographics were also very different. The French colonial population in North America was far smaller than that of Britain, with about 56,000 inhabitants in French Canada by 1740 compared with nearly a million people of European background in British North America. Indeed, British emigration to North America had been seen as a threat by French diplomats.[38]

Political contexts established particular strategic issues. In the case of the War of American Independence, it was unclear to the British how to translate military outcomes into political results, and also whether the best outcomes related to supporting Loyalists or bringing down Patriots in what was also an American civil war. If the latter was the policy, it was uncertain whether it was to be achieved by winning control over territory or by defeating Patriot armies. The British government did not want, and could not afford, a large occupation force. Instead, like that of most imperial powers, its rule depended on consent, and the solution to the rebellion was seen as political as much as military. The understanding of this may make British warmaking seem modern, involving as it did hearts and minds, but, in practice, this technique was common to counter-revolutionary warfare when the revolution, far from being restricted to marginal groups in society, included the socially prominent. However, the availability of a linked political–military strategy did not guarantee success in North America, or elsewhere. The Continental Congress, the Patriot government, rejected negotiations, notably in 1776 and 1778, and the British found it difficult to build up the strength of the Loyalists. Indeed, John Adams, a prominent revolutionary, suggested that the very act of revolution led to its success.

As with other revolutionary struggles, the war was a political as much as a military struggle; therefore, the revolutionaries had to convince themselves, and the British, that there was no alternative to independence. Adams' point could not be made of such conventional wars as that of the Bavarian Succession between Austria and Prussia (1778–9). Adams was certainly accurate as far as his base of New England was concerned, for it contained few active Loyalists; but the colonists were less unified elsewhere and, in particular, there was much Loyalism in Georgia, North Carolina, and in sections of the Middle Colonies, such as Long Island and the eastern shore of the Chesapeake. Indeed, divisions among the colonists meant that winning over the middle ground was significant for each side for both military and political reasons.

The politicisation of much of the American public, to which Adams referred, and the motivation of many of their troops[39] were important aspects of what was conventionally seen as 'modernity' when this state was understood in terms of mass mobilisation and citizens' armies. Today, in contrast, modernity is more readily understood in terms of often only partly engaged publics and relatively small, volunteer professional armies. Ironically, this description was truer of the British in 1775–83 than of the Americans. Such comparisons between the situation in the eighteenth century and later ideas of development and progress can be misleadingly ahistorical; but these comparisons also demonstrate the possibly questionable nature of the tendency to ascribe probable victory to a popular fight for independence. Until 1778, when France officially entered the war on their side, the Americans fought alone. They had no formal allies, although, seeking to harm Britain, both France and Spain provided aid, especially munitions and money, for the Americans were short of both. The Americans also fought alone because Britain was not committed to any other war, ensuring that the British could devote their undivided attention to the colonies.

There was no major capability gap in the Americans' favour. Indeed, their cause was greatly handicapped by the problems of creating an effective war machine, including mobilising and directing resources. The revolution's anti-authoritarian character and the absence of national institutions made it hard to create a viable national military system.

The Americans failed to win the war with their offensives in 1775. Boston, the main British base, was too tough a nut to crack, while the American invasion of Canada, although initially successful, led to the Americans closing the year with an intractable siege of Québec. In 1776, the British evacuated Boston, when their anchorage became exposed to American cannon fire, but also hit back; and the Americans lost New York (1776) and Philadelphia (1777), after defeats at Long Island (1776) and Brandywine (1777). In 1776, they were driven from Canada.

Nevertheless, the Americans avoided decisive defeat. This was a key achievement given Britain's ability to focus on America. Moreover, at Saratoga in the Hudson valley in 1777, a British army under Burgoyne was forced to surrender at the end of a campaign characterised by poor strategic insight, operational folly, and an inability to cope with the tactical needs of the battlespace.[40] Furthermore, the British failed to create an effective pacification policy in the area they controlled.[41]

Once France officially came into the war in 1778 (in place of earlier providing secret assistance), it was also unclear to Britain which enemy should be the prime target. Indeed, few new units were subsequently sent to North America. Instead, much of the focus for the British and French was on seizing the Caribbean colonies of the other, a task where amphibious capability was linked to the profit to be gained from such seizures. France's entry into the conflict on the American side in 1778 transformed the war, pushed naval considerations to the fore, and shifted the geographical focus to encompass the West Indies, home waters, and even India. From 1778, Britain lacked the initiative overall. It launched offensives, such as those in Georgia (1778), South Carolina (1780), and Virginia (1781), but, on the whole, Britain's opponents were able to take the initiative in North America, the West Indies, and the Indian Ocean.

This multi-pronged attack caused major problems for British force-availability. Once the British lacked naval dominance and the initiative, they had to spread their troops out on defensive duties. It was difficult to take units from garrisons and assemble an expeditionary force. Moreover, in the face of French and Spanish attacks, the weaknesses of British positions were exposed. Britain's need to confront a number of challenges around the world placed considerable burdens on its ability to control and allocate resources and to make accurate threat assessments. This need also raised issues of strategic understanding that were exacerbated by poor communications. Before the telegraph produced the nineteenth-century communications revolution, instructions could go no faster than the swiftest horse or the speediest boat.

French entry changed the nature and politics of the war, but did not have the immediate effects on land that were, or might have been, anticipated. French entry did not oblige the British to abandon New York, nor did it lead to another American attack on Canada (which was discussed in 1778), nor to the postponing of British operations in the South. Instead, having captured Savannah, the major town in Georgia, in late 1778, the British successfully besieged Charleston, South Carolina, the major town in the South, in 1780. The return, after its fall, of many of the more prominent citizens of Lowland South Carolina to their loyalty appeared to be a vindication of the British policy of combining military force with a conciliatory policy. This policy had already been tried with some success in Georgia. However, like the Chinese in Burma, the British were affected by disease, in this case yellow fever.[42]

Spanish entry into the war in 1779 was important in the Caribbean, the British losing the colony of West Florida in 1779–81, Pensacola, the major position, falling in May 1781 to a much larger force. However, Spanish entry was not significant elsewhere in North America, except in so far as British forces were diverted to counter the reality and threat of Spanish efforts elsewhere, both in the Americas and in Europe.

The British failure of 1781 at the hands of the Americans and the French was not yet apparent. Instead, in January 1781, short of pay, food and clothes, and seeking discharge in the face of unclear enlistment contracts, both the Pennsylvania Line and three New Jersey regiments mutinied. The Pennsylvania mutiny was ended only by concessions,[43] which is a reminder of the precarious nature of the Revolution militarily even at this stage. George Washington had professionalised the Continental Army and imposed collective discipline, but his achievement was still uncertain.[44]

Prior to the Revolution, the colonists had developed what has been presented as a distinctive American way of war.[45] However, in conflict with France and the Native Americans, the British army had also crafted a marked capacity to operate successfully in North America, including in the interior.[46] Thus, the War of Independence did not feature one modern and developing military system defeating an anachronistic one; rather, two modernising systems competing with each other. Each was operating as fit for purpose, and this situation helps explain the difficulties facing the American revolutionaries. This observation can be extended to the prospects for other rebellions and revolutions, because, with armies and navies having to be fit for purpose for warfare that was neither limited nor indecisive, that situation made them more capable of acting against such insurrections.

Nevertheless, along with the geographical scale, the war's political dimension distinguished it from much *ancien régime* warfare. The difference in force–space ratios meant major contrasts in staff work, logistics, and operational concepts, while the politics of the revolutionaries' widespread commitment to independence fundamentally affected strategy. This was also true operationally in the case of the militia's major contribution to the American cause, including partisan warfare.

Conclusions

The approach taken in this chapter is scarcely the standard one for this period. The usual emphasis is not only heavily Western-centric, but also organised around the idea that the American Revolution was a key moment of novelty in world military history, a moment that was at once pregnant with future possibilities and also linked to a debate in Europe about how best to introduce major changes in order to fight effectively in a self-consciously modern and reforming fashion. The latter idea joins the American and French Revolutions and thus structures events around a clear narrative and analysis.

Instead, the argument here is that this approach is invalid. It makes little sense of conflict across much of the world, and also misunderstands the situation in the West. First, the emphasis on America and France downplays the vitality as military systems of the leading Western powers, Britain and Russia. Secondly, there is a misleading tendency to link military change to political radicalism. Thirdly, there is a failure to consider what was happening outside the West at the time. This chapter has demonstrated that, in a period in which the non-West appears less active, with no dominant narratives to match those of China versus the Zunghars or the career of Nadir Shah, nevertheless there were both important developments and ones that revealed the range of military capability.

The struggle between China and Burma is of particular significance because it indicates the difficulties faced by major powers in deploying their strength in hostile environments against determined opponents. The number of factors that played a role thus contributed to the range of military capability. The relationship between the China–Burma conflict and the other struggles of the two powers was significant, notably the Second Jinchuan War in the case of China and the war with Siam in that of Burma. Again, there was a parallel in the West, especially with France being able to act against Britain because it was not involved in the War of Bavarian Succession. Similarly, Turkey fought Russia and Persia in a sequential fashion. The role of choice, and the extent of skill involved, in relating policy to international systems involving a number of powers was highly important to the military history of the period.

6 1780–1800

These years are conventionally dominated by developments in Western Europe, the French Revolution, which broke out in 1789, and the outbreak of the French Revolutionary Wars which followed in 1792 and lasted until 1802, although, after Napoleon came to power in France in 1799, these wars are sometimes grouped with the Napoleonic Wars which lasted, with two brief intervals in 1802–3 and 1814–15, until 1815. Linked to this focus, this period is usually discussed in terms of a clear teleology. These developments are considered in this chapter, but the central themes of the chapter are different from the conventional account. Again, the perspective is global, with global, crucially, not only understood, as it so often is, in terms of conflict between Western imperial powers. Moreover, there is an engagement in this chapter with a range of issues that cannot be assessed in terms of the teleology already referred to.

The approach here aims to cover all the world at the end of the century, not only in order to assess important trends, but also so as to be able to compare them with the situation at the start of the century. In some cases, it is possible to make direct comparisons, as in assessing Russian and Austrian wars with the Turks between 1787 and 1792 alongside those of the 1710s. Other themes for 1780–1800 include the problems of sustaining and enforcing success, and translating victories into victory, as with the British in North America in 1780–1, the Burmese and Siamese in South-East Asia, and Napoleon in Egypt and the Near East. This issue overlaps with that of the mixed success of imperial pressure on weaker states, for example the Chinese on Vietnam and Nepal, as well as the very differing results of the British in their three wars with Mysore in this period.

Lastly, French debates in the 1780s (and earlier) over military techniques can be considered, alongside the actions, from 1792, of the French Revolutionaries, as an attempt to increase the effectiveness, and change the nature, of Western warfare. However, the serious problems the French encountered in the 1790s, notably, but not only, in 1798–9, suggest the need for caution about the assessment of French activity in terms of effective sweeping change, let alone military revolution.

China

By the end of the century, China was at peace with all its neighbours, and essentially on China's terms. China was not threatened at this point on her land or sea frontiers by any power with significant offensive capability. Russia accepted China's treaty boundaries, but not those of Turkey or Persia as each agreement with the latter two was seen as the basis for further advances. As far as China's other frontiers were considered, the eastern (Khalka) Mongols were part of the Chinese system; the Zunghars had been destroyed; Eastern Turkestan had been conquered; and other neighbours were tributary states. The next powerful Central Asian people to the west, the Kazakhs, were divided. Nevertheless, important elements among the Kazakhs accepted tributary status and remained under Chinese influence until it was supplanted by that of Russia in the mid-nineteenth century.

There was failure, however, for China against Vietnam in 1788–9. In 1786, a successful peasant revolt against the Le dynasty, the Hanoi-based rulers of northern Vietnam, had been followed by the flight to China of the new Le ruler where he sought Chinese backing. This cause was backed by Sun, governor of the frontier provinces of Guangxi and Guangdong, and he persuaded the Qianlong emperor to support a new Chinese-dominated order in Vietnam. However, the Chinese attempt to capture Hanoi was defeated by Nguyen Hue, the unifier of Vietnam, as the result of a surprise attack on Chinese forces in January 1789. Rejecting advice for a renewed invasion, the Emperor dismissed Sun and accepted Nguyen Hue's effort to negotiate peace, which included the acceptance of vassal status.

The campaign had not been helped by the lack of domestic (Vietnamese) support for the incompetent Le ruler, while the Vietnamese were well familiar with the use of firearms. At the same time, there was no Chinese tradition of sustained attempts at conquest in South-East Asia, the area was not of crucial strategic interest, and the heavily-forested environment was unsuitable for Manchu cavalry.[1] Having reunited Vietnam after nearly two centuries of division, Nguyen Hue proclaimed himself Emperor as Quang-trung (r. 1788–92).

Elsewhere, the Chinese were more successful. Gurkha incursions from Nepal in 1788 had led the Tibetans in May 1789 to agree to pay an annual tribute. In 1791, the Gurkhas invaded anew. These developments challenged the Chinese position in Tibet. As a result, the Chinese dispatched about 15,000 troops, mostly from nearby Sichuan and Tibet, but including bannermen from more distant Beijing and Mongolia. The invasion force led by Fukang'an, the most prestigious Chinese general of the period,

suffered heavy casualties once it crossed into Nepal and was also challenged logistically and by the approaching winter. Nevertheless, the Chinese
advanced to near Katmandu in Nepal and the Gurkhas offered terms which
the Chinese accepted. The Gurkhas entered into a tributary relationship,
and thus recognised Chinese authority. The British in Bengal had refused to
come to the aid of the Gurkhas. The Chinese advance, a formidable and costly
logistical undertaking, owed much to financial support from the major salt
merchants who provided much of the money for Qianlong's operations. The
opportunity to increase Chinese authority in Tibet was also taken.

This account of the Nepal/Tibet crisis presents it in terms of coherent
national units, but, as so often, the situation was more complex and there
was a question of the co-operation across such boundaries. A dispute
between the two brothers of the dead third Panchen Lama over his inheritance became bound up with institutional and sectarian divisions within
Tibet, and Samarpa, the tenth Shamar tulku, the Red Crown lama, fled
to Nepal in 1788 seeking support. He swore to become a Nepalese subject
rather than backing the Tibetan government, which he presented as
Chinese. Samarpa was then alleged to have provided the invading Gurkhas
with necessary information about the route. Samarpa died after the
Chinese victory, allegedly of hepatitis or suicide, and the recognition of any
more Shamar tulkus was banned, ending that line of lamas.[2]

Two campaigns against the Gurkhas, that in 1789, which had not in fact
led to conflict, as well as the 1791 campaign, were included in the list of
ten victorious campaigns to which Qianlong lay claim in his treatise *Yuzhi
shiquan ji* [*In commemoration of the ten complete military victories*], composed in
1792. This treatise was misleading in that it also included failures, notably
the campaigns against Burma (1760s) and Vietnam (1780s), while the 1791
Nepal expedition was less successful than was suggested and also reflected
the limitations of Manchu imperialism. These limitations included the
serious costs and logistical problems of frontier operations as well as the
strength of opposition.[3] At the same time, the treatise testified to the strong
association between monarchical prestige and military success.

The Chinese army also devoted much attention to suppressing domestic
risings. Some were mounted by Han Chinese subjects, notably the huge
and very costly millenarian White Lotus rebellion of 1796–1805 in the Han
River valley and beyond, especially in western Hubei, southern Shaanxi
and northern Sichuan. Non-Chinese subjects also posed serious problems,
particularly with the Miao revolts in the provinces of Hunan and Guizhou
in 1795–7. The diversion of troops to deal with these revolts helped encourage the White Lotus leaders to rebel. The Yao revolt in eastern Guangxi in
1790 was also significant, as was a Taiwanese rebellion in 1787–8, the Lin

Shuangwen Rebellion, in which migrants from one part of China feuded with those from another. Regulars and militia were used to suppress the rising.

As with Spanish resistance to Napoleon from 1808, the White Lotus rebels made extensive use of guerrilla tactics and benefited from the hilly character of their core area. The rising was only put down with brutal repression and after a formidable military effort. While Green Standard (Han Chinese) troops were especially used for such 'pacification' duties, in this case Manchu banner troops from Manchuria were also employed, as were local mercenaries and militia.[4] As a reminder of the continuity of military commitments, the adopted son of Mingrui, who had been defeated and committed suicide in Burma in 1768, died in the White Lotus War in 1797 (Mingrui did not have a biological son). When the news reached the Qianlong emperor, he became sentimental, remembering Mingrui's death.

The Miao revolt was in response to the spread of Han settlement and the attempt to increase government power, a counterpart to the opposition of the Native Americans to American expansion. In turn, the Chinese army responded by creating more garrisons, building a wall, introducing military–agricultural colonists, and using brutal repression.

The scale of the risings in China means that they should be no mere postscript to the military history of the period, especially as the White Lotus rebellion is frequently seen as a key event in the history of Manchu China. The rebellion indicated the importance of religious commitment as a source of opposition, in this case millenarian sectarian Buddhism, a belief that it was possible and necessary through violence to usher in a better world. At the same time, the pressures of unprecedented population growth were significant, notably in leading to land shortage.

The strains linked to the conflict and caused by it were readily apparent, not least because more than 117,000 regular troops were deployed as well as hundreds of thousands of militia, and the war indicated the shrinking power of the central government. The failure of the emperor to control his generals and governors, who profited greatly from the war, was a major factor in the protraction of the conflict which, in total, cost 120 million taels of silver. This failure indicated the ability of the military leaders to impose their will on the new Jiaqing emperor (r. 1796–1820). However, the key point was that the rebellion was suppressed. The main rebel force in Hubei was destroyed in 1798, and the focus then moved to eastern Sichuan, but the rebels were unable to gain the initiative. By 1800, the rebellion was weak. The dates generally given for it, 1796–1805, are therefore misleading.

China focused on rebellions in the 1790s while Western powers, although faced by rebellions, notably in Vendée and Saint-Domingue for France, and, more briefly Ireland for Britain in 1798, concentrated on war with other powers. The scholarly focus on international conflicts then affects the treatment of rebellion elsewhere, for example in China and Turkey. However, the rebellions faced by the Chinese were greater in scale than those that Britain and France suppressed. On the other hand, the latter rebellions were linked to foreign powers (France and Britain respectively), which gave the rebellions strategic importance.

South-East Asia

The scale, tempo and intensity of conflict in South-East Asia matched those across much of Europe. Burma, Siam (Thailand) and Vietnam all saw a mixture of external warfare and statebuilding by force. Burma was unwilling to accept its failure in Siam and launched new offensives in 1785 and 1786. In 1785, there was an advance on Siam from the north as well as a pincer offensive on southern Siam focused on Junk Ceylon/Phuket Island. In the latter, one force moved overland from Tenasserim through the Kra Isthmus while a second force proceeded by sea from Tavoy. However, the Burmese occupation of Junk Ceylon was very brief, and the 1785 campaign failed because of Siamese attacks on Burmese communications. The 1786 offensive was defeated in battle. The scale of the Burmese military was indicated by the conscription of about 200,000 men for each of the 1785 and 1786 offensives.

Meanwhile, Tashin had been overthrown in Siam, having launched an unpopular invasion of Vietnam. As with Persia in the 1720s for Russia and Turkey, and North America in the 1770s for France, instability in Vietnam encouraged intervention by outside powers, for China was also to intervene in Vietnam. Tashin's growing insanity led Chakri, a general, to mount a coup in 1782, and Tashin was killed in the resulting street fighting. Chakri became ruler as Rama I (r. 1782–1809). The Siamese also expanded into the Malay peninsula, reasserting suzerainty over the northern Malay sultanates. Indeed, both Siam and Burma were central players in a wider-ranging pattern of competitive statebuilding, a pattern in which China played an episodic role as far as the other powers were concerned, but an insistent one in the case of peoples in its border regions.

In contrast, the Western role in the region was limited. The British East India Company established a presence in west Malaya at Penang in 1786, but the Company was unwilling either to expand this presence or to help the Sultan of Kedah, with whom the Penang negotiation had been conducted, against Siamese pressure. Meanwhile, in 1785, a Dutch squadron captured Kuala Selangor and Riouw, the island that controlled the eastern approach to the Malacca Strait, but this success made little difference to the regional powers.

Demonstrating the link between statebuilding and civil war, Vietnam was to become a more powerful state as it was unified. French arms and advisers played a role from the late 1780s, but to the benefit of the expansionist schemes of Nguyen Anh, who captured Saigon in 1789. Based in southern Vietnam around the Mekong delta, he was the rival of Nguyen Hue, Emperor Quang-trung (r. 1788–92). After he died, Nguyen Anh conquered all of Vietnam by 1802 and proclaimed himself Emperor Gia-Long. Although interested in Western military technology, the Vietnamese did not really Westernise.

Aside from attacking Siam, the energetic Bo-daw-hpaya of Burma (r. 1781–1819) expanded westward, overrunning the smaller kingdom of Arakan in 1784, and creating a tense situation in relations with the neighbouring position of the British East India Company in Bengal. Burmese expansion was read by the British as a threat related to French schemes. There was concern about links, including a possible Franco-Burmese-Vietnamese invasion of Siam, and Bo-daw-hpaya certainly negotiated with the French at their Bengal base of Chandernagore in his search for Western arms.[5]

The commitments on Burma's western frontier help explain its failure against Siam, serving as a reminder of the need to consider a state's military effectiveness and strategic choices by looking at the totality of its commitments. At the same time, Burmese failure against Siam also reflected leadership factors on both sides as well as the development of effective defensive strategies by the Siamese. Chakri mounted a more effective resistance to Burmese attacks than his predecessors had done.

This case indicates the flaws with analyses that allocate the causes of success or failure to only one factor, an approach that is overly common in social science accounts relying on metrics and/or seeking schematic explanations. However, the exigencies of space ensure that accounts of warfare generally simplify and this book cannot be free from the process. At the same time, it offers the central argument that the standard analysis in terms of a Western-driven early-modern military revolution is not only overly simplified but also misleading.

India

The standard narrative for India focuses on British activity and the attempts of Indian rulers to respond, culminating, for this century, in the successful British advance on Seringapatam, the capital of Mysore in southern India, in 1799. This advance, in which attacks by Mysore forces were beaten off by firepower in a battle at Malavelly on 27 March, was followed by the storming of the city on 4 May through its breached walls, with Tipu Sultan dying in its defence.[6]

The resulting end to the Mysore issue, with territory annexed and a pliant new ruler installed, becomes a key stage in an apparently now-inexorable process of British advance. As a reminder of the folly of taking a century as a rigid divide, the fall of Seringapatam was followed, albeit in a different war, by the victories of Arthur Wellesley, later Duke of Wellington, over the Marathas at Assaye and Argaum in western India in 1803. These three successes are then grouped together militarily by seeing them as triumphs for the British use of disciplined infantry firepower and by posing the question of why the Indians did not match this proficiency.

As with most analyses, this one is not without a basis, but it is also less than a complete account. Proposing that the threat from the British was the organising theme of Indian warfare fails to address the variety of developments within India, the extent to which the British faced serious difficulties there, and the degree of British dependence on Indian assistance.

At a broader geographical perspective within South Asia, there were other non-Indian states that were a threat besides Britain. The Burmese conquests of Manipur and Arakan were only a regional challenge, but campaigning in Siam and Laos demonstrated the range of Burmese operations, and there was an apparent threat to Bengal, which was to lead Britain to war with Burma in 1824. Again, the Chinese advance to Katmandu brought the Gurkhas into line as far as Chinese power in Tibet was concerned. The Chinese did not press on, but alongside their ability to intervene, albeit unsuccessfully, in Burma in the 1760s, they had provided a significant display of capability.

More centrally, with Timur Shah (r. 1773–93), a less bellicose and far less popular ruler than his father, the Afghans did not repeat their advances of the 1750s and early 1760s. Timur faced a number of opponents, and the imperial inheritance he had received was weakened both by serious opposition from within his family and because a sense of vulnerability encouraged opportunistic rebellions and attacks. To the east, in Punjab, there was continued opposition by the Sikhs. In Sind, to the south-east of Afghanistan, in 1779, the Amir, a vassal of Timur Shah, was driven out by a rival chief, Mir Fath Ali Khan, leading Timur to intervene. He drove Mir Fath out, but such successes frequently proved ephemeral unless secured by the presence of the ruler, and so in this case. Mir Fath regained Sind and, in 1786, Timur Shah accepted this on condition that tribute was paid. However, Mir Fath refused to provide the tribute in 1789, and Sind thus became independent.

To the north, Timur Shah was challenged by opposition from the Uzbeks under Emir Murad of Bukhara (r. 1785–1800, the founder of the Mangit dynasty), in modern Uzbekistan, who sought to exploit the weakness of Timur's authority north of the Hindu Kush mountains in Central Afghanistan. Having encouraged Balkh in northern Afghanistan to rebel, the Emir crossed the River Amu Darya (Oxus). In the event, Timur moved to oppose the advance and the Bukharans retreated, but Balkh and northern Afghanistan became in effect autonomous. In Khurusan in modern north-east Persia, Timur had to send three expeditions in order to end rebellions against the rule of his vassal, Shahrokh.

Opposition closer to the centre of Afghan power was more serious. In 1791, while the court was at Peshawar (in modern Pakistan), Timur Shah only narrowly survived a serious court conspiracy supported by many Peshawaris. In 1793, he died, with rumours that he had been poisoned. His successor was Zaman Mirza, his fifth son, and the son of a favourite wife. Governor of Kabul, the key point to control, Zaman was challenged by Timur's eldest son, Humayun Mira, who advanced from Kandahar, where he was governor, only to be defeated at Kalat-i-Ghilzai.

Rivalries within the royal family, notably near continual opposition to Zaman Shah (r. 1793–1800) from his brothers, greatly complicated relations with foreign powers, providing an obvious contrast with the situation in China which also did not follow primogeniture but which avoided such conflict. In the case of Persia, Agha Muhammad, the Shah, pressed for the cession of Balkh as a prelude to a Persian attack on Bukhara. Zaman Shah agreed, but Agha Muhammad turned west to deal with the Russians in the Caucasus, and Bukhara, encouraged by Zaman's half-brother Mahmud, Governor of Herat, seized Balkh. In turn, Zaman defeated Mahmud and captured Herat, and Bukhara returned to peace with Zaman. Similarly, Zaman advanced across the Indus to tackle a rebellion in Punjab, only to return to face a rebellion by Humayun Mirza who was backed by the Baluchi chiefs. When the Afghan army advanced, Humayun was betrayed, captured and blinded. Again, an invasion of Sind was abandoned due to renewed opposition by Mahmud, who was defeated near Girshk, only to be offered reinstatement when Zaman's attacks on Herat failed.

Despite these serious problems, the Afghans remained a factor in the power politics of northern India. In 1796, Zaman Shah invaded Punjab, retreating, however, when Agha Muhammad of Persia occupied Khurusan. In 1797, Zaman Shah invaded again, reaching Lahore and being promised the support of the Rohillas, only to turn back because his brother Mahmud rebelled again. In 1798, it was feared by the British and their allies that the Afghans would advance across north India as far as Oudh, which was a

British protectorate. There was concern about Afghan links in Oudh and more generally among the Muslims of northern India.

In response, the British looked at the idea of an Indian alliance against the Afghans involving in particular the Marathas, sought to persuade Persia to raise its level of military activity in order to dissuade the Afghans from advancing, and also anticipated supplying cannon and munitions both to Persia and to principalities south of the Punjab that might resist the Afghans, notably Sind. In the event, there was no Afghan advance. Fath Ali Shah (r. 1797–1834), Agha Mohammad of Persia's nephew and successor, backed Zaman's rebellious brothers and moved his army towards Khurusan in 1799, which led Zaman Shah to pull back to Peshawar. He was the last Afghan ruler to capture Lahore. This episode scarcely suggests an agenda of British dominance of India, let alone South Asia. However, it also demonstrated the range of British attention.

Zaman was faced by a major rebellion by Mahmud who enjoyed support from the powerful Durrani clan. Defeated in 1800, Zaman was blinded and replaced as ruler by Mahmud who, in turn, was overthrown in 1803 by Shah Shuja', the seventh son of Timur Shah. In 1809, the latter was defeated and replaced by Mahmud.

Leaving aside these external forces, it was again the case that the British were not necessarily the most dynamic element in India. Indeed, for much of the period, that position seemed rather to belong to the Marathas, who made major territorial gains in India and pressed for tribute from other states, such as Marwar, putting pressure on their finances and social cohesion.[7] Maratha proficiency was demonstrated in 1790 in victory over the Rajputs at Merta and in 1795 when the Nizam of Hyderabad, whom the British had wanted as an ally against the Marathas, was easily beaten. He was defeated at Kharda on 11 March, in large part because he retreated after his artillery and infantry were unable to prevail against the Maratha cannon and infantry. The terrain was not conducive for use of the cavalry of either side, which led both sides to rely on their Westernised infantry. As a result of this defeat, in which casualties were low,[8] much of the western half of the Nizam's dominions were lost to the Marathas.

Aside from success in battle, the Maratha military, especially the army of Mahadji Sindhia, was developing in size and weaponry. From mid-century, the Marathas had felt it increasingly necessary to supplement their cavalry with infantry and artillery, notably in order to be more effective against fortresses and so as to counter the advantages of British-trained infantry and artillery. However, this development greatly increased the cost of their more numerous armed forces, and thus disrupted the political economy of Maratha states, as well as slowing down their armies and exposing them to defeat by forces focused on infantry. Moreover, the Marathas could not counter the advantages the British derived from control of the resources of Bengal and thanks to dominance of coastal and oceanic waters.[9]

Hyderabad and Mysore also developed their infantry and artillery. Indeed, when the British took the major fortified city of Bangalore from Mysore in 1791, they found over 100 cannon. Indian military proficiency helped cause serious military problems for the British. In 1781, Colonel Thomas Goddard advanced from Bassein on Pune, overrunning the Bhore Ghaut, but failed to defeat the Marathas. Affected by attacks on his supplies, Goddard was forced to retreat with serious losses. In this campaign, the British suffered not only from the problems of terrain and logistics, and from Maratha effectiveness, but also from the need to fight Mysore at the same time. Thus, the multi-polar (divided) nature of Indian states after the fall of the Mughals did not always work to the benefit of the British. Indeed, the following year, Tipu Sultan surprised and defeated a British force just south of the Coleroon river. In this battle, the British held off the Mysore cavalry until their ammunition ran out.

Individual successes and failures had different causes, but the overall lesson was that Indian military systems were not foredoomed to failure. In particular, the light cavalry of Britain's opponents could best be thwarted only if the British recruited local allies. Hence, alongside their reliance on *sepoys* – Indian troops trained to fight with the weapons and tactics of their European counterparts – came the need for Indian cavalry campaigning in their own units. The British use of allied Indian military forces went back to Stringer Lawrence in the Carnatic in the 1740s, and put a premium on the political skill of British leaders, on the financial resources of Britain's Indian possessions, and also on the factors encouraging Indian rulers to help Britain, notably the search for assistance against other rulers. Political skill was a two-way process.

This help proved very important. In 1781, Goddard was able to recruit Mughal and Pathan cavalry, and in 1782 the Company's success in settling differences with the Marathas thwarted Haidar Ali's request that the latter send a force to threaten Bengal. The 1792 and 1799 advances on Seringapatam, the Mysore capital, were more successful than that of 1791 largely because local allies had been secured. In 1792, the *Peshwā* (the leading Maratha ruler), the Nizam of Hyderabad, and Britain all gained territory from Mysore in the peace treaty. The backing of the Nizam's forces was especially important in 1799.[10] He had been obliged to sign an alliance treaty with the Company the previous year.

Thus, the failure of Hyderabad, Mysore and the Marathas to make common cause against the British was crucial. Indeed, in 1784–7, Mysore and the Marathas fought a war, with Mysore victorious at Nargund in 1784. Divisions among the Marathas were also crucial. They were greatly weakened by periods of civil war that in general reflected disputed successions.[11] Moreover, the major shift in power from the centre to the peripheral Maratha states made the British task easier because it hindered co-operation between their opponents.

Rivalry between the leading Maratha dynasties and leaders, notably the *Peshwā*, Shinde (Sindhia), Holkar and Bhonsle (rulers of Nagpur), led to political instability as well as conflict, such as Mahadji Shinde's victory over Tukoji Holkar at the battle of Lakheri in May 1793, a struggle largely settled by the superior quality of the former's infantry under Benoit de Boigne. Holkar's *sepoys* fought to the end, unlike his cavalry which was driven from the field. Mahadji, however, died in 1794 and his successor, his nephew Daulatrao, lacked his ability. Daulatrao's attempt to gain control of the Maratha confederacy was a particular cause of instability. His forces were engaged with opponents within Mahadji's family and clientage system, as well as the Holkars and the Rajputs. The aggression of the volatile Daulatrao encouraged Baji Rao II, the *Peshwā* from late 1795, to look for British help and, in return, to provide support for the British against Tipu Sultan of Mysore.

It was the ability of the British to benefit from these problems and divisions within India that helped give them victory at a time of acute problems for Britain; and this was an achievement that was military, political and financial.[12] There were important structural factors aiding the British, not least the institutional continuity of the East India Company, and the ability of a profitable global trading system (the leading such system) to generate profits and provide credit that would enable the waging of sustained, large-scale conflict. Linked to this trading system came the importance of sea power. The British understanding of how best to campaign effectively in India, notably through improved logistics that helped in the combination of mobility with firepower, was also highly significant. At the same time, the British campaigning there from 1778 to 1806 amply illustrated the role of contingency and the crucial primacy of political factors, especially the lack of unity among the Indian princes.

The Persian and Turkish empires

General military history covering the close of the century continues its longer-term pattern of ignoring Persia. However, Persia remained of regional consequence while also suffering the consequences of the internal conflict that had been a factor from mid-century. The late 1780s and early

1790s saw the Qajar tribe under Agha Muhammad (r. 1779–97) take over the entire country, destroying the Zands. From the Qajar tribal base south of the Caspian Sea, the capital, Isfahan, was captured in 1785, while the city of Tehran accepted Agha Muhammad's power in 1786. Zand disunity was significant in his success. Failure exacerbated tensions among the Zands and in 1789 their leader, Ja'far Khan, was assassinated, after which internicine conflict flared up until Lotf Ali Khan Zand seized power in the important southern city of Shiraz that year. He held off Agha Muhammad from Shiraz, but the city rebelled in 1791 when he unsuccessfully advanced on Isfahan. Lotf Ali then besieged Shiraz without success, defeating a Qajar relieving force, but in 1792 Agha Muhammad advanced with a larger army. This army was attacked at night by Lotf Ali, but initial success was not maintained and Lotf Ali had to flee.[13] Moving east, he captured the city of Kirman, only for it to be besieged by Agha Muhammad and taken by treachery in October 1794. The surviving men were all blinded. In turn, Lotf Ali was betrayed and tortured to death. In 1796, Agha Muhammad advanced to Khurusan, taking the submission of Nadir Shah's grandson Shahrokh, who was then tortured to reveal the location of jewels. They were important to Agha Muhammad, who liked them but also saw them as totems of authority and legitimacy.[14]

A capacity for power-projection had already been demonstrated in 1795. Agha Muhammad advanced in the Caucasus in order to reconquer former Persian territories and to assert sovereignty. Georgia, abandoned by its Russian ally, was overrun by Persian cavalry. After a bitter battle, the capital, Tbilisi, was sacked, with heavy casualties, and 15,000 Georgians were then taken away as slaves; a brutally dramatic instance of the extent to which the Caucasus region was used as a source of slaves for the Islamic world.

Agha Muhammad's achievement was limited, however, because in June 1797, while campaigning in the Caucasus, he was stabbed to death by servants whose execution he had ordered but which had not yet been carried out. Already, his achievement had been challenged by Russia, which was not prepared to accept a Persian advance into the Caucasus. Advancing into Persia, the Russian forces captured Darbent, Baku, Shirvan and Gandja in 1796, although Paul I, the new ruler, then recalled the Russian troops. The Russian advance into Georgia, where troops were stationed in 1799, proved more lasting. After the death of its king, George XII, Russia annexed most of Georgia in 1801. In 1800, Georgia had rejected Persian pressure to send George's eldest son as a hostage, and an invasion by Daghestanis had been defeated by the Georgians.

To the east of Persia, the interest of the Durranis of Afghanistan in Khurasan remained an issue. Nevertheless, although much of Persian government was in effect devolved and a matter of eliciting co-operation,[15] Persia remained far more united than had been the case after Nadir Shah's assassination. Agha Muhammad had planned his succession, and his nephew, Fath Ali Shah (r. 1797–1834), duly gained power, readily suppressing opposition. Indeed, Persia was to prove an important player in the international relations of the early nineteenth century.

There had been no resumption of conflict with the Turks after the peace of 1779, but discussion of its possibility indicated the degree to which Persian expansion was still seen as a prospect. In the early 1780s, there was Russian interest in the idea of a partition of the Turkish empire by Austria, Russia and Persia. In opposition, France, which had long supported Turkey as a counter-weight to Russia, sought to thwart Russian influence in Persia, sending an embassy to Isfahan in 1784 that angered Catherine II (the Great) of Russia. This interest prefigured significant French, Russian and British rivalry for influence in Persia in the 1800s. Moreover, this rivalry was more similar to competition in the sixteenth and seventeenth centuries over winning the alliance of strong non-Western states than the late nineteenth-century case of Western powers contesting spheres of influence in these states.

The same was still true of Turkey, but, nevertheless, there was a growing sense, from the time of the 1768–74 Russo-Turkish War on, that there had been a major change in the balance of power between Turkey and its Christian neighbours. This change meant that these neighbours had to compete, both in order to maintain Turkey against their rivals and so as to ensure their own goals within the Turkish empire.

The latter issue slackened in the late 1770s as competition focused instead on rivalries within Christian Europe, notably with the Austro-Prussian War of the Bavarian Succession (1778–9). However, Catherine II shifted her attention in the late 1770s to ambitious anti-Turkish schemes, including the Greek Project, the bold plan for the expulsion of the Turks from the Balkans, and the creation, instead, of an empire ruled by her grandson born in 1779 who was symbolically christened Constantine. These schemes were supported by Prince Gregory Potemkin, an influential former lover of Catherine, who was closely associated with the development of Russia's recent gains from the Turks, not least the build-up of naval capacity on the Black Sea. Potemkin also had ambitions to be a successful general. In the meanwhile, Russia was led to advance by developments on the frontier. Russian intervention in the Crimea in support of a client khan, Sahin Giray, who came to power in 1777, was affected when he both proved an unreliable client and faced rebellion. This led to the dispatch of Russian troops in 1782, and the annexation of the Crimea the following April.

In many respects, a pattern of incipient Turkish collapse appeared clear. Indeed, there was growing French influence in Egypt and diplomatic chatter about the French being ceded the Mediterranean islands of Crete and Chios by the Turks.[16] However, it would be mistaken to prefigure the serious Turkish failure that was to be seen in the 1820s–30s. Moreover, although the Russians had done well in the war of 1768–74, they had failed then to obtain their territorial goals in the Danubian principalities (Moldavia and Wallachia), while their naval expedition to the Aegean had not led to the benefits Russia hoped for in Greece.

In addition, the Turks displayed considerable resilience in the 1780s. In 1786–7, they reimposed a measure of control over the Mamluk beys who wielded effective power in Egypt.[17] In 1786, an expeditionary force landed in Egypt and defeated the beys, capturing Cairo. However, the rebel beys retreated to Upper Egypt and, unable to impose a settlement, the Turks had to negotiate terms in 1787.

Despite the costs of the 1768–74 war, the Turks also displayed considerable determination in resisting the extension of Russian power. The latter had upset the balance of power in the Caucasus and, in 1785, Russia and Turkey were drawn in to support competing protégés among the local rulers. Negotiations between Russia and Turkey failed, and it was the Turks who declared war in 1787. Moreover, they decided to fight until the Russians had been driven from the Caucasus and the Crimea and a new Crimean khan had been appointed. The loss of the Crimea had been a major blow to Turkish military manpower as well as marking the loss of a large population of Muslims to non-Muslim rule. The bold Turkish plans, combined with the Russian Greek Project, indicated the extent to which military activity was not based on a modest, incremental path toward territorial expansion. Instead, warfare, far from being limited, rested on a determination to pursue major gains.

The war was to prove a disaster for the Turks. In 1787, the Turks took the initiative, launching an attack on the Russian fortress of Kinburn, part of the Russian defensive system on the Black Sea. In the first battle of the war, however, on 2 October 1787, the Russians under Count Alexander Suvorov defeated the Turkish force that had landed near Kinburn, although it took nine hours for the Russians to prevail, and only after bitter hand-to-hand fighting. In 1788, the Russians moved to the attack, focusing on the powerful fortress of Ochakov which overlooked the entrance to the Bug and Dnieper rivers and was an important base on the route to the Crimea along the northern coast of the Black Sea. After a long siege and lengthy bombardment, the fortress was stormed on 16 December, with both sides suffering heavy casualties and the population mostly put to the sword.

In 1788, the Turks focused their attention on Russia's ally Austria, which entered the war that year, and against which it was easiest to deploy Turkish forces. Deploying 140,000 troops, the Austrians had hoped to conquer Belgrade, Serbia, Moldavia, Wallachia and most of Bosnia, but the Emperor Joseph II proved a poor commander-in-chief, the Russians did not provide help, disease debilitated the Austrians, and, by concentrating their forces against them, the Turks were able to put the Austrians on the defensive. Invading the Banat in southern Hungary in July, they captured the fortress of Mehadiye and defeated the Austrians at Slatina on 20 September.

In 1789, however, the Turks lost the initiative. The main Russian army under Potemkin advanced to the Dniester river, capturing the fortresses of Akkerman and Bender. The Turkish position north of the Danube collapsed, with the Austrians and Russians able to co-operate as they had not done in 1788. A joint Austro-Russian army was victorious at Fokshani and Martineshti (22 September), and both Belgrade and Bucharest fell to the Austrians. Turkish morale collapsed.[18] In 1790, the Russians under Suvorov took forts in the Danube delta such as Izmail (10 December) and Tulcha, and in 1791 they advanced south of the Danube. Victories that summer at Babaday and Machin revealed Turkish vulnerability and the army was largely destroyed.

Separately, to the east of the Crimea, Anapa, the major Turkish fortress near the Kuban, fell in June 1791 after a short siege. The Turks had relied on the help of Battal Hüseyin Pasha, son of a key Anatolian notable, and conferred the province of Trabzon on him. He wanted to recover the Caucasus, but instead was driven back in 1790, leaving Anapa exposed.[19] The Turks came to terms by the Treaty of Jassy of January 1792, which left Russia with the Crimea, Ochakov, and the territory extending as far as the Dniester.

The Russians had demonstrated an impressive battlefield and siegecraft capability and had largely solved the serious logistical problems of deploying large forces across the steppe.[20] Moreover, in the Ochakov Crisis of early 1791, the Russians had felt sufficient confidence to see off the threat of war with Britain and Prussia unless they agreed to end the conflict with the Turks and without territorial gains. This was a demand designed to prevent an apparently imminent transformation of the European system through Turkish defeat. A similar threat of Prussian attack had led Austria to leave the war in 1790, but the Russians proved more determined, and successfully so. They had also seen off Gustavus III of Sweden who had declared war in 1788 in the hope of reconquering some of Sweden's former territories ceded to Russia in 1721. He signed a subsidy treaty with the Turks in 1789, and was part of the coalition Britain and Prussia sought to assemble against

Russia, but Gustavus negotiated peace with Russia in 1790 having failed to win victory.

Turkey was left weakened by her defeat, and this encouraged her to look to Western expertise. For example, François Kauffer, a French engineer, was asked to produce plans for strengthening fortresses exposed to Russian attack, such as Akkerman and Izmail.

Russia focused in the mid-1790s not on exploiting its advantage against Turkey, but rather on seeking to settle the Polish question by ending Polish independence (see pp. 156–7). However, French ambitions found the Turkish empire vulnerable in 1798–9. Evading the British navy, Napoleon invaded Egypt in 1798, defeating the Mamluks at Shubra Khit and Embabeh, and capturing Alexandria and Cairo; although, after he had landed, the French fleet had been defeated at the Battle of the Nile by the British. A French force advanced up the Nile to Aswan, but resistance continued in Upper Egypt, being supported by volunteers from Arabia.

Napoleon did not use the linear formations common to Western European battlefields. Instead, he deployed his infantry in squares, as Rumyantsev had done against the Turks in 1770. This enabled Napoleon to combine the firepower of densely-packed infantry with a tactical flexibility of formations that could not be put at a disadvantage by being attacked in flank or rear by more mobile cavalry. In the battles, French cannon and musket fire repelled cavalry attacks, inflicting heavy casualties. These battles reflected the weakness of the Egyptian military system, which had little experience of Western-style conflict. Non-Western forces tended to be most effective when able to rely on their mobility and, therefore, not vulnerable to the firepower and tactical flexibility of Western units.

In 1799, Napoleon pressed on into Turkish-ruled Palestine, winning a number of successes before being held at Acre where the defence was helped by British naval gunners, a shift in the firepower equation. Moreover, Napoleon's logistics were affected by the British navy. Napoleon then returned to Egypt where, at Aboukir, he defeated a newly-landed Turkish army only to abandon his troops, in the face of British naval power, and flee back to France.[21]

By this stage, it appeared clear that powerful centres of the Islamic world were vulnerable and could only be protected from Western conquest by the support of Western forces. Indeed, the French army in Egypt was to surrender and be repatriated to France in 1801 only after being defeated by a British expeditionary force.[22] Egyptian and Turkish military action had not achieved this end. A focus on vulnerability, however, is an overly simplistic conclusion. Indeed, the next British force sent to Egypt, that in 1807, was to be defeated. Nevertheless, there had been a major change in the position from that of mid-century.

As a reminder of the need not to put Western pressure so far to the fore that non-Western issues are ignored, the Turks were also under pressure from the Al-Saud state in Arabia. Under Abdul-Aziz bin Muhammad (r. 1765–1803), Saudi power was greatly extended. The Shia of al-Hasa, the area on the Persian Gulf to the south of Iraq, were particularly hard hit, with ancestral shrines destroyed. There were also advances into the Hejaz, where Mecca and Medina were occupied in 1805, and into Turkish-ruled Iraq, where the Shia holy places of Nejf and Kerbela were attacked, the latter being sacked in 1802.[23] The Saudis also raided into Transjordan. In response, the Turks and their local agents both organised defensive measures and launched expeditions. In 1790, the Sharif of Mecca sent one against the Al-Saud heartland of Najd, but it eventually failed. The defensive measures were also aimed against the Bedouin, notably building new forts on the route of the Hajj from Damascus to the Holy Cities of Mecca and Medina.

For the Russians, conflict with Islamic forces was not only a case of warfare with Turkey and Persia. The Russians also faced opposition on their borderlands. In the North Caucasus, a rising under Mansur Ushurma, a Chechen Naqshbandi sheik who launched a holy war in 1785, posed serious problems. That year, a Russian force was encircled and destroyed on the banks of the River Sunja.[24] Nevertheless, in 1785, Mansur failed in his attacks on the forts of Kizliar and Grigoriopolis and, after defeat at Tátartoub, his support collapsed. This struggle was bound up in the greater rivalry with Turkey, and Mansur was captured when the Turkish fort of Anapa was taken in 1791. East of the Caspian, however, there was no major expansion of Russian power in this period.

Africa

Similarly, in Africa, the European impact remained minimal. Indeed, this was dramatically displayed with the failure, in 1775 and 1784, of two expeditions launched by Spain against the major privateering base of Algiers. Moreover, expansion from the Dutch colony of Cape Town and from the Portuguese colonies of Angola and Mozambique was limited. Having failed in 1744, as in 1683, in a campaign against the kingdom of Matamba to the east of Angola, Portugal became more cautious in its military activity and focused on gaining slaves by trade, not war.[25]

The Dutch were the most dynamic Western power. Expanding east from Cape Colony, they overran the San and Khoekhoe peoples with few difficulties, but then encountered the Xhosa, leading to a war between 1779 and 1781. The Xhosa mounted serious resistance, but were defeated on the Fish river. In West Africa, the British established a colony for freed slaves at Sierra Leone in 1787 but, inland from their coastal bases, the European presence was slight. The French base on Madagascar at Fort Dauphin had been abandoned in 1768.

There was also conflict between Africans and Westerners in the West Indies with *bossales*, recently-arrived slaves, playing a key role in the rising in Saint-Domingue from 1791 against French rule. Many of the *bossales* were experienced in the methods of African warfare, notably ambushes and mass attacks. These tactics, however, proved fruitless against the coastal cities, while in regular battles the insurgents' shortage of firearms helped ensure that their casualties were far heavier.[26]

None of the Western powers had the military impact in Africa of the *jihad* launched by Usuman dan Fodio and the Fulani against the Hausa states in modern northern Nigeria. Militarily, this *jihad* was not dependent on firearms. Instead, its tactics were based on mobility, manoeuvre and shock attack. Ideology, in the shape of marshalling some spiritual drives in order to ensure group coherence, also played an important role in the success of the Merina ruler Adrianampoinimerina (r. *c*. 1783–*c*. 1810), who spread his power in Madagascar.[27]

The *jihad* launched by Usuman dan Fodio was part of a process of territorial change in the interior of West Africa that was not linked to Western pressure. For example, the pashalik of Timbuktu on the River Niger declined under pressure from the Tuareg and was destroyed by them in 1787. In its place, the Bambara people, whose principal town was Segu, extended their power down the Niger.

Also in 1787, an Ethiopian army equipped with cannon and thousands of muskets was defeated by the cavalry of the Yejju at Amed Ber. Ethiopia was no longer under Turkish pressure as it had been in the sixteenth century. The Turks, however, continued to have a presence on the Red Sea coast and the Nile Valley, providing firearms as a key trade good.

More generally, the use of firearms was limited in regions distant from coastal and trans-Saharan contact with Westerners, North Africans and Turks. In West Africa, there was diffusion of Western arms without Western political control, although the traffic in firearms developed more slowly at a distance from the coast. Muskets, powder and shot were imported in increasing quantities, and were particularly important in the trade for slaves.[28] For example, in the Senegal valley, gifts of guns were used to expand French influence. There is little evidence that Westerners provided real training in the use of firearms, but rulers showed a keen interest in seeing Western troops and their local auxiliaries exercise in formation. The auxiliaries were crucial to the security of the Western positions and to the offensive capability of Western forces, and were probably the key figures in the transfer of expertise. Since they often worked seasonally for the Westerners and were trained to use firearms, for example in the riverboat convoys on the River Senegal, these auxiliaries had ample opportunity to sell their expertise to local rulers.

There is evidence that the troops of some African kingdoms trained in formation. Further, there are a few cases of Africans capturing Western cannon and putting them to use, but field pieces were normally not sold to them, although some were given as gifts. Casting cannon was probably beyond the expertise of West African blacksmiths, although they could make copies of flintlock muskets.[29] This weaponry could be significant in conflict, but it scarcely defined the causes, course or consequences of warfare. The Westerners benefited as the purchasers of large numbers of those enslaved in the frequent warfare of the period.[30]

The Americas

In Amazonia, the Muras were undefeated but could never stop the Portuguese, and the peace they sought in 1784 appears to have reflected the need to reach an accommodation with colonial power.[31] Meanwhile, the diffusion of European weaponry and horses continued to be important in North America, and, indeed, became more significant as the range of trade increased. Moreover, these arms contributed to a situation in which the Europeans were not necessarily the dominant party. For example, in 1776, there were only 1,900 troops to defend the frontier of Spanish North America. Goods and trade were used by the Spaniards to keep the peace with the Natives, but the idea of Comanche subjugation through external manipulation by Spanish officials in the 1780s ignores the nature of Comanche political culture. The Comanche co-operated with the Spaniards in attacks on the Apache in the late 1780s, but only to suit their own goals. Spanish attempts to direct and manipulate Comanche warmaking were repeatedly unsuccessful.[32]

Even east of the Mississippi, the Natives remained formidable, notably the Creeks in the south-east. However, there was a change in the Ohio Valley. The end of the British presence and the absence of strong government encouraged frontiersmen to seize Native lands in the mid-1780s. In 1787, there was an attempt by the Confederation Congress to create a more orderly situation, but relations with the Natives were characterised by mutual distrust.[33] Initially, the Americans found it difficult to prevail. In 1790, there was a failed invasion of Native territory designed to end the violence stemming from Native hostility to what were seen as extorted land cessions in treaties of 1785–9. The following year, a Native army killed 647 men when it successfully attacked an American force at Kekionga. The Native capacity to mount a major attack was abundantly demonstrated.[34] However, in 1794 the Natives were heavily defeated at Fallen Timbers. In part, this defeat indicated the significance of political factors, notably the Anglo-American treaty of 1794 which led Britain to abandon its Native allies. Linked to this, the Natives agreed by the Treaty of Greenville in 1795 to cede much of Ohio to the Americans.[35]

In terms of control over most of North America, this campaigning was as, if not more, significant than the struggles over dominance between Europeans that had left the British in control by 1763 over the eastern seaboard and part of the hinterland, for this control to be partly lost in 1775–83 (the British retained their position in Canada and the Spaniards regained Florida). The War of Independence was important to the issue of control over the North American interior: the war disrupted relations between the British and the Natives, many of whom backed the British during the war. Moreover, Patriot campaigning against the Natives, campaigning which drew on a harsh racism,[36] proved very damaging, notably for the Iroquois,[37] but also for Native societies that were not devastated, for instance the Creek.[38] The war also affected African American slaves, many of whom had sought to escape under its cover while some backed the British.[39]

The British failure that helped transform the situation for the Natives in North America owed much to France, a key instance of Washington being the 'happy beneficiary'[40] of a series of events he could not control. By 1781, the French government was looking for a way out, but French naval power and French troops proved crucial in forcing the surrender of the poorly-situated British army in Virginia at Yorktown on 19 October 1781. This failure did not mean the end of the war, as Britain still controlled New York, Charleston and Savannah, and it proved impossible to co-ordinate American and French operations in 1782, but, after Yorktown, the political consensus in Britain shifted against continued war, and the resulting change of government in 1782 led the British to settle. As the Americans were not in a position to invade Britain, the war could only come to an end when the British decided to cease making an effort.

American dependence on France and (to a lesser extent) Spain underlines the mistake in thinking of this war in teleological terms of the defeat of an *ancien régime* army by a revolutionary new force. The French military scarcely conformed to this model, while, indeed, the Continental Army owed its tactics and structure to the general Western model. Guerrilla warfare tended to occur only when American regular forces were very weak, as in the South in 1781 after defeats at Charleston and Camden in 1780. Moreover, the war indicated the extent to which *ancien régime* warfare was neither limited nor static. Instead, it spanned much of the world, with bold attempts at power projection, such as the French fleet and army sent to India in 1780. British resilience was also a key aspect of the war. This resilience, like the global range of the conflict, linked the French Revolutionary War with what came earlier.

A number of issues remained unsettled between Britain and America in 1783, and were to help lead to renewed war in 1812. There were also to be issues in dispute between America and its wartime allies, France and Spain. Nevertheless, the striking feature of the post-war situation was that the Americans did not try to spread their control and export their revolution anew to the British colonies, notably Canada. Instead, disputes with the European powers were handled without conflict until 1812. The 'Quasi War' with France in the late 1790s remained only a naval conflict in which attacks on American merchantmen were used by France to try, unsuccessfully, to force the USA to accept French views on America's role in the global trade system.[41]

The lack of war with Britain, France or Spain between 1783 and 1812 did not mean that the Americans were pacific, as the Native Americans were well aware, while there was also growing and successful pressure on Spain's possessions in Florida and on the Gulf Coast. Moreover, rebellions within the new state, Shays's Rebellion of 1786–7 and the Whiskey Rebellion of 1794, led to military action in order to maintain order.[42] Pressure to build up a professional army linked this action to a key division in American politics, that between proponents and opponents of a stronger state, the former the Federalists under Alexander Hamilton, and the latter the Democratic Republicans under Thomas Jefferson. However, the implications of such an army for the American state remained latent because there were no external or internal challenges to match those that were to face France in the 1790s.

One of the challenges that faced France involved conflict in the West Indies. Instability linked to the French Revolution helped lead to a large-scale slave rising in France's leading Caribbean colony, Saint-Domingue, in August 1791. After a complex and bitter war in which the French were also hit hard by yellow fever and malaria, Saint-Domingue became, in 1804, the independent black state of Haiti.

Europe

European warfare in the 1790s saw the bringing to fruition of longer-term terms, including calls for military change, alongside the particular pressures stemming from the French Revolution and the reaction to it. The longer-term sources of change were threefold. First, widespread demographic and economic expansion in Europe from the 1740s produced the resources for military expansion, just as expansion in China did. The early-modern 'Little Ice Age', with all its attendant problems in terms of lower temperatures limiting agricultural yields, morphed into a period that was not always as difficult.[43]

Secondly, the emphasis on the value of reform and the consciously rational approach to problems that characterised Enlightenment thought encouraged a call for the new rather than the traditional. There was less of a comparable call outside the West. Thirdly, the impact of the protracted warfare of 1740–62, as well as of subsequent conflicts, led to a determination to replace what had been found deficient and to ensure that armies and societies were in a better state for future conflicts. The last were seen as likely. In the 1780s, Europe's rulers were not planning for the French Revolutionary War, but they were preparing for major conflicts, such as that which nearly broke out in 1790–1 between the Anglo-Prussian alliance system, and that of Austria and Russia.

Frederick II, the Great, of Prussia (r. 1740–86), who had the leading military reputation in Europe, was willing to consider change, for example more flexible tactical ideas in 1768, in particular an advance in open order. In general, however, there was little change in Prussian methods after the Seven Years' War. Instead, it was in France, humiliated by the armies of Prussia and Britain at Rossbach (1757) and Minden (1759) respectively, that there was the most experimentation in theory and practice, and a willingness to challenge the operation, organisation, equipment and ethos of the army. Thus, the pressure for change owed much to the experience of failure, part of the action–reaction cycle of military development, rather than being due to the product of intellectual enquiry which is the usual approach to the subject.

Nevertheless, the latter was important, and there were several significant works proposing change. In his *Essai général de tactique* (1772), Hippolyte de Guibert stressed movement and enveloping manoeuvres, advocated living off the land in order to increase the speed of operations, criticised reliance on fortifications, and urged the value of a patriotic citizen army. In France, interest in different fighting methods developed earlier ideas by writers such as Marshal Saxe, whose *Mes rêveries* criticised reliance on firepower alone, advocating, instead, a combination of firepower and shock. Saxe was important because of his prestige and because he encouraged fresh thoughts about tactics and strategy. He was not alone in this: two other French writers, Jean-Charles Folard from the 1720s and François-Jean de Mesnil-Durand between 1755 and 1774, stressed the shock and weight of forces attacking in columns rather than the customary deployment of firepower and linear tactics. Folard developed his ideas as a discussion of the lessons he learned from serving in the War of the Spanish Succession. Artillery also attracted attention. In *De l'usage de l'artillerie nouvelle dans la guerre de campagne* (1778), the Chevalier Jean du Teil argued that the artillery should begin battles and should be massed for effect, rather than being dispersed among the infantry units.

Doctrine, organisation, training and weaponry reflected the new ideas, although, again, more than theoretical concepts played a role. Ideas were tested. French manoeuvres in 1778 designed to compare the value of columns and lines failed to settle the controversy, but the new French tactical manual in 1791 incorporated both ideas. Meanwhile, the concept of the division, a standing unit maintained in peace and war, and including elements of all arms and, therefore, able to operate independently, was developed in France. Such a unit could serve effectively, both as a detached force and as part of a co-ordinated army operating in accordance with an operational prospectus. The divisional plan evolved from 1759, and in 1788 regiments were organised as brigades and divisions, although these were not combined-arms units.[44]

In the kingdom of Sardinia (Savoy-Piedmont), as a parallel process, the army was organised in 1775 into four departments, essentially divisions, one composed of cavalry and three of infantry. Each was divided into two 'wings', each of which was composed of two brigades. Each of the latter was composed of two regiments. The word 'division', meaning a unit including two brigades, appeared officially in the 1786 organisation when the army was divided into two lines or wings, each composed of two departments, each of which was composed of two divisions.[45]

An improvement in France's artillery added a major change in capability in what was increasingly a more important arm of battle. Jean-Baptiste Gribeauval (1715–89), who had served during the Seven Years' War with the Austrian army, then the best for artillery in Europe, standardised the French artillery from 1769, and was appointed inspector-general of artillery in 1776. He used standardised specifications: 4-, 8-, and 12-pounder cannon and 6-inch howitzers in eight-gun batteries. Mobility was increased by stronger, larger wheels, shorter barrels and lighter-weight cannon, and by more secure mobile gun carriages. Horses were harnessed in pairs instead of in tandem. Better casting methods helped accuracy, which was also improved by better sights, the issue of gunnery table, and the introduction of inclination markers. The rate of fire rose as a result of the introduction of pre-packaged rounds. Thanks to Gribeauval's reforms, Revolutionary France had the best artillery in Europe.

Breaking out in 1789, the French Revolution was in part a product of military humiliation. First, the French government had badly lost domestic prestige as a result of military failure, both defeat in battle, notably Rossbach in 1757, and an inability to confront Prussia and Britain in the Dutch Crisis of 1787. The latter was an episode that fell short of war, but where equations of military strength, international support and political resolution all proved mutually supporting. The French backed down rather than fight a British-encouraged Prussian invasion that rapidly overthrew the weak resistance of France's Dutch protégés.[46] In part, indeed, the French Revolution arose from a competitive system of global power politics in which, due to this crisis, France was doing badly.[47] Successive wars had also left France with very heavy debts.[48]

Second, despite considering doing so in 1789, the French government did not use the army to suppress disaffection and opposition. Instead, the opposite occurred: the army was unable to maintain order and prevent violent insurrectionary episodes, and notably so in the centre of government, Paris, in 1789 and 1792. An increasingly radical government and politics in France led to the mustering of a counter-revolutionary coalition, and war broke out in 1792.

Both narrative and analysis appear clear. Pre-Revolutionary changes were brought to fruition in the French Revolutionary Wars, at the same time that the Revolution offered a powerful addition of popular enthusiasm and national mobilisation.[49] There is much to say for this account, some aspects of which are discussed in what follows. However, as the subsequent section makes clear, alternative views can be advanced.

Rather than assuming that radicalism led to pressure for war, and then to war, the pressure owed much also to the strategies of moderate groups, including the *Feuillants*, who hoped to strengthen the monarchy. However, the course of events overtook and destroyed the moderates.[50] Furthermore, it is important not to assume that the improvement in French capability was the sole or even the dominant theme in the 1790s. As ever, there is the question of what to emphasise and how to analyse developments. For example, in 1745–8, the French under Saxe overran the Austrian Netherlands (Belgium) before pressing on into the United Provinces (Dutch Republic), taking two major frontier fortresses, Bergen-op-Zoom in 1747 and Maastricht in 1748. In 1792, in contrast, although the initial French attempts to invade the Austrian Netherlands met with disaster, an invasion in November met with overwhelming success and the country fell in only a month. The comparison with the length of time taken by Saxe appears clear evidence of a greater effectiveness and one that can be related to the new tactics that were to be associated with the French. Victory at Jemappes on 6 November 1792 played a key role, and the French there, having advanced in columns, defeated the less numerous Austrians. However, both the time-scale discussed and the account offered can be varied. In 1792, unlike in 1745–8, the French benefited from fighting only Austrians in the Low Countries and from the hostility to Austrian rule stemming from the 1787 revolution in the Austrian Netherlands, which had only recently been suppressed.

In 1793 British and Dutch entry into the war altered the situation. The Austrians made major gains after their victory at Neerwinden and in 1794 the Austrian Netherlands had to be conquered anew by France. Amsterdam fell to the French the following January. The timescale, therefore, does not appear too different from that in the 1740s, and if the United Provinces were conquered in 1795, it was a sign of the success of the French Revolutionaries; on the other hand, in 1748 the Dutch inability under French pressure to sustain their war effort helped lead to peace.

The French benefited in the 1790s from numbers, tactics, command and organisation. Superiority in numbers was important in a number of key battles, including Valmy (1792), Jemappes (1792) and Wattignies (1793). The *levée en masse* decreed in August 1793 and the general conscription ordered under the Jourdan Law in September 1798 were significant in raising these numbers, as was the size of the French population. French armies were able to operate effectively on several fronts at once, to sustain heavy casualties, to match the opposing forces of much of Europe, and to put earlier ideas about combat and conflict into practice.[51] Franz von Thugut, the leading Austrian minister, complained in 1794, 'Reduced to the defensive, we are continually harassed … by innumerable [French] hordes … our army is vastly weakened by [its] partial victories while the enemy repairs its losses with the greatest ease.'[52]

The large number of inexperienced French soldiers that resulted from mass conscription created a problem of organisation. Independent attack columns were the most effective way to use these soldiers, and this method was also best for an army that put an emphasis on the attack. Column advances were far more flexible than advancing lines. Moreover, the French combination of artillery, skirmishers and assault columns proved a potent *ad hoc* use of tactical elements that was matched to the technology of the time. Columns were preceded by skirmishers who disrupted the close-packed lines of opponents and were supported by massed cannon.

The greater dispersal of units ensured that command and co-ordination skills became more important, and, in organising their army anew with a committed professionalism,[53] the French benefited from young and determined commanders. Talent flourished and both ordinary soldiers, such as

Jean-Baptiste Jourdan, and junior officers, including Napoleon, were able to rise to the top. Aside from offering energy and talent, Napoleon skilfully promoted an image of successful heroism,[54] indicating the continuity of *gloire* from the *ancien régime*, but also its new idiom in a more populist age.[55]

The armies were systematised by Lazare Carnot, head of the military section of the Committee of Public Safety, who brought a measure of organisation to the military confusion that followed the Revolution. Success in forming, training and sustaining new armies was instrumental in the transition from a royal army to a nation in arms.

The new logistics brought about by the partial abandonment of the magazine system or reliance on fixed depots helped the aggressive style of war – in tactics, operations and strategy – of the revolutionary armies, which relied on numbers and enthusiasm. The way was open for the ruthless boldness that Napoleon was to show in Italy in 1796–7, not least in suppressing popular opposition there once opposing Sardinian and Austrian armies had been defeated, notably the Austrians at Castiglione, Arcola and Rivoli in 1797. In the British Parliament in April 1797, Richard Brinsley Sheridan, the most famous author of English comedies of his day and an opposition spokesman, mocked governmental assurances about the ease with which the French would be abandoned, 'I will not remind those gentlemen of their declaration so often made, that the French must fly before troops well disciplined and regularly paid. We have fatal experience of the folly of those declarations; we have seen soldiers frequently without pay, and without sufficient provisions, put to rout the best-paid armies in Europe.'[56] The greater scale of the French army was to be organised in the field with the development of the corps system and this was to pave the way for the development of operational art, at least as understood in the modern West.[57]

At the same time, while noting links, it is necessary to differentiate between the 1790s and what followed under Napoleon in the 1800s. Focusing on the 1790s, the politics – military, diplomatic, financial and social – of the Revolution were more important than its tactical innovations. It has been argued that the French soldiers were better motivated and, hence, more successful and better able to use the new methods. This is hard to prove, but, initially at least, revolutionary enthusiasm does seem, by its nature, to have been an important element in French capability. It was probably necessary for the higher morale required for effective shock action. Patriotic determination was also important to counter the limited training of the early Revolutionary armies.

At the same time, it is necessary to consider the complexity of warmaking in the 1790s, the limitations of French Revolutionary forces, and the extent to which they could be defeated. This scholarship is not simply a case of the revenge of the particular on the general, of detail on theory, but also raises profound questions about the way in which the image of military change frequently serves as a substitute for reality. This point is also pertinent for views in the past. Alongside the theory of a radical break with the Revolution comes the extent to which the French army was already changing prior to that and also the extent to which Revolutionary forces often reprised earlier situations. For example, having rapidly conquered Nice and Savoy (on the French side of the Alps) in 1792, the French failed to break through the Alps in the face of Sardinian and Austrian opposition. In 1796, in contrast, the French exploited the same route used in 1745 when they entered Piedmont via Genoa.

Moreover, because the indecisive War of the Bavarian Succession (1778–9) was a far shorter struggle than those involving the French Revolutionaries and Napoleon, and it found Frederick the Great aligned against only one power (Austria), the implications of the decline in relative Prussian effectiveness seen in this war were not developed prior to the French Revolution. These implications serve, however, as a reminder of the difficulties of model building. French success over Prussia in 1792–5 and 1806 is seen as evidence of the *ancien régime* system's passing, and of its replacement by French Revolutionary warfare and its Napoleonic successor. Yet, this pattern of ready transference of leading position and fitness for purpose[58] can be queried. Austria's ability to hold off a Prussian attack in 1778, to succeed against the Turks in 1789, and to end rebellions in Belgium and Hungary in 1790, indicates that the situation was much more complex and looks toward Austrian successes against the French in the 1790s, notably in Belgium in 1793 and in Germany in 1795 and 1796, including battles such as Amberg and Würzburg in 1796. Like the Russians, the Austrians displayed an impressive multiple capability. Against the French, the Austrians proved to be tough opponents while the Russians were repeatedly to show impressive staying power and fighting quality. For example, in 1799 the French under Jourdan were defeated by the Austrians at Ostrach and Stockach and driven back across the Rhine, as well as being initially beaten in Switzerland by the Russians.

Napoleon's victories in Egypt did not match the Russian achievement in taking on and beating major Turkish armies (and fleets) and capturing key positions. The Russians not only beat the Turks in the 1790s, but also conquered Poland. The latter success tends to be overlooked in the focus on French warmaking, but Russian success in Poland indicates the degree to which revolutionaries could be defeated by *ancien régime* regulars. The Polish rising in the spring of 1794 led to the driving out of Russian garrisons from Warsaw and Vilna. However, Russian, Prussian and Austrian forces were soon able to defeat their opponents and capture all the cities. The Russian advance under Suvorov proved particularly effective. Victories at Krupczyce, Terespol, Maciejowice and Kobilka in September–October 1794 were followed by the capture of Warsaw in November.[59]

Polish failure reflected the superior military resources of the partitioning powers, as well as the geographical vulnerability of Poland to attack from a number of directions, and the extent to which the first two partitions, in 1772 and 1792, had already removed much of the Polish room for manoeuvre that had been enjoyed in previous years. Each war therefore is specific to its circumstances, and the same point can be made about the British defeat of an Irish rebellion in 1798, a rebellion belatedly supported by a French landing.[60] Nevertheless, Polish failure helps contextualise French success, underlining the significance of particular political alignments and developments in affecting the fate of Revolutionary forces.

Moreover, the range of the Russian military was also demonstrated against the French. In 1799, Russia entered the War of the Second Coalition (versus France), and Suvorov advanced into northern Italy, the first time the Russians had operated there. His victories, especially at Cassano d'Adda, Trebbia and Novi, were brutal battles in which repeated attacks finally found weaknesses in the French position. Like Napoleon, Suvorov was a believer in the tactics of attack and in campaigning through taking the initiative, and he had little time for sieges. Just as Wellington in 1808–13 was to repeat in Portugal and Spain methods he had developed and used in India, notably against the Marathas in 1803, so Suvorov employed against the French techniques developed earlier in conflict with the Turks. Willing to accept a high rate of casualties and to mount costly frontal attacks, Suvorov relied on bayonet attacks, not defensive volley firepower, and showed that an emphasis on aggression, attack and risk was not restricted to the French. Rather than the wastage of ammunition seen with unaimed volley fire, Suvorov preferred aimed firepower.[61]

Tactical proficiency and command skill therefore were scarcely restricted to the French. The Russians also were capable of devising aggressive tactical and operational methods. The British navy abundantly demonstrated the value of professionalism and the extent to which success was not dependent on radicalism, in politics or in war. Moreover, as always, the political context was central. The Second Coalition against France did well initially in 1799, but divisions within the Coalition gravely weakened it and helped the French regain the initiative. Outnumbered and short of supplies, Suvorov had to abandon Switzerland. At the same time, France was under great strain. Discredited by division and unpopular, its government, the Directory, rapidly succumbed to a coup mounted by Napoleon in November and he became First Consul and General-in-Chief.

At this stage, however, it was far from clear that Napoleon would prove able to defeat Austria in 1800, as he was to do at Marengo in northern Italy that June, nor, more conclusively, dominate Europe through repeated successes in 1805–9. It is important not to read back from these successes to the Revolutionary armies of the 1790s. It is also necessary to note the repeated failures of Napoleonic warmaking in 1812–15. The eventual triumph of the *ancien régime* armies over Napoleon, then, does not demonstrate their superiority in the 1790s, but it again indicates the folly of drawing clear lessons about respective effectiveness and the nature of military proficiency and progress in this period. Despite this caveat, professionalism, the key merit of *ancien régime* militaries, was to emerge as the vital principle of military organisation.[62]

Conclusions

The pace of activity toward the close of the eighteenth century was clearly in favour of major states, what Adam Smith had referred to in 1776 as 'the opulent and civilised' in contrast to 'the poor and barbarous'. The conquest of the Crimea in 1783[63] was symbolic of this wider development as Edward Gibbon had seen the Crimean Tatars as the likely source of any future onslaught on Christian Europe. Russian resources, firepower and determination were also crucial in the Kuban, to the east of the Black Sea. When, in 1783, the Nogais there resisted being incorporated into the expanding Russian state, they were defeated at Urai-Ilgasi and the River Laba by a small, disciplined force under Suvorov. The ability to force battles on nomadic and semi-nomadic peoples was important to their defeat.

Separate but related to this, there was also conflict between Smith's 'opulent and civilised'. They benefited more than 'the poor and barbarous' from the rise in population and the improvement in climate that helped agriculture. However, the natural disasters of the 1780s, notably a major volcanic explosion in Iceland, affected the climate, creating problems for farming around the world. More specifically, military operations on land and at sea were dependent on climate and weather. In addition, fear of bad weather affected military planning. For example, the difficulty of moving artillery made sieges uncertain.[64]

There was also a major change in the relationship between Europe and its 'dark side' of the Earth. Whereas there had been relatively few voyages in and across the Pacific in the seventeenth century, the pace markedly picked up in the eighteenth. Russia became active in the Aleutian Islands and Alaska,

Spain developed a colonial presence in California, and the British and French both launched voyages of exploration in which scientific research sat alongside geopolitical competition. Whereas the Dutch expedition sent in 1696–7 to explore the west coast of Australia had reported that the 'southland' offered little for the Dutch East India Company (a reasonable assessment compared with the opportunities of Java) and the Dutch had not established a base there, the British rapidly developed a presence from 1788. The Australian Aborigines were not in a position to mount sustained resistance in areas where the environment encouraged large numbers of European settlers, because they lacked the numbers, firepower and large-scale organisation of the settlers and were also being exposed to deadly new diseases.

The ability to overcome the 'poor and barbarous' was scarcely limited to Westerners, as was shown by the strength of the Chinese position on the steppe. However, the lack of non-Western long-range naval capability and interest in maritime power-projection, themes discussed in the next chapter, meant that overseas expansion at the expense of the 'poor and barbarous' was only achieved by Westerners. The impact of this had long been apparent in the Americas, was now clear in Australia, and was to be a major factor in African history by the mid-nineteenth century.

If the relation between different types of civilisations was an important factor, there was also the case of the contrasting military cultures of the major civilisations. In 1792, a Russian request to Japan to open diplomatic and commercial relations led a hostile Japan to order the establishment of coastal defences, although nothing happened in part because the Russians did not pursue the matter.[65] The key developments were at the expense of Turkey and in India. In the wars of 1768–72 and 1787–92, the Russians pushed the Turkish frontier back to the Balkans and challenged the Turkish position there. Just as the British in India drew on local military traditions, especially in hiring light cavalry, so the Russians also adapted to the circumstances of steppe warfare, notably by developing particular tactical techniques and logistical practices, ranging from deployment and advancing in hollow squares, to looser uniforms, improvements in mobility, a focus on annihilating the enemy in battle, and the practice of covering sieges with a field army.[66]

India is possibly the most interesting area of military change, due in large part to the need there to respond to a variety of challenges. Alongside those of external forces, notably Afghans and Europeans, came the challenges posed by the highly-competitive nature of post-Mughal politics. India was certainly an area of rapid changes in weaponry and military organisation. Western-style infantry were created by a number of powers, especially the

Nizam of Hyderabad and the Marathas,[67] although it is mistaken to assume that disciplined and drilled infantry could not also be found in the Indian tradition. Furthermore, it is inaccurate to see the West as the sole factor influencing South Asian military developments.[68] In 1781, John Bristow, the British Resident in Lucknow, estimated that the forces of Alam II, the Mughal emperor, not generally noted then as a major military power, included thirty battalions of *sepoys* (regular infantry) and 5,000 rocket men, as well as infantry and cavalry, 73,000 strong, supplied by dependent lords. Eleven years later, a British officer commented on Mysore forces: 'the enemy fire heavily at the rate of about 800 shot a day'.[69] Although there was a lack of standardisation, Tipu had a significant artillery, as well as powder magazines and musket factories.[70]

In hindsight, such forces can seem obsolete, and foredoomed to defeat by the British because of deficient weaponry and organisation, including unsatisfactory command practices and a lack of unit cohesion.[71] Pejorative remarks can readily be cited, for example about the cohesion and weaponry of Indian infantry or the lengthy supply-trains of Indian units. Yet, aside from a lack of any clear Western technological edge on land,[72] there was also Western praise for Indian units, notably, but not only, in describing the Mysore forces in 1791. Moreover, there was little doubt about Maratha proficiency. For example, Mahadji Shinde's army proved successful in campaigns in Rajputana in the 1780s and 1790s, and its artillery contributed to the fall of the major Rajput fortress of Chitor in only a matter of weeks. Shinde was the Maratha leader most determined to train his infantry and artillery along Western lines in order to complement the traditional Maratha cavalry.

Benoit de Boigne, a Frenchman whom he hired in 1784, initially raised a force of about 1,700 troops, but, under a new contract in 1790, he was given a large *jagir* (land grant), the province of Aligarh, that enabled him to raise a far larger force. The troops he trained in Western methods were 27,000 strong with 130 cannon in 1793, and were known as *Fauj-e-Hind*, the Army of Hindustan. Alongside heavy artillery, de Boigne developed a light artillery capability generally lacking among Indian rulers. Each of de Boigne's battalions had a battery of six cannon. As well as muskets, gunpowder and shot, the cannon were produced in five factories established by a Scotsman, Sangster, while the officer corps were nearly entirely Western.[73]

Domination of Rajputana produced the resources for this military build-up. In 1784, Mahadji had had himself appointed Regent Plenipotentiary by Alam II, which enabled him to demand that the Rajputs pay the traditional taxes and tribute due to the Emperor.[74] At Laslot in 1787, de Boigne's cannon and infantry routed a far larger body of Rajput cavalry which foolishly attacked the defensive square without preparatory fire. The following year, outside Agra, the cavalry charges of Ismail Baig, a Mughal noble opposed to Mahadji, were similarly defeated, although, in an echo of Robert Clive's victory at Plassey in 1757 (see p. 83), he was also affected by the deserting of a key supporter who had been bribed by Mahadji. In 1790, there were victories over Rajput cavalry at Patun and Merta. At Patun, de Boigne's infantry advanced firing by platoons. At Merta, Rajput attacks on de Boigne's square were beaten off. Rajput opposition came to an end. As a result, Mahadji was left in control of Hindustan. The Rajputs had not significantly changed their means of fighting, and, instead, remained focused on heroism and frontal attacks.

These victories were comparable to Napoleon's triumphs over the Mamluks in Egypt in 1798, but were different in that they led to a political outcome. In turn, Tukoji Holkar raised a *sepoy* force under a French mercenary. That these forces were to be defeated by the British in 1799 (Mysore) and 1803 (Marathas) does not make their defeat inevitable. De Boigne himself had resigned in December 1795, due both to poor health and to the replacement of the dead Mahadji by his more volatile nephew, Daulatrao.

It may seem unsatisfactory to end this section both on a note of caution and a long way from the battlefields of Napoleonic Europe. Yet, this is necessary in order to re-create the uncertainties of the period. At the close of the 1790s, it appeared unclear how far the French presence in Egypt would threaten power-relationships all the way to India, and notably the British situation there. In July 1797, the month in which he became Foreign Minister, Charles-Maurice de Talleyrand told the *Institut de France* that the Egyptian expedition would lead to a French conquest of India. Conversely, it was also unclear whether the Directory government in France would survive the assault of the opposing Second Coalition. These were questions about 'Which West?' and, more specifically, the struggle between Britain and France outside Europe and between France and its rivals within, a question that had broadened out with American independence.

Yet, alongside 'Which West?' came questions about the relationship between the West and the non-West. In the Americas and Africa, there was no fundamental transformation as the trends of the previous century were maintained: advancing frontiers of Western control and settlement in the New World, and no real changes in the situation between Westerners and non-Westerners in Africa. There were major, if very different, changes, in Australia and the Turkish empire, with significant gains for Britain and Russia respectively, and a sense of more major change as possible, indeed imminent.

In India, the situation was less clear, and this, and the importance of developments there, focuses attention. Failed modernisation on the part of the Indian states is one of the themes of discussion, and the subject is addressed in part in terms of the detrimental military and political conse-quences for these states. Warren Hastings, British Governor-General of Bengal from 1773 to 1785, was content for Indian states to try to emulate Western infantry formations because he was confident they would never succeed and that such emulation would take resources away from their cavalry and slow them up in the field. As Maratha armies became more professional, so the strategy based on living off the land became less feasi-ble. Furthermore, the new infantry and artillery formations proved expen-sive, leading to developments in revenue administration, banking and credit that created serious political problems, while, at the same time, there was not a centralised fiscal system comparable to those being developed across much of Christian Europe.

These problems were linked not only to the new force-structure but also to a political culture that suffered from an absence of bureaucratic method and stable governance, and that, indeed, has been described as feudal,[75] with all that that implies in terms of being well behind the West in development. British administrative goals and methods are then contrasted with those of Indian states,[76] not least because it is claimed that the British benefited from the degree to which they were less willing than earlier conquerors to absorb Indian political and military values.[77] The greater continuity and institutional stability of the East India Company seems particularly signifi-cant. The contrast with Indian states appears both readily apparent and significant for respective military success. In Mysore, the death of Haidar Ali in 1782 was temporarily kept secret so that civil war should not break out before his son Tipu could become the Sultan.

Yet, there is a danger that the analysis of British success in India conforms to a standard approach that misleadingly attributes to winners all the strengths of superior political and military systems and greater resources, and all the skills of vision, strategic know-how, preparation and back-up; whereas losers tend to lose because they lose. There is a need, in contrast, particularly but not only at the operational level, for continued reference to chance, notably individual leadership and alliance dynamics. As a result, there should be a frequent use of terms such as 'perhaps' and 'maybe', and also a measure of scepticism about the attribution of inevitability to long-term military history.

It is particularly important to be wary of judgements that assume a ready superiority in Western governmental systems as a result of fiscal demands generating institutional development. Indeed, the East India Company was nearly bankrupted by the campaigns of 1803–4 against the Marathas. Successive wars saw the number of Indian and British troops at the disposal of the Company rise from about 54,000 in 1773 to 70,000 in 1794 and 160,000 in 1801, and ensured that the Company's debts trebled between 1793 and 1808.[78] As a result, the Company recalled Richard Wellesley, the bellicose Governor-General in 1805, and sought peace with the Marathas.

This clash is a reminder of the role of competing interests and ideas in the formulation of policy; in short, of the dynamic nature of strategic culture. British territorial gains in India coincided with the declining influence of the Company vis-à-vis the British government and Parliament. The Company repeatedly found that commanders in India did not do as expected.

Whatever the inevitability of British success in India and of the financial benefits of its position there,[79] and this inevitability did not seem obvious even after the victories of 1799 and 1803; there was no such clarity in the case of the West and China,[80] or Japan. At the same time, the clear contrast between Britain and these powers rested on the strength of the Royal Navy and the ability, as a result, for British policymakers to think on a geographical scale the Chinese could not match nor indeed conceive. The far-flung nature of Western empires had long encouraged such thinking, as in 1705 when Portugal sought British help in Indian waters against Omani and other attacks,[81] but wide-ranging planning and implementation became more common later in the century.

This scale was demonstrated in 1798–1801 when, in response to the French invasion of Egypt, the British abandoned plans for an expedition from India to Batavia (Djakarta), which was ruled by France's Dutch ally, and instead moved first ships, and then troops, to the Red Sea in order to support pressure from the Mediterranean. Batavia was not to fall until 1811. Already, in 1795, the British had conducted a preliminary reconnaissance of the Red Sea. A base was established in 1799 on the island of Perim in the Straits of Bab-el-Mandab at the mouth of the Red Sea, but, as the island was waterless, it was evacuated. The British plans for the Red Sea included seeking to extend British influence into the Hijaz (western Arabia) in order to thwart any French use of the Red Sea to advance into the Indian Ocean.[82] Similarly, in 1796, troops and warships were concentrated on Cape Town from Britain and India in order to prevent a Dutch plan to regain the position which had been captured the previous year.[83] The Dutch did not regain it until the Peace of Amiens in 1802 and then it fell anew to the British in 1806.

No non-Western state could make plans for operations of this range. Tipu Sultan sent four warships to Basra in 1786 in an attempt to seek Turkish support, but the failure of the mission was matched by the disastrous fate of most of the squadron.[84]

Aside from the unique nature of Western warmaking on the world scale, the range of British power suggests that narratives of military modernisation should focus on Britain, and not France. Linked to this, the key revolution was economic (the Industrial Revolution led by Britain), and not political (the French Revolution). Each revolution was linked to war, the Industrial Revolution being moulded by British warmaking, just as it moulded it; and the same was true of the French Revolution.

Yet, if politics is to be emphasised, the sophistication of a British system capable of ensuring funds, consistency and outcomes, and without the political instability seen in France, deserves emphasis. This system was particularly apparent in the case of the Royal Navy. Had the Irish rebellion of 1798 been successful, or more successful, then the situation might have seemed less benign for Britain, but it was rapidly suppressed, and there was no comparable opposition in England, Scotland and Wales. However, the cost and economic disruption of the war pressed hard throughout society, leading to inflation, the collapse of the gold standard under which paper currency was met by the Bank of England (1797), the successful introduction of income tax (1799), the stagnation of average real wages, and widespread hardship, especially in the famine years of 1795–6 and 1799–1801.

The response, including the Act of Union with Ireland in 1800, indicated that Britain in 1800 also exemplified the development of state forms and political institutions, a development that had great consequences for military activity. It could be seen in the process of strategy as governance and politics that was readily apparent in the reforms of the late 1790s and early 1800s. As the latest iteration of the fiscal developments that, from the Glorious Revolution of 1689, had strengthened Britain as a state and as a military power,[85] the introduction of income tax helped reduce the need for financing war through borrowing. Income tax was a response to the liquidity crisis of 1797, and made it easier to endure setbacks, as borrowing was very dependent on confidence. Parliamentary union with Ireland was regarded as a key way to reduce another vulnerability of the British state.[86]

By then, Britain was a state with social and political practices and organisations designed to try to control violence, in order to ensure that it was directed only against foreign powers. Although this monopolisation of violence was challenged by the persistence of piracy and smuggling in the British world,[87] and had been confronted by rebellion in Ireland in 1798, it was relatively effective. Supporting this monopolisation was important to British state development and modernisation. Across the world, attempts to monopolise violence and sustain the military helped provide the backdrop to much of nineteenth-century politics and warfare.

7 Naval Capability and Warfare

When Captain James Cook, British naval officer and famed explorer, visited the Pacific island of Tahiti for the second time in 1774, its fleet was preparing for a punishment expedition against the neighbouring island of Mocorea. Cook and William Hodges, the expedition painter, took great interest in these war preparations, as did the general public when Hodges' painting *The War Boats of the Island of Otaheite* [*Tahiti*] was exhibited in London in 1777. Cook estimated that the expedition involved 160 large war canoes, 170 smaller ones and no less than 7,760 men.

Cook's three voyages to the Pacific, which were supported by the Admiralty, were also highly impressive examples of naval organisation, but it is a mistake to let the Royal Navy crowd out other activity. The focus on Western navies is more understandable and appropriate than that on Western armies explicitly or implicitly decried over the previous six chapters. However, adopting a different perspective provides an opportunity to rethink the topic and also to consider whether there are any instructive parallels with the situation on land.

The naval history of the period is generally told not in part but in whole in terms of the Western powers. There is no discussion of non-Western naval activity and, instead, the story resolves into one of Britain and its leading opponent, France, which had the world's second largest navy. Such an account is understandable, not least because only the major Western powers controlled fleets of deep-draught vessels able to operate at great distances. Indeed, the acquisition, first, of a major galley fleet and, then, of a large deep-sea fleet was one way in which Russia signalled its emergence as a great power.

Nevertheless, non-Western powers could also take a naval role, including an amphibious one. This activity, however, has not been studied systematically, and there is a tendency to glance at it only when there was a clash with Western naval forces, which leads to a failure to judge the goals and capability of non-Western powers other than in terms of such a clash. Moreover, the very limited discussion of non-Western naval forces at times suffers from a misleading teleology that assumes the need for development on the Western model, as indeed occurred in the late nineteenth century, most notably with Japan.

Asia, Oceania and Africa

Non-Western naval activity was significant at sea in Asian, Pacific, African and Mediterranean waters, and less so in the New World. These waters of course cover much of the globe and its coasts, and it is unsurprising that there was a great variety in naval activity, notably in scale and range, but also in purpose and social, economic and political contexts. The key point was that the use of naval force was similar to that of much Western naval power in that it was an aspect of combined operations. Amphibious attacks were more important than the battles between fleets discussed later in terms of concepts of command of the sea, which were inappropriate for the naval capabilities of the period. A focus on such amphibious attacks meant that there was scant need for deep-sea capability unless, as with Western powers, there was a requirement to sail across the oceans in order to reach the coasts where amphibious attacks could be mounted. In practice, however, such attacks often required the use of numbers of troops, who were best transported along coasts in order both to meet their requirements for food and water, and to provide shelter from storms.

There were non-Western naval forces that could deploy strength a considerable distance, notably Oman on the east of the Arabian peninsula. However, most were not deep-sea. Instead, shallow-draught boats whose crews fought with missile vessels were found across much of the world, including on the coasts of Africa, the Pacific, New Zealand and in Pacific North America. As with land warfare in some non-Western societies, and in marked contrast to the situation in the West, the divide between fighting humans and the hunting of animals was not too great at this level of weapon technology and military organisation.

At the same time, non-Western naval and amphibious forces not only were hunters or raiders, but also could achieve operational goals. Particularly along the African coasts and those of India, South-East Asia and the East Indies, there were polities that controlled flotillas operating in inshore, estuarine, deltaic and riverine waters. These boats were shallow in draught, and therefore enjoyed a local range denied Western warships which had a deeper draught.

Indeed, the problems facing the latter were shown in 1799 when British warships, sent into the Red Sea to operate against the French in Egypt, both nearly suffered the loss of a large frigate which ran aground and found that they could not approach the new French base at Suez because the waters were too shallow.[1] This operation has already been mentioned in the previous chapter (see p. 163), and the differing ways in which it can be considered show the varied nature of historical episodes and evidence and the role of the historian in deciding what to emphasise. At the same time, the 1799 operation provided a useful preparation for the expeditions of 1801 when British units from India and Cape Town were moved into the Red Sea before marching across the desert to the Nile and then sailing down the river as part of the British assault on French forces in Egypt. Moreover, Western forces could develop a shallow draught capacity by building, purchase, seizure or co-operation. In Bengal in 1757, Clive's force advanced on Cutwa in part by water.[2]

The crews of non-Western boats usually fought with missile weapons, which in the eighteenth century increasingly meant muskets. A small number of canoes also carried cannon. In the 1780s, a free Black from Brazil introduced brass swivel guns in the canoe fleets of the coastal lagoons of West Africa.

The use of sizeable fleets to pursue operational, indeed strategic, goals was seen in conflicts among both the polities along the south shore of the Persian Gulf and the New Zealand Maori, and also in the unification of the Hawai'ian archipelago. By 1789, in the last case, Kamehameha I was using a swivel gun secured to a platform on the hulls of a big double canoe. Soon after, he had a large double canoe mounting two cannon and rigged like a Western schooner. Double-hulled sailing canoes were also found in New Zealand. Such boats helped Kamehameha as he expanded his power across the archipelago. His power was based on the west coast of the island of Hawai'i, a coast frequented by European ships, and he both acquired guns and cannon, and used Europeans as cannoneers. The key clashes occurred on land. Kamehameha won dominance of the island of Hawai'i in 1791 and of the islands of Manui and Oahu in 1795. The battle of Nuuanu (1795) was particularly important. Guns replaced spears, clubs, daggers and sling-shots. In 1796, however, the difficult waters between Oahu and Kauai as well as disease ended Kamehameha's plans to invade Kauai. More generally, long-range, inter-archipelagic travel by canoes had declined from the sixteenth century, possibly due to climate change associated with the Little Ice Age.

Canoes were also important in inland waterways, for example on the rivers Niger and Senegal in West Africa. Birchbark canoes played an important role in Native American conflict in North America, the canoes providing vital mobility.[3] The 'brown water' element of naval history, however, has received little attention for the eighteenth century, and notably because there was no repetition of the conflicts within China seen in the previous century. Instead, the Chinese wars with the Zunghars were entirely waged on land. However, in 1769, the Chinese forces preparing for their invasion of Burma sought to take advantage of the waterways. Several thousand sailors were moved there from the coast, while hundreds of boats were built locally.[4] In the event, they were not to be significant in the unsuccessful invasion, and the boats were burnt before the Chinese withdrew.

Burma itself made much use of warships: large canoes with sixty oars, that were equipped with swivel guns and also able to ram their opponents, which operated on rivers and in inshore waters. These warships competed in the 1750s in the war between the Mons of Pegu in southern Burma and 'Alaungpaya who was based further north. The use of fire-rafts was important to naval conflict. When 'Alaungpaya first campaigned against the southern port of Syriam, where the Mons were linked to the French, his canoes were beaten off by gunfire from two French ships, but the town fell to a surprise attack in July 1756 after its garrison had been weakened by starvation as the result of a siege. Later that year, he was able to capture two French warships near Syriam because they were both led aground by a Burmese pilot and attacked by the Burmese galleys and fire-rafts. As a result, 'Alaungpaya gained a valuable addition of cannon that helped against Pegu. Pegu itself fell to 'Alaungpaya in 1757 as a result of attack by land and water. His boats thwarted his opponents' fire-rafts.

The Chinese used Green Standard troops for their navy rather than Manchu bannermen. This reflected a range of factors including the lower prestige of naval service and differences in relevant expertise. As ever, issues of cause and effect are not easy to disentangle, and this point is especially valid for Chinese naval forces as they are a much understudied element of the Chinese military. It appears that the numerous patrol craft, many armed with small cannon,[5] were reasonably effective in maintaining order on China's extensive rivers, but less so in defending coastal waters against pirates. However, the conquest of Taiwan in 1683 greatly reduced the pirate challenge by removing local bases. Moreover, there was no recurrence until the end of the eighteenth century of the large-scale pirate attacks of the sixteenth century, some of which had been based in southern Japan.

Thus, the naval situation had been transformed by the consolidation of state power. Japan had been unified in the late sixteenth century, and, thereafter, Japanese-based piracy had declined. Similarly, the eventual establishment of a powerful Manchu state stopped the twin-challenge of large-scale piracy and Ming *revanchism* from maritime areas, notably Taiwan. Both these processes had been largely achieved as a result of operations on land, which helps explain the relative neglect of the naval history of East Asia in this period, but, even so, there is more to say both about the seventeenth-century creation of a new order and about the eighteenth-century consequences. The weak state of the Chinese navy reflected the lack of any serious challenge from the sea.[6] In addition, rebellions did not pose a major naval issue. For example, there was no naval battle in the White Lotus rebellion of 1796–1805. Piracy again became a serious problem starting from the end of the eighteenth century, although so far studies of the subject are relatively limited. No real and significant measures against the new pirate challenge were adopted in China before the mid-nineteenth century.[7] Meanwhile, Japan responded in 1792 to an apparent threat from Russia by planning coastal fortifications, rather than by developing naval strength.

Also rowed, galleys were the nearest equivalent at a large scale to canoes. Galleys were particularly appropriate for shallow waters and also where winds were light or the availability of any wind was unreliable and navigation difficult, and less appropriate in stormy deep seas. Such ships were used by important regional naval powers, notably in the East Indies. For example, the Illanos of the Sulu Islands in the southern Philippines deployed large fleets of heavily-armed galleys. They were able and willing to attack the warships of the Dutch East India Company. The Buginese state of Bone also mounted major raids by sea, and, in the 1720s and 1730s, a Bugi pirate of royal descent, Arung Singkang, conquered part of east Borneo.

In India, the Marathas had a measure of naval strength, including many galleys, and conducted guerrilla-style raiding attacks on the Portuguese and the British East India Company. The shallow draught of their ships was more appropriate for the waters of the west coast than that of the larger British warships.[8] As a result, the East India Company built a series of lighter, shallow-draught vessels, including *galivats*, sailing rowboats armed with cannon. Under Kanhoji Angria, the Maratha warships had considerable success, but his four sons did not co-operate and, in 1739 and 1742, Sambhaji Angria's fleet was defeated by the Portuguese, while, in 1749, Tulaji Angria's fleet was beaten by the British. In 1755–6, his fleet and his fortress of Gheria were destroyed by the British supported by a Maratha fleet and army.

Under Haidar Ali and Tipu Sultan, Mysore developed a navy from 1763. In 1765, it contained 30 warships while, in the 1790s, Tipu established a Board of Admiralty and planned to build 100 warships. The larger frigate-sized warships of the navy were strong, and the fleet was able to help in operations. In 1780, Mysore troops were transported for the invasion of the Carnatic. Moreover, in the 1790s, Tipu embarked on a policy of fixed coastal defence batteries and forts designed to deal with the serious vulnerability of Mysore's harbours to naval attack. Thus, in 1766 and 1780, the

British launched destructive attacks on the Mysore ships in the harbour at Mangalore. Despite his plans, Tipu did not build the forty larger ships mentioned in 1796, and he was overthrown in 1799 without his fleet playing any significant role in that campaign. In the resulting territorial settlement, Mysore lost its coastline.[9] More generally, no non-Western power emulated the seventeenth-century naval moves of Coxinga and the Omanis, which, albeit only in a regional context, had both thrown the Western powers onto the defensive, taking Fort Zeelandia in Taiwan (1662) and Mombasa (1698) respectively.

The wood available in the west of India, notably on the Konkan coastline around Maharashtra, the part of the Deccan where the Maratha ships operated, was good for shipbuilding. The British started using this wood for their own warships, notably in the early nineteenth century, but also earlier. Offshore and littoral warfare had forced the British to build ships with a smaller draught, and the west Indian shipwrights were put into use by the East India Company. The flexibility brought by British seapower was shown in December 1767 in the Bay of Bengal when an amphibious force landed in the Northern Circars and then marched inland, helping lead the Nizam to negotiate peace in February 1768.

Islamic navies

The naval strength of the North African powers – Morocco, Algiers, Tunis and Tripoli – relied on galleys but also used sail-powered galleons. The *chebeck*, a light sailing vessel with auxiliary oars, was important. In line with the privateering economies of these territories, of which all bar independent Morocco were autonomous Turkish provinces, the warships were used for commerce raiding, not fleet engagements.[10] The North Africans sought to avoid clashes with other warships. The Moroccans captured the crew of a Dutch frigate in 1751, but only after it had been driven ashore during a storm.

In turn, Western powers dispatched expeditions to show the flag and deter the North Africans from privateering. Their attacks led the Dutch to send men-of-war twice yearly to escort merchantmen to Italy and the Near East. Formal conflicts involving the Dutch included war with Algiers in 1716–26 and 1755–9, and with Morocco in 1751–2 and 1774–7. The French had a naval show of force against Morocco in 1765–6. Venice, which acted repeatedly against Algiers and Tripoli between 1768 and 1774, did so successfully against Tunis and Tripoli in 1784, 1785 and 1786.

However, conflict with the North African states was generally fruitless other than in encouraging the latter to show restraint. Occasionally, privateering bases were attacked, but they usually proved difficult targets, not least because deep-draught warships risked running aground on uncharted rocks off their approaches. The French bombardment of the Moroccan privateering bases of Larache and Salé in 1765 achieved little. In 1784, when a large combined Spanish, Portuguese, Neapolitan and Maltese fleet attempted to destroy the privateering base of Algiers, a line of Algerian warships prevented the Spaniards from coming ashore. An earlier attack in 1775 had been repelled on land when exposed Spanish troops were subjected to heavy fire and their artillery was delayed by the coastal sand. Having seen off attack, Algiers was able to send privateers to attack the shores of the northern Mediterranean, including the seas off Genoa, Nice and Sardinia in 1787.

The Turks were a far more formidable power than the North Africans, but their naval activity did not range as far as it had in the sixteenth century; and notably not to the Arabian Sea nor off the coast of East Africa. However, the Turks remained significant in the Black Sea and the eastern Mediterranean, and continued to have a river fleet on the Danube. At the turn of the seventeenth and eighteenth centuries, the Turks abandoned their traditional dependence on galleys and built a new fleet of sail-powered galleons that carried more cannon. This was part of a general pattern of development in Mediterranean warfare, although galleys continued to have a role until 1814 when they were discarded by the Royal Sardinian Navy. In the first two decades of the century, the Turkish fleet was believed capable of influencing Italian politics, as with the rumours circulated in Venice in 1708 that it would be sent to the Adriatic.[11]

The Turkish fleet proved particularly effective against Venice in 1715–18, helped by the extent to which Venice was a weaker and more vulnerable power than in the seventeenth century. In 1715, when the Turks benefited from not being at war with any other power, they were extremely successful in using amphibious power to support the rapid conquest of the Morea (Peloponnese) from the Venetians. For example, on the Mani, the southernmost peninsula of the Morea, the fortresses of Kelefa and Zarnáta surrendered in August 1715 to a Turkish squadron which was able to bring force to bear against weak positions. In 1716, the Turks went on to invade the island of Corfu, the main protection for Venice's position in the Adriatic, but the fortifications of the main position there proved too strong. This might seem a major failure for Turkish amphibious power, but the same had occurred in Corfu in 1538, while Western powers during the eighteenth century, at Algiers and elsewhere, also found amphibious operations very difficult. Victor Amadeus II of Savoy-Piedmont was sufficiently concerned to issue orders for the defence of his new territory of Sicily against Turkish attack.[12]

Moreover, in the first half of the eighteenth century, the Turks were able to hold off Christian naval forces in the eastern basin of the Mediterranean. In 1718, off the island of Cerigo, a key location on the maritime route between the Aegean and the Mediterranean, the Turkish fleet had the advantage over an opposing Christian fleet, principally consisting of Venetian warships, and the Christians lost nearly 2,000 men in a battle on which relatively little scholarly work has been done. Peace with the Turks from 1718 encouraged a reduction of the well-administered Venetian fleet, and, thereafter, it essentially served to protect trade from privateers, and did not wage war.

The Turks also reduced their navy, and understandably, as their major challenge in the 1720s and early 1730s was that of Persia. The focus in the Turkish war with Russia and Austria in the late 1730s was on land operations, while in the 1740s war with Persia resumed.[13] The Turks were no longer mentioned as threatening or potentially influencing Italian politics, although good relationships with them were sought by Naples and Venice, both in order to help trade and because in theory the Regencies of Algiers, Tunis and Tripoli were part of the Turkish empire. In practice, Turkish authority there declined markedly.

In the 1770s, the Turks had to face a new version of the longstanding northern European presence in the Mediterranean. The English and Dutch had deployed ships in the 1700s, 1710s, 1720s, 1730s and 1740s, essentially in order to protect trade and fight France and Spain, although, in 1706, Robert Harley, one of the English Secretaries of State, thought that French influence in Constantinople could be countered 'when the Turks know we have so powerful a fleet in those seas, which can safely visit them'. This belief was doubted, not on the grounds that the Royal Navy lacked sufficient strength, but because the Turks would be informed by the French that it was too busy fighting France in the War of the Spanish Succession.[14]

In the event, during the Russo-Turkish war of 1768–74, Russia sent a fleet from St Petersburg in the Baltic in order to attack the Turks, and, therefore, into the eastern Mediterranean. Having over-wintered at Livorno in Tuscany in 1769–70, the Russians attacked the Turkish fleet at Cesmé off the Aegean island of Chios on 5 July 1770. The closely-moored Turkish fleet, of twenty ships of the line and frigates, and at least thirteen galleys, was outmanoeuvred, and almost totally destroyed by fireships. About 11,000 Turks were killed. However, although the Russians landed troops in many locations, for example the Mani in the Morea, they were unable to exploit the situation in order to drive the Turks from the Aegean. Moreover, the balance of Turkish concern was shown by the lack of major repairs at the Dardanelles fortresses between 1770 and 1784.[15] There was greater Turkish sensitivity about the situation to the north of the Black Sea. Russia's longstanding interest in establishing a naval base on Malta proved fruitless.[16]

Turkish authority meanwhile continued to decline in North Africa. In 1783, Algiers pursued direct negotiations with Western powers, Tunis following immediately. The Turkish fleet was no longer considered a threat and did not intervene when Western navies attacked Algiers, Tunis and Tripoli in 1784–6.

In the next Russo-Turkish war, that of 1787–92, the British feared that the Russians would be able to send a fleet to the Red Sea via Madagascar in order to open up a new sphere of naval operations against the Turks. However, the Russians focused on the Black Sea where they now had a naval base, and wanted both to prevent the Turks from mounting attacks on the Crimea and, instead, to use their fleet to support operations on land. The Russians were victorious at the battles of the Dnieper (1788) and Tendra (1790). The Turks lost twelve warships in the two battles; the Russians only one. Russian naval success was important in order to ensure that the Turks were unable to re-supply besieged coastal fortresses. Turkish warships were poorly constructed, inadequately caulked and difficult to manoeuvre, and the reliance on impressment (seizure for compulsory service) was accompanied by a lack of a large cadre of experienced sailors.[17]

The threat from Revolutionary France, notably after the annexation of the Ionian Islands off western Greece from Venice in 1797 and Napoleon's expedition to Egypt in 1798, led Turkey and Russia to sign an alliance in January 1799. As a result, a joint fleet, provisioned by the Turks, occupied the Ionian Islands in early 1799, successfully besieging Corfu. The French seizure of Malta from the Knights of St John also showed how traditional geopolitical alignments had been transformed by the French Revolutionary War. In the event, the subsequent Napoleonic Wars were to end with Britain in control of both the Ionian Islands and Malta.

There were no battles comparable to Tendra, let alone Cesmé, marking the demise of Omani naval power in the western basin of the Indian Ocean. Indeed, the Omanis remained the key power on the Swahili coast of East Africa. The Portuguese lost their base of Fort Jesus at Mombasa to the Omani Arabs in 1698 and again (after retaking it in 1728) in 1729, when, although the besiegers had no artillery and very few firearms, the garrison surrendered as a result of low morale and problems with food supplies. A Portuguese attempt to regain Mombasa in 1769 failed. As a result, the Portuguese presence was restricted to Mozambique further south.

The Omanis were also active in the Persian Gulf, where, in 1717, they conquered Bahrain, Qishm and Larak, and raided Bandar Abbas. They also met with checks: the Omanis were repelled by the Persian forces on Bahrain in 1715, and were repulsed from Hormuz in 1718. That year, the Persians regained Bahrain, only for the Omanis to retake it, killing allegedly 6,000 Persian troops. The Persians were reduced to seeking British and Dutch help, and unsuccessfully so, and in 1720, the Persians felt obliged to negotiate with the Omanis.[18]

The Omanis, however, proved less successful than in the late seventeenth century in pressing on the west coast of India.[19] In large part, this was because the British had taken over the protective role previously fulfilled by the Portuguese. The East India Company ran an efficient fleet of its own, the Bombay Marine, and this was able to counteract local pirates, notably the Angrias, deter Omani attacks, and protect British trade into the Persian Gulf. As a result, Bombay's profitable status as an entrepot was preserved. Most of the Bombay Marine's ships were not large warships but, instead, vessels better adapted for inshore waters. Nevertheless, the Bombay Marine could deploy considerable firepower. Western naval potential was also demonstrated at the coffee port of Mocha in Yemen in 1737 where moves against French trade had led to the dispatch of a squadron from Pondicherry, the major French base in India. Having bombarded the port, the French landed troops and, in response, their commercial privileges were restored.

The Persian Gulf also witnessed the use of Persian naval power, notably when Nadir Shah intervened in Oman. He sought to create a navy based at Bushire, with a supporting cannon foundry at Gombroom. Nadir forced the sale of ships by the Dutch and British East India Companies, and, by 1737, had a fleet that included four sizeable warships, two of which he had obtained from the British. After an unsuccessful attempt by the Persians to capture Basra in 1735, Bahrain was seized in 1736, while in 1737 the fleet carried 5,000 Persian troops to Oman, 6,000 more following in 1738. However, as with many conflicts elsewhere in the world, that in the Persian Gulf was not a struggle between two clearly separated powers, but rather a war in which elements on both sides co-operated. Indeed, in 1737 and 1738, the Persians invaded Oman in alliance with the ruler, the Iman of Oman, and were resisted by his rebellious subjects under Bal'arab ibn Himyar Al-Ya'riba, who was defeated in both years. However, each year the allies fell out. The Persian expedition also suffered from a serious shortage of food and money, and, in 1740, the Persian navy, which had defeated the Arab fleet the previous year, mutinied.

A fresh attempt to build up the fleet was made from 1740. Nadir Shah sought to purchase foreign ships, in 1741 ordering eleven from Surat in India, a centre of Western commercial activity, and more ships were built at Bushire from that year. After being reduced to a precarious hold on the port of Julfār in 1739–42, the Persians benefited from a fresh civil war in

Oman in 1742. However, alternative commitments, especially against the Turks, led to a shortage of funds and provisions, leading the Persian troops to desert and surrender, and the Persian commander rebelled against Nadir. A lack of reinforcements resulted in the abandonment of the Persian presence in Oman in 1744.[20] This presence was not only a marginal one, but also one that was difficult to sustain through Nadir's standard methods of raiding foreign lands and extorting supplies from his own dominions.

The Persians did not persist with their maritime schemes after Nadir was killed in 1747. Moreover, he had used his army, not a navy, to attack the Mughals in 1739. Nor was there a Persian fleet on the Caspian Sea.

The Turkish naval presence in the Persian Gulf was even less significant than its Persian counterpart. When, in 1735, the Pasha of Turkish-ruled Basra defeated a Persian naval attempt to seize the port, he did so by commandeering British ships. Basra was no longer a significant naval base while it had also become less important as a trading centre. The British were unsuccessful in 1765 when they attacked the piratical Banu Ka'b of Khizistan at the head of the Persian Gulf.

Although there were shared functions, notably amphibious operations and overlapping types of ships and armament, nevertheless there were also significant contrasts between non-Western and Western navies. In particular, the North African, Omani and Maratha ships were commerce raiders whose emphasis was on speed and manoeuvrability, rather than strength and durability. A shortage of timber appropriate for masts was an additional problem in North Africa.[21] In contrast, the heavy, slow, big ships of the line of Western navies were designed for battle and emphasised battering power. Such a comparison, however, needs to note the considerable variety in the specifications and goals of these ships of the line.[22] Furthermore, there were several types of ships in the Western navies that were not ships of the line, for example the cutters used to help customs services in the incessant war against smugglers. More generally, 'small war' at sea requires more work comparable to that recently done for 'small war' on land.

Western navies

Western navies continued the pattern of development begun in the mid-seventeenth century, with a concentration on specialised warships instead of armed merchantmen, and with a related specialised organisation and infrastructure. In the mid-seventeenth century, there had also been an increase in naval firepower, notably thanks to the replacement of bronze cannon with cheaper cast-iron guns. Heavier shot was fired and, as a result of the number of cannon being carried, the firepower of many individual ships of the line now surpassed that of entire armies. English broadside firepower increased with the development of improved tackles which used the gun's recoil to speed reloading inboard. Linear tactics were adapted by all navies in order to maximise firepower. Warships could not fire straight ahead, so were deployed to fire broadsides against a parallel line of opposing vessels.[23]

The growth of Western naval power was not simply a matter of developments afloat. In addition, naval bases were founded and existing ones enhanced, so that a new geography of naval power, based on ports such as Brest and Plymouth, was created. Both these ports had direct access to the Atlantic, which became more important to Britain and France than locations on the North Sea and the Mediterranean, such as Chatham and Toulon respectively.

The conflicts between these two powers comprised the key naval struggle of the period. The decisive English victory at Barfleur/La Hogue in 1692 ended the threat of a French invasion of England that year, while the subsequent French decision to focus on the army ensured that Britain was able to develop a major lead in naval tonnage. After the somewhat indecisive battle of Malaga in 1704 enabled the British to consolidate their newly-won position at Gibraltar, the French navy languished.[24] Despite an invasion scare in 1731 and British concern about French naval moves and plans in 1733 and 1740, the French navy did not mount a serious challenge to the British again until 1744 when a storm in the English Channel thwarted an attempt to invade southern England. The Dutch navy was affected by a lack of willingness to invest sufficiently in the navy or to reform its institutions,[25] and, in part, by a focus on the army; and, as a result, the Dutch played a smaller role against France in the 1700s than had been envisaged in the 1689 agreement with Britain.[26] This issue recurred as a problem in Anglo-Dutch relations in the 1740s and 1790s.

An age of British naval hegemony had clearly begun with the moves of other powers in the Mediterranean seen as depending in part on the Royal Navy.[27] Moreover, in 1747, two impressive British victories off Cape Finisterre revealed that the French navy was unable to protect its long-distance trade. Having failed to fulfil expectations in the early stages of the war with Spain and, later, France (1739–48), the Royal Navy had become an effective strategic force by 1747.[28]

The British position, however, was challenged by the Bourbons in 1746–55, as France and Spain then launched more warships than Britain. Fortunately for Britain, Spain did not join the Seven Years' War (1756–63) until 1762, and, by then, her ally France had been defeated at sea. The crucial campaign was that of 1759. Choiseul, the leading French minister, planned a naval concentration to cover an invasion of Britain, prefiguring Napoleon's plan in 1805. However, the division of the French navy between the far-apart bases of Brest and Toulon made a concentration of strength difficult, and the British benefited from their division to defeat them separately in bold attacking actions at Lagos (Portugal) and Quiberon Bay. All possibility of a major French invasion of Britain was now gone, and the British were confirmed in their view that they were *the* naval power. In 1762, Havana, the leading Spanish naval and military base in the West Indies, was captured by a major amphibious operation.

British assumptions were to be challenged in the next war, the American War of Independence. Thanks to much shipbuilding in the late 1760s and 1770s, especially by Spain, then one of the most dynamic states in Europe, by 1780 France and Spain combined had a quantitative superiority in naval tonnage over Britain of about 25 per cent. Partly as a result, the British were unable to repeat their success of the Seven Years' War. The British had control of neither European nor American waters, and were unable to defeat the French navy in 1778 when war began with France before Spain entered the conflict the following year. As British naval strength was concentrated on defending home waters, and thus countering moves by the French fleet in nearby Brest, the Toulon (French Mediterranean) fleet was able to sail to North America in 1778, although when it arrived it achieved relatively little. In 1779, France and Spain planned an invasion of England only for it to be thwarted by disease and poor organisation rather than by British naval action. The British position in the Mediterranean was also challenged.[29]

It was not until the battle of the Saints on 12 April 1782 that there was a decisive British naval victory to rank with Barfleur (1692), Lagos (1759), and Quiberon Bay (1759). It was a testimony to the rising importance of colonies and trans-oceanic operations, and the failure of the British to maintain an effective blockade of France, that this battle was fought in the Caribbean. Breaking through the French line of warships, George Rodney captured five of them. More generally in the War of American Independence, British failure in the Thirteen Colonies of North America was not matched by a wider collapse of the empire, in part due to the resilience of the Royal Navy. This achievement was readily apparent in the Indian Ocean as the naval struggle between Britain and France was connected to the war between Britain and Mysore. Albeit in more difficult circumstances, the combination of France and Mysore did not have the same destructive impact for Britain as that of France and the American Patriots.

The importance of naval strength encouraged a shipbuilding race in the 1780s in which Britain and France launched a formidable amount of tonnage. Spain remained the third leading naval power,[30] an indication of the misleading tendency to underrate its strength; while Russia became the fourth. The Dutch, who had been in that position, or higher, until the early 1750s, before dropping to fifth in 1755–65 and to sixth in 1775–80, expanded their navy to regain, with a greater size than before in that century, the fifth position from 1785.[31] Partly as a result, it was important for Britain and France to compete for influence in the Dutch Crisis in 1787. The two powers competed anew, this time with Spain on France's side and the Dutch on Britain's side, in the Nootka Sound Crisis of 1790, although, in each case, the French backed down. Denmark, Sweden, Naples, Portugal and Turkey also all increased the size of their navies in the 1780s. In 1792–3, Britain moved towards war with Revolutionary France in part in order to protect the Dutch. They did not fight until 1793, by which time the French fleet had been badly affected by the political and administrative disruption stemming from the French Revolution. In 1793, the British were invited into Toulon by French royalists, before being driven out again by Revolutionary forces benefiting from the well-sited cannon of Napoleon, then a young artillery officer.

The following year, the British defeated France's Brest fleet at the battle of the Glorious First of June. Having gained the weather gauge, enough British ships broke through the French line to bring superior gunnery to bear at close range. The French lost seven warships, but showed a willingness to fight bravely for the new republic.[32] British success indicated the broad-based nature of command ability on the eve of Nelson's triumphs, as well as the extent of fleet cohesion.

The British had grasped the controlling maritime position, only to see it collapse in 1795–6 when the French forced Spain and the Dutch into alliance and gained the benefit of their fleets. Once more able to threaten invasion of the British Isles, indeed sending troops into Ireland in 1798 (where they were rapidly defeated), France confronted Britain in a struggle for her survival, notably in 1797–8 and 1805. The result of this struggle was decisive in the defeat of the attempt to subvert Europe to one hegemonic power.

Success is easier to describe than to explain. The British benefited from a range of factors, although these would still have been in play had they lost or simply lacked success, which is a reminder of the need for caution in explaining victory. The size of the British navy was clearly important. Thanks to the capture of French ships and to shipbuilding, by 1760 it had a displacement of about 375,000 metric tonnes, at that point the largest navy in the world, although this advantage was lost when opponents combined, as in 1779 when France and Spain, the second and third leading naval powers, sought to mount a joint invasion of England.

The greater effectiveness of the British navy was largely due to its having more ships, to its extensive and effective administrative system, to the strength of public finances, and to good naval leadership. Britain had a more meritocratic promotion system and a more unified naval tradition than those of France, and a greater commitment of national resources to naval rather than land warfare, a political choice that reflected the major role of trade and the character of the national self-image.[33]

The British situation contrasted greatly with that of China. Thus, the two strongest powers of the period, both of which greatly expanded territorially around 1760 after victorious campaigns, were very different, politically, geopolitically, and militarily. The French financial system lacked the institutional strength and stability of its British counterpart, and this lack badly affected French naval finances in 1759. The French also did not have an effective chain of naval command, and trade was less important to their government and their political culture.[34] The points about financial systems and chains of command can also be made when contrasting British and Indian warmaking on land at the close of the century. Moreover, British naval efficiency increased from the 1790s with the introduction of more effective attitudes and practices of financial and administrative control. This introduction reflected a more general openness to new thinking and a readiness to consult those with expert knowledge.[35]

Britain's commercial position was enhanced by the protection offered by the Royal Navy.[36] Similarly, the ability to wreck the foreign trade of rivals could cripple their imperial system and greatly hamper their economy. Even if it was not possible to inflict this degree of damage, higher insurance premiums, danger money for sailors, and the need to resort to convoys and other defensive measures, could push up the cost of trade. Vessels were seized by warships and by privateers – private vessels given licences to take enemy ships. Privateers were smaller and less heavily-gunned than ships of the line, but they were more manoeuvrable and of shallower draught, and were thus more appropriate for commerce raiding. Largely thanks to the British, nearly 1,800 ships and barges insured at Marseilles, France's leading Mediterranean port, were captured in the War of the Spanish Succession, a major blow to the French economy. In turn, French privateering bases, especially St Malo and Dunkirk, proved difficult to contain, and the British suffered from the *guerre de course* (privateering war). At the same time, Britain's relative success against French and Spanish privateers owed much to the size of the navy.

In contrast to differences in size, Western navies were similar in their ships and weapons. Indeed, the thesis of the contemporary British historian Edward Gibbon that a similarity in weaponry would prevent any one

Western power from achieving a position of hegemony[37] was inaccurate as far as the maritime world was concerned, and also with regard to the trans-oceanic rivalry between Britain and France. For example, Sir Thomas Slade, Surveyor of the British Navy from 1755 to 1771, designed a series of two-decker 74-gun warships that were both manoeuvrable and capable of holding their own in the punishing close-range artillery duels of line of battle engagements, and he did so working from French and Spanish warships captured in the 1740s. Benefiting from the general increase in long-distance naval capability that stemmed in part from changes in ship design, the British used weapons and tactics similar to those of their Western rivals.

That, however, does not mean that there were no contrasts in effectiveness that would help explain British success. Instead, the British benefited from a series of advantages that, although modest in comparison with the contrasts between Western and non-Western warships, were still significant. Superior gunnery was a key point. Progress in British metallurgy linked to what was to be described as the Industrial Revolution improved their gunnery towards the end of the century, and the impact of British naval gunfire on enemy hulls and crews markedly increased during the years of conflict from 1793 to 1815 when enemy ships were reduced to wrecks in a comparatively short time. Britain had an advantage in technology and industrial capability, as well as having good seamanship and well-drilled gun crews who could deliver a formidable rate of fire.

Britain, France, Spain and the Dutch did not exhaust the nature of Western naval power. Indeed, there was a separate naval world in the Baltic where, alongside clashes between deep-draught warships and the deployment of British, Dutch and French warships, there were also engagements between local galley fleets, in contrast with the Mediterranean where galley warfare became less significant.

The major expansion of naval power was less significant for Russia than its growing strength and effectiveness on land, and its key conflicts were all waged on land. Nevertheless, the naval expansion was important to both Peter the Great (r. 1689–1725) and Catherine the Great (r. 1762–96), and they clearly saw naval power as an aspect of Russia's modernisation. Under Peter, this was linked to the foundation of St Petersburg as capital, 'window to the west', and port on Russia's newly-conquered Baltic coastline. In 1703, Peter himself laid the foundation stone of the Peter-Paul Fortress. The following year, he founded the Admiralty Shipyard on the bank of the River Neva opposite the fortress, and in 1706 its first warship was launched. A naval academy followed in 1715. By 1720, Russia was the strongest naval power in the Baltic. The previous year, Russian galley-borne forces had ravaged the eastern coast of Sweden.

Galleys were particularly useful in shallow and island-strewn waters such as those in the Gulf of Finland, the approach to St Petersburg. Lake, lagoon and river warfare could also be important. In 1702, the Swedish flotilla on Lake Ladoga was defeated by a far larger Russian squadron. Similarly, in 1776, the British and the Americans clashed on Lake Champlain as the British tried to advance south from Canada, destroying the American squadron. The previous year, Benedict Arnold had used river boats for his advance on British-held Québec, across largely trackless Maine.

The Russians made extensive use of shallow-draft ships, as in 1737 when allegedly 1,000 boats were used to transport 40,000 troops across the Sea of Azov so that the Crimea could be invaded, greatly expanding the potential axes of attack. In 1790, a Russian flotilla played a role in the successful siege of the Turkish fortress of Izmail on the Danube.

Russian galley-borne forces proved particularly useful in operations against Swedish-ruled Finland in the 1710s and 1740s. The British envoy, Sir Cyril Wych, reported in 1742 that there were 130 galleys in St Petersburg in 'constant good order', each with three cannon and able to carry 200 troops, and that 'with these they can make great and sudden … irruptions'.[38] Such a force was not a threat to Britain, but it was to allies and potential allies, notably Sweden, Denmark and Prussia. Naval power served to intimidate and was discussed in these terms, as in the Baltic crises of 1749–50 and 1772–3 when Russian naval strength was a factor in considering Sweden's options.

When war between Russia and Sweden resumed in 1788, each side attempted to match or thwart the naval capability of the other. The Swedish ship designer Fredrik Henrik af Chapman had studied in France and Britain. He developed oared archipelago frigates whose diagonal internal stiffenings enabled them to carry heavy guns in a light, shallow-draught hull, and oared gunboats, small boats with great firepower and a small target area; the guns were moved on rails and used as ballast when the boats sailed in open waters. In 1788–90, both navies constructed a large number of oared vessels, the Swedes focusing on gunboats, while the Russians built a large number of oared frigates as well. In the battles of 1790, Russia was able to hold off the Swedish attacks.

Programmes of naval construction indicated not only the resources of European governments, but also the capability of their military-industrial complexes. Fleets were powerful and sophisticated military systems, sustained by mighty industrial and logistical resources based in dockyards that were among the largest industrial plants, employers of labour, and groups of buildings in the world. These dockyards were supported by massive storehouses, such as the vast Lands Zeemagazijn in Amsterdam, which was destroyed by fire in 1791. These naval bases required considerable investment. Even minor naval powers developed an infrastructure, Savoy-Piedmont establishing yards and other building at the naval headquarters, Villafranca, as well as at Nice and on the island of Sardinia. A naval school was established.

Although there were no intimations of the radical changes that were, by 1870, to supersede the age of wooden, wind-powered warships firing solid shot from smoothbore (unrifled) cannon, the age of sail had a capacity for change, matching the situation seen on land in the West. There were numerous innovations at sea, and they were put to good use. Improvements in seaworthiness, stemming in part from the abandon-ment of earlier top-heavy and clumsy designs, increased the capability of warships, both to take part in all-weather blockades and to operate across the oceans. However, expeditions could be greatly delayed[39] or dispersed as a result of the weather. Adverse winds helped thwart French invasion attempts directed against England in 1744 and Ireland in 1796. Many ships, moreover, were shipwrecked in storms, often with heavy casualties.[40]

After the War of American Independence, the French adopted recent British naval innovations, such as the copper-sheathing of ships' bottoms in order to discourage barnacles and so increase manoeuvrability. There was also the carronade, a new powerful short-range cannon named after the Scottish ironworks where it was manufactured. Standardisation was increasingly apparent in the period, and in 1786 the French adopted stand-ard ship designs for their fleet.

Despite the limitations of naval technology, greater capability encour-aged the projection of power. The British navy played a major part in Mediterranean politics from the 1700s to the 1750s,[41] and then again in the 1790s. Rumours in 1741 that the Habsburgs would let Britain establish a naval base at Livorno in Tuscany reflected the belief that naval support was important to the Austrian cause in Italy. In the War of the Austrian Succession (1740–8), British naval activity in the western Mediterranean proved very important as it cut Spanish supply routes and prevented the Spaniards in Italy from receiving any significant reinforcements.

Effectiveness in power-projection, however, depended in part on the availability of troops and on skill in amphibious operations; a skill that owed much to experience. In January 1704, John Chetwynd, the English envoy in Turin, noted that an English fleet was due in the Mediterranean that summer, but added 'unless there are 10,000 soldiers aboard the fleet it will not have that respect paid to it which it deserves',[42] and thus be able to encourage allies, influence neutrals, and intimidate and weaken opponents. In the event, the availability of troops was important, as in the English capture of Gibraltar that year and of the island of Minorca in 1708. The very presence of the fleet, moreover, was seen as significant in influencing opinion in Spain where there was a civil war in progress.[43] Naval power was also important in convoying troops, as in 1713 when the British navy carried Victor Amadeus II of Savoy-Piedmont and 6,000 of his troops to take possession of Sicily in accordance with the peace settlement.

Moreover, naval warfare could be decisive, although, under the strain of conflict, navies found it difficult to fulfil their tactical potential. The essential resilience of wooden ships (wood floats) ensured that they were difficult to sink by gunfire, although they would sink if the magazine was detonated. At the outset of wars, even Britain, the leading naval power, found it difficult to ensure victory, as was shown in indecisive clashes with the French off Malaga (1704), Toulon (1744), Minorca (1756), and Ushant (1778), the last a serious failure off Brest as it left the French able to project power into North American waters. Especially in the case of the last two battles, the individual ships' companies were newly-recruited or pressed, their captains were still working up the sailing capabilities of their ships and crew, and the admiral was still working up and determining the capacities of his captains, who were equally unsure of their commander. More generally, thanks in large part to the combination of the wind and the poor manoeuvrability of warships, naval battles frequently did not develop as suggested by fighting instructions, and admirals had only limited control once battles had begun.

Nevertheless, cannon firing at short range could devastate rigging and masts, and effectively incapacitate the ships. So battles in which no ships were sunk could, nevertheless, be hard-fought and decisive. Thus, the French failure to defeat an Anglo-Dutch fleet off Malaga in 1704 ended with the latter holding the initiative in the Mediterranean. The battle off Rügen between the Danish and Swedish fleets in 1715 left the Danes able to cut supply lines to Stralsund, the last Swedish base in Germany. The French were unable to repair damage sustained in the action off Porto Novo in 1759, so leaving the British in command of Indian waters. No warships were sunk or captured in the five Anglo-French battles in Indian waters during the War of American Independence, but, as the British force was built up by reinforcements, this outcome represented a failure for France.

Warships could be deployed against coastal positions, which led to a relevant literature, as with John Ardesoif's *An Introduction to Marine Fortifications and Gunnery* (Gosport, 1772). However, success was mixed. When, in 1745, the British squadron in the Mediterranean under Vice-Admiral Rowley tried to bombard Genoa they found the Genoese galleys deployed in line, sufficiently close in to remain protected by coastal artillery but far enough out to prevent the British bombarding the city. After firing about sixty shots, Rowley left.

As a central aspect of developing the oceans as a 'manoeuvre space', the Europeans also took their naval military-industrial capability outside Europe, with major shipyards at colonial bases, notably Havana (Spanish) and Halifax, Nova Scotia (British). In the West Indies, the British had two naval bases on Jamaica – Port Royal and Port Antonio – as well as English Harbour on Antigua, begun in 1728 and still impressive. Port Royal was able to careen the larger ships of the line sent there. Moreover, the growing British naval and mercantile presence in the Indian Ocean owed much to shipyards in India, where ships could be built and repaired, especially Bombay (Mumbai). By the mid-1770s, Bombay's dry dock, the sole one available to the Royal Navy outside Britain, could take three third-rate warships.[44]

Overseas naval forces supported European trade. In 1725, when French merchants were expelled from their new base at Mahé on the south-west coast of India, the French sent a squadron from Pondicherry on the east coast, forcing the return of the merchants and obtaining new commercial benefits. They were less successful in protecting their commercial position at Syriam in Burma against attack by 'Alaungpaya in 1756.

In the colonies, the lack of siege trains of heavy artillery led frequently to a reliance on the cannon of supporting warships when attacking coastal positions. These weapons were either fired from the ships or manhandled ashore and fired by sailors. Both options were important to the success of numerous British sieges and were eased because most centres of colonial power were ports, on rivers or the coast, notably Québec and Havana which were successfully besieged in 1759 and 1762 respectively.

The potential for operations outside Europe was increased by the role of European navies in organising the charting of coastlines, to the benefit of trade as well as the assertion of power. In 1764–81, George Gauld was instructed by the British Admiralty to chart the waters of the Gulf of Mexico, which was seen as a means to consolidate the recent British acquisition of Florida.

Naval operations outside Europe, however, especially in the Indian Ocean and the Caribbean, remained greatly dependent on climate and disease. The British expedition sent from Madras in October 1756 to recapture Calcutta from the Nawab of Bengal was hit by the weather, by sickness, and by running aground.[45] More generally, despite improvements in some spheres, the conditions of service at sea continued to be bleak. Disease led to high mortality from, for example, yellow fever in the British and Spanish fleets in the 1720s, and from typhus in the British and Dutch fleets in the 1740s. The situation was exacerbated by cramped living conditions, poor sanitation, and inadequate and inappropriate food. In particular, there was a shortage of fresh food, fruit and vegetables, and hence a lack of vitamin C. The cumulative impact was to make naval service unattractive and to ensure serious losses among those already in service.

Conversely, improved conditions, notably the supply of vitamin C, which was very important to sailors' health, could lead to greater effectiveness. As an instance of the administrative underpinning of such conditions, the British Navy Board, Victualling Board and Ordnance Board were able effectively to direct a formidable re-supply system, including on the far-flung East Indies Station.[46] The Ordnance Board also proved successful and pro-active in arming the navy.[47]

Effectiveness, however, was challenged by the problems of command and control posed by operations outside Europe. These problems were related to the difficulties of deploying ships so as to match the moves of opposing fleets. In 1740, Thomas, Duke of Newcastle, the British Secretary of State for the Southern Department, informed Edward Vernon, the naval commander in the Caribbean:

> the King [George II] does not think it proper to prescribe any particular service to be undertaken by you, but leaves it entirely to your discretion to act against the Spaniards, in such manner, and in such places, as shall appear to you best to answer the ends proposed by His Majesty's orders to you, which were to distress and annoy the Spaniards in the most effectual manner, by taking their ships, and possessing yourself of such of their places and settlements as you should think practicable to attempt.

Vernon was told that he would be kept 'greatly superior to any force that either is, or may be sent by the Spaniards to the West Indies'.[48] The failure to do so in North American waters led in 1781 to the British inability to relieve by sea the British army besieged at Yorktown. The French blockade of the mouth of Chesapeake Bay could not be forced, and, as a result, the British army at Yorktown surrendered.

The West and the Rest

Much of this book owes its importance to a determination to contextualise Western developments and to give due weight to non-Western powers and peoples. At sea, however, there was no balance, and no frontier of capability and control. This situation was dramatically demonstrated as Western warships, notably under James Cook, Jean-François de la Pérouse, Antonio Malaspina and George Vancouver, explored the Pacific. Western expeditions established the first Western colony in Australasia – the British position at Botany Bay in 1788 – considered where to establish naval bases, charted and (re-)named the world, and in 1790 came close to conflict in the Nootka Sound Incident over trade on what would later be called Vancouver Island.

There was still much of the world's land surface where Western military strength was unknown, but the warships that ran out their guns around the globe were the forceful edge of the first real integration of the world, an integration made by Westerners and to their own ends and profit. The significance of this at the time (as opposed to for the future) is, however, less clear. John Corneille noted that when Muhammad Ali Khan, Nawab of the Carnatic, a British ally, visited HMS *Kent* in 1755, he was 'greatly surprised at its size and number of guns'.[49] A foreign source for the views of an Indian ruler is perforce unreliable, but there is no direct information on the latter. Moreover, no Indian state had a warship comparable to the *Kent*.

The contrast between the West and the Rest became even more marked in the last decades of the century as the total displacement tonnage of Western navies rose from 1.07 million tons in 1770 to 1.21 million by 1780 and 1.6 million in 1790.[50] Thus, there was a major expansion of naval capability within the existing technological constraints. The long-term and growing stress on firepower affected fleet structures, with warships becoming bigger and carrying heavier guns.

The major qualifications of Western dominance were those offered by another European power, Turkey, and another Western power, newly-independent America. The Turkish navy increased in size in the 1780s and 1790s, and there were also technological innovations, notably the copper-bottoming of ships from 1792, and the building of the first dry dock in the Golden Horn. British, French and Swedish influence and experts played a role, but, by training Turkish shipbuilders, the direct dependence on Western expertise was lessened.[51] Nevertheless, the Russian victory in the war of 1787–92 owed something to naval successes over the Turks in the Black Sea.

American experimentation with new naval technology, in the shape of the submarine and underwater munitions, was not brought to fruition due to operational difficulties, although it captured the risk to existing powers posed by bypassing existing capability. During the War of Independence, the Americans, instead, offered a new version of a more traditional challenge, as their privateering attacks on the British[52] were supplemented by fleet action by the French and, less prominently, the Continental Navy of the new state.[53]

The loss of the support of the Thirteen Colonies was not significant for Britain in terms of the arithmetic of ships of the line. However, it was important for the manpower that had been contributed to the Royal Navy, both directly and indirectly, through the role of the merchant marine of the colonies in British imperial trade, notably the supply of food to the West Indies. Indeed, manpower issues, as the Royal Navy struggled to meet its needs in the context of contrasting British and American legal and political assumptions, helped lead to the outbreak of the War of 1812 between Britain and the USA. This point serves as a reminder that statistical measures of naval power in terms of numbers of warships need to be complemented by analysis of the manpower situation.

Once they were independent, the Americans did not match the Europeans in developing a large fleet. Indeed, the initial absence of a federal revenue base helped ensure that there was no navy, for, once independence was won, the Continental Navy was disbanded, its last ship being sold in 1785. The lack of the necessary infrastructure of bureaucracy and naval dockyards was a key problem, and contrasted with the situation in Europe.[54]

Nevertheless, in 1794, the Federalists reconstituted a navy, and this was then built up from 1797 in the Quasi War with France as the Americans had to protect their trade from French attacks. The limiting consequences of federal financial weaknesses ensured, however, that the construction of ten frigates was financed by subscriptions raised in the major ports. Clashes between American and French warships from the summer of 1798 were largely won by the Americans.[55] In 1801, Thomas Jefferson, the new President, informed Congress that he was sending a squadron against the Barbary States of North Africa.

These developments were pregnant with future significance, but in 1812 the Americans had no ships of the line and their total navy, although including the most powerful frigates of the age, comprised only 17 ships. The Europeans retained a naval dominance that helped ensure the spread of their power and influence over the seas of the world.

8 War and Society

In 1776, the Scottish economist Adam Smith offered, in his *Inquiry into the Nature and Causes of the Wealth of Nations* (which was to prove the foundational work for modern economics), an analysis of the sociology of warfare in which he adopted the standard Western stadial (stages) approach, and contrasted nations of hunters and shepherds with the 'more advanced state of society', in which industry was important. These advanced societies were seen by Smith as providing a hierarchy of military organisation and sophistication in which 'a well-regulated standing army' was vital to the defence of civilisation. Firearms, Smith claimed, were crucial in the onset of military modernity and as a measure of military capability:

> Before the invention of fire-arms, that army was superior in which the soldiers had, each individually, the greatest skill and dexterity in the use of their arms … since the invention … strength and agility of body, or even extraordinary dexterity and skill in the use of arms, though they are far from being of no consequence, are, however, of less consequence. … In modern war the great expense of fire-arms gives an evident advantage to the nation which can best afford that expense; and consequently, to an opulent and civilised, over a poor and barbarous nation. In ancient times the opulent and civilised found it difficult to defend themselves against the poor and barbarous nations. In modern times the poor and barbarous find it difficult to defend themselves against the opulent and civilised.[1]

Although exaggerating the military advantages of the 'opulent and civilised', Smith, like his British contemporary the famous historian Edward Gibbon, had captured an important development. He also drew attention to the question of why there were different 'types' of society and military systems, and what the consequences were.

Comparative discussion provided, and provides, a way to identify and dispute these differences. In this chapter, this issue will be discussed in terms of the related topics of war and society, and war and statebuilding, some aspects of which were covered in chapter 1. Each of these topics takes on the most meaning in the global context while also offering an important way to consider this context, and thus to advance comparative discussion.

The global context should not be seen from a Western perspective, nor with effectiveness and capability assessed largely in those terms. Warfare in much of the world was planned and waged without reference to Western weaponry, methods or politics. The West made a major impact in this period in India and (less successfully) Sri Lanka, but elsewhere in South Asia this was definitely not the case, and even less so in East Asia.

There, the advance that had taken Western power to the Philippines, Taiwan, Siberia's Pacific coast, and the Amur Valley, had already been partially reversed, the Dutch being driven from Taiwan in 1662, and the Russians from the Amur Valley in the 1680s. There was no resumption of the pace of Western advance in this region, the most populous in the world, in the eighteenth century. Indeed, Taiwan was never again to be a Western colony, while Russia did not regain control of the Amur Valley until the late 1850s.

This failure was not simply a result of Western states meeting or being unwilling to face resistance from powerful non-Western counterparts, the latter being other versions of the 'opulent and civilised'. Instead, in northeast Siberia, the native Chukchi were also formidable, serving as a reminder that Smith's dichotomy did not really hold up at the imperial margins, a point also true for the Spaniards in both Chile and northern Mexico. The Chukchi defeated a Cossack expedition in Russian service in 1729 and resisted genocidal attacks in 1730–1 and 1744–7. The Russians eventually stopped the war, abandoning their fort at Anadyrsk in 1764, although it had successfully resisted siege as recently as 1762. Trade links developed and the Russians finally recognised Chukchi rights to their territories. On the other hand, there was no risk that the Chukchi would advance to sweep the Russians from eastern Siberia.

In the case of China, in contrast, Westerners were certainly faced by the 'opulent and civilised'. Andreas Ly reported from Sichuan in 1748, 'Everywhere it is rumoured that a war has broken out between the Europeans and the Cantonese, and therefore the officials of that province have added guards to the maritime coastline: which seems false to me, but perhaps they have heard of fighting between European princes, and for that reason are on their guard, lest the Europeans make trouble in the province, which seems unlikely to me.'[2] In the event, Ly was correct on both counts. Whereas competition between Westerners played a major role in India in the 1740s and 1750s, and was also a factor (albeit a lesser one) in West Africa, the Chinese were not drawn into the rivalries, let alone conflicts, between Western states. China was simply too powerful, and the Western powers too weak.

It is tempting, but unnecessary, to explain this lack of Western advance as a failure, indeed by reference to a structural limitation of the Western military system. There were, of course, weaknesses and limits, but it is more appropriate to note that the Western powers concentrated, first, on war with each other in Europe itself, and secondly, on attacks on other Western colonial possessions. Conflict with non-Western powers, particularly those (not including Turkey) that were not close neighbours, came a long way behind. Thus, in 1762, a British expedition from Madras captured Spanish-ruled Manila. There was no comparable British expedition against any non-Western target in East or South-East Asia, although the situation in India was very different.

Conflict with non-Western powers measured the relative military and political prowess of Western powers in the global theatre, and their adaptability to radically different situations. Also, just as with the wars between the armies and navies of Western powers, conflicts with non-Westerners were forcing-houses for tactical innovations and developments in weaponry that informed warfare throughout the world in the nineteenth and twentieth centuries.

The extent to which the West was already distinctive in 1800, let alone in the rate of progress in land (as opposed to sea) military technology, is unclear, as, if so, is the cause. It has been argued that the West already had a particularly high productivity growth in military production due to a continued high rate of military competition matched by the political possibilities of centralising the fiscal system; with the first not matched in China and the second in India.[3] This argument has the advantage of combining military fitness for purpose and structural considerations, but may also underplay the developments in both China and India while, moreover, exaggerating the West's relative capability on land by 1800.

The West was certainly to become the major innovator of weapons and methods, and Western military and political power were eventually to dominate the world, albeit not lastingly and, in the meanwhile, often precariously. The Western achievement owed much to the greater, or possibly different, ambition of Western nations that was indicated, at least in part, by the failure of sophisticated East and South Asian states to develop any, let alone comparable, oceanic naval power. Maritime links, moreover, produced military benefits, ensuring, for example, that Britain could turn its dominance of Bengal into control of much of the world production of saltpetre, a key constituent of gunpowder.[4] Nevertheless, major land empires, particularly China, also shared in the ability of maritime empires to draw on wider resources in responding to opposition including rebellions. Indeed, this ability proved an important cause in the failure of many rebellions.

In contrast, indigenous peoples and states outside Europe, when confronted by Western aggression, tended to have two advantages. The first was superior numbers, at least locally in the zone of contact, and the second was greater knowledge of, cultural identity with, and administrative control over, local territory. The differences in their military practice could also lessen the advantages of the Western military, although 'lessen' was not necessarily the same as 'negate'. For example, the pattern of Cherokee activity in 1776 was fairly typical of Native American conflict with Western regulars and colonists. Following attacks on the Virginia and Carolina frontier, the Cherokee lands were invaded by columns of American militia. Instead of resisting, the Cherokee largely abandoned their towns to be burned by the militia, disappeared into the mountains, and repeatedly returned, once the militia had departed, to cause sufficient trouble to provoke repeated militia incursions.

This style of war had become a standard pattern, as Natives had come to appreciate that defending any given point against a large force was dangerous, and instead had developed alternative strategies reliant on the likelihood that the militia would not remain for long. The Natives had abandoned their traditional fortification systems in the face of Western siegecraft capabilities. They lacked the numbers to man any fortification system, and individual positions could, justifiably, be seen as traps, presenting targets for their opponents' cannon. In turn, Western forces focused on destroying crops and shelter, which made life difficult for the Natives in the long run, and made them more likely to negotiate.[5]

Western success, where it occurred, can be explained by a variety, and varying combination, of factors; and the way in which the combination held, or was held together, was in itself important. In India, the British East India Company, despite its frequent internal disputes, was a corporation of seamless continuity that competed with personalised native autocracies that were dependent on strong leadership and vulnerable to recurrent succession crises. More generally, Western powers, especially outside Europe where their royal leadership and courtly politics were at a distance, benefited from the relatively post-feudal and non-personalised nature of their military command systems and command philosophy. There was a degree of bureaucratisation, notably with navies, although that did not preclude many practices that scarcely matched later bureaucratic ideas.

In contrast to the West, many non-Western powers had a more, often a far more, personalised system of command which helped create problems if rulers lacked success and funds, a lack that was frequently linked. However, the degree of administrative consistency and political continuity among these powers varied greatly, with China enjoying more than did the Mughal empire, and Turkey less than China, but far more than Persia or Afghanistan.

Publications and war

The application of reason and science to weapons development and tactical theory was also important. From the Renaissance, this factor was more apparent in the West than elsewhere in the world. In particular, the number of manuals and speculative works on warfare seem to have been far greater in the West than elsewhere, and this availability helped change aspects of warfare that were hidebound, instinctive and traditional, although it would be mistaken to ignore works elsewhere, including in Japan, China and India. Mir Zainul Abedeen Shushtari, a general in the army of Tipu Sultan, produced one discussing the military reforms introduced in Mysore under Haidar Ali and his son, Tipu, including standardisation and improvements to both infantry and artillery.[6]

At the same time as encouraging consideration of change, printed works were related to the characteristics of consistency, regularity and uniformity linked to permanent forces and bureaucratic support. Information encoded these characteristics and replicated them. It was most apparent in drill manuals, with their depiction of troops operating in a predictable fashion. Moreover, fortification diagrams and manuals were also at once descriptive and predictive.[7] Like drill manuals with their diagrammatic depiction of military formations, these diagrams and manuals captured the spatial characteristic of force, the deployment of power, and its operation in terms of controlling space.

Publications were linked directly to the idea and practice of military education. This could be seen, for example, in P. Bardet de Villeneuve's *Cours de la Science Militaire, à l'usage de l'infanterie, de l'artillerie, du génie, et de la marine* [*Military Science Course*, The Hague, 1740–2], and in works by Thomas Simes: *The Military Guide for Young Officers, Containing a System of the Art of War* (London, 1776), and *The Regulator: or Instructions to Form the Officer, and Complete the Soldier* (London, 1780). Officers read widely, in the history and art [theory and practice] of war, and this reading was linked to a more self-conscious professionalism in which continuous training rested on accessing accumulated wisdom through the culture of print. Contemporary writings on war reflected the sense not only that there were lessons to be learned but that they needed learning.[8]

In the case of the British army, there was a shift in mid-century from reading military history, including both the influential Classical (Ancient) tradition, for example Julius Caesar's *Gallic Wars*,[9] and recent military history, to reading works on the art of war. This shift, which has been linked to French success in the Low Countries over the British in 1745–8 during the War of the Austrian Succession, success that contrasted markedly with

French failure in the last struggle between the two powers, the War of the Spanish Succession (1702–13), represented a new way of inquiring for knowledge.[10] Publications also contributed to the development of common Western ideas of military professionalism, as did service together in coalition forces.[11]

Thanks to the world of print, there was also a changing character and intensity in public interest in conflict. In Britain, where the press developed greatly, in size, sophistication and freedom, from the 1690s, it devoted much attention to war, a process encouraged by Britain spending most of 1689 to 1720 at war. This attention led to animated discussions in coffee-houses, which were a centre of newspaper reading.[12] There was a similarly active press in the United Provinces (modern Netherlands), but nowhere outside the West.

Science and war

The use of publications was linked to the utilisation of scientific developments, and, over a long time-scale, this utilisation changed the potential of Western warfare. Scientific experimentation, and the quantification on which it rested,[13] involved a different process from scrutinising Classical (Ancient) texts for the wisdom of the past. This process proved particularly important with firearms and shipbuilding. For example, in 1779, General Thomas Desaguliers, Chief Fire Master at the British Royal Arsenal at Woolwich, carried out comparative tests of the accuracy of a smoothbored musket, a New York rifle, and a carbine. Different variables were then tested: weight of shot, amount of powder used, greasing and coating of the barrel and shot, distance to target, and the material from which the targets were constructed. The tests demonstrated the rifle's accuracy.[14]

The century witnessed the linkage of Newtonian science to military engineering, artillery and military thought in the West. Ballistics were revolutionised in the West, especially between 1742 and 1753 by Benjamin Robins and Leonhard Euler. Robins invented new instruments enabling him to discover and quantify the air resistance to high-speed projectiles. He also furthered understanding of the impact of rifling on accuracy. 'The central figure of the ballistics revolution',[15] Robins died in 1751 while serving as Engineer-General and Captain of the Madras artillery for the British East India Company. The author of *Neue Gründsatze der Artillerie* (1745), Euler also solved the equations of subsonic ballistic motion in 1753 and summarised some of the results in published tables. As a result, his data and conclusions could be more widely used. The application of theoretical advances helped improve firing tables. French gunners used faulty ones until Bernard Forest de Bélidor's *Le Bombardier françois, ou nouvelle méthode de jetter les bombes avec précision* was published in 1731.

Translations increased the impact of publications, but, again, reflected the significance of the particular cultural spheres within which translations occurred. If inter-adoption was a key element of military and other modernisation,[16] then the potential for adaptation was eased by translation as it provided more information than simply copying weapons. Euler was translated into English and Robins into German. Furthermore, wanting to be up-to-date led to emendations. For example, the changes between the 1756 and 1774 editions of the mathematician Francis Holliday's *An Easy Introduction to Fortification and Practical Gunnery* also included material on the theory of projectiles. Publications brought publicity to debates over best practice, as in controversy over fortification techniques, controversy that included criticism of the best practice of a former generation.[17] Again, this process was not matched outside the West.

Theoretical and empirical advances greatly increased the predictive power of ballistics, and helped turn gunnery from a craft into a science that could, and should, be taught. These developments affected the use of artillery, and influenced military education, which was encouraged by both major and minor powers. For example, the School of Mathematics and Navigation, opened in Moscow in 1701, was intended to assist the rise of Russian naval power. The technical nature of navigational skills and ballistics made formal education particularly important for naval and artillery officers.[18] The *Reali Scuole d'Artigliera e Genio* (Royal School of Artillery and Engineering) was opened in 1739 and the *Collegio Militare* (Military College) of Verona in 1759.[19] An artillery school was opened in Naples in 1744, and an engineering academy ten years later, and, in 1769, they were amalgamated into the *Reale Academia Militare*. It taught ballistics, tactics, experimental physics and chemistry to officer cadets, all of whom were supposed to attend classes. However, in general, military academies involved educating noble officers, rather than encouraging social mobility through the military by educating others.

Science could be significant to military effectiveness. For example, a better understanding of hydrostatics contributed to advances in the theory of shipbuilding.[20] Moreover, in response to Britain's dominance of the Indian sources of saltpetre from the late 1750s, the French developed domestic production, turning to Antoine Laurent de Lavoisier, their leading chemist. His *Instruction sur l'establissement de nitières et sur la fabrication du saltpêtre* (1777) and *Recueil de mémoires sur la formation et sur le fabrication du saltpêtre* (1786) provided detailed instructions on relevant processes, and Lavoisier also helped ensure improvements in the saltpetre refineries. French production increased, and the American Revolutionary cause benefited.[21] It would be naïve to explain success or failure simply with reference to the availability of saltpetre, but it was significant.

Another successful use of science was seen in George Washington's decision to have the Continental Army inoculated against smallpox, which had badly affected the American invasion of Canada in 1775. Moreover, underlining the threat from disease, in 1777, a British officer, Major Robert Donkin, had suggested using smallpox against the Americans; although this course was not pursued. Washington's policies proved very important to his forces' effectiveness, notably in 1780–1.[22] Publications increased the circulation of ideas about how best to confront disease, as with John Hunter's *Observations on the Diseases of the Army in Jamaica* (1788), an important work given the heavy losses to tropical diseases.

Recruitment and conditions

The rationalism and order applied to military organisation and activity[23] were not only seen in the West, but were particularly apparent there. The Western armies and navies of the period were 'standing' (permanent) forces under the direct control of the rulers. The spread of conscription greatly altered the politics of military service and war; although systems of conscription were less effective than in the late nineteenth and twentieth centuries, not least because of the limited amount of information at the disposal of the state and the weakness of its policing power.

In 1693, each Prussian province was ordered to provide a certain number of recruits, a number which was achieved by conscription, largely of peasants. The same year, French militia were sent to fight in war zones; from 1688 they had been raised by conscription among unmarried peasants. Conscription was imposed in a number of states, including Denmark in 1701, Russia in 1705, and Austria and Bohemia (Czech Republic) in 1771. Savoy-Piedmont developed a militia system from 1713, with ten 'provincial regiments' based on the main districts of the state. In Prussia, a cantonal system was established between 1727 and 1735: every regiment was assigned a permanent catchment area around its peacetime garrison town, from where it drew its draftees for lifelong service. Such systems increased control over the peasantry, which was, anyway, less able than volunteers to adopt a contractual approach towards military service. The peasantry was also a social group particularly vulnerable to conscription as it lacked exemptions on the grounds of valued economic activity or social status.[24]

Lack of consent on the part of most soldiers was not the same as an absence of willingness, but it frequently was linked. Moreover, this situation often proved an aspect of a disparaging view, by rulers, commanders and officers, of common soldiers. The latter were frequently seen as untrustworthy individuals, devoid of honour, best controlled with fear, and requiring constant supervision. Although codes of military justice existed and, in the West, were humanised from mid-century, in line with Enlightenment values, actual practice remained inconsistent as well as severe and was affected by patronage and personal prejudice.[25]

An emphasis on control, supervision and discipline seemed the best way to maintain unit cohesion in the face of the punishing nature of conflict. In the case of Christian Europe, drill helped secure this cohesion, which was related to a 'battle culture of forbearance' that emphasised the psychological significance of advancing in unbroken order under fire and closing on an enemy who would thereby be mastered.[26] This practice, however, did not invariably work, as defenders were not always overawed. It would be convenient to argue that the heavy casualties inflicted on advancing British troops by American Patriots at Bunker Hill in 1775 demonstrated the failure of the social politics of this type of conflict, but then the British had encountered a similar fate at the hands of French regulars at Fontenoy in 1745, and at Bunker Hill the British carried the position, which they did not at Fontenoy. As ever, examples have to be set alongside others that lead to differing conclusions.

The social parameters of military service varied greatly, both across the world and also within particular cultural areas and even within individual states and armies. Societies varied in how they dealt with the question of who should fight and what status they should be accorded. In particular, there was a tension in some states between appointment as a result of noble status and as a consequence of wealth. The role of purchase was widespread, for example in Britain and Spain,[27] and created particular tension in France, notably in the 1770s and 1780s. This tension arose because of pressure from nobles to end the sale of positions and, instead, leave them to those who could demonstrate their aristocratic background.[28] Nevertheless, there was a common stress on the particular responsibilities and privileges of the social élite, both in terms of avoiding undesirable service and in being far better treated if they served.

It is possible to emphasise a common hierarchical model, with officers drawn from the social élite, who, while bound together by conventions of honour, commanded troops in a harsh, disciplinary fashion. Yet, there were also important variations in command, both formal and informal. The formal focused on whether there was conscription, for military service was generally less harsh and more conditional when troops were volunteers. This variety in discipline overlapped with the significant informal variations in military service seen in the practices of obedience. Some units resorted to passive disobedience, strike action, or even mutiny, in the face of what were regarded as unreasonable conditions.[29] This situation was not only true of the West, but can also be seen elsewhere, for example in the Turkish army.

An emphasis on diversity subverts attempts to present troops as automata. That uniformity might have been the objective of drill that focused on repetitive movements and formulaic tactics,[30] but patterned behaviour did not define what was a more varied military experience, both on and off the battlefield.[31]

Aside from the circumstances of battle, conflict also called for considerable physical toughness and stamina. The conditions of warfare, ranging from accommodation and food to medical attention and the weight of weaponry, were bleak by modern standards. Exposure to the weather was particularly harsh as troops marched and often slept in the open, frequently without adequate footwear, dry clothing, or cover. These factors helped ensure that campaigning in the winter was more dangerous. Moreover, the campaigning day was also shorter in the winter and there was a lack of forage. The seasonal character of much (but by no means all) warfare therefore had functional roots rather than reflecting some propensity for limited conflict.

Due to their exposure to the weather, and because of the vulnerability of close-packed groups to infectious diseases, troops suffered seriously from disease, greatly lessening their operational effectiveness as well as their stamina in battle. Even with increased attention to disease, and developments in military medicine,[32] death rates remained high. However, as the circumstances of civilian life and work for much of the population were also fairly bleak, the conditions of the military were less exceptional; while in many cultures there were also social, economic and cultural factors encouraging military service, and notably so with steppe peoples.

Recruitment practices were as important an aspect of rising state military power as the number of troops in armies, which is sometimes employed in a somewhat crude fashion as the sole indicator of such power. In Christian Europe, new recruitment systems were mediated by aristocratic officers[33] and military entrepreneurship persisted,[34] but control by government had been enhanced from the mid-seventeenth century, and there was no longer a figure equivalent to Albrecht von Wallenstein, the independent entrepreneur who raised and commanded armies for the Emperor Ferdinand II in the 1620s and 1630s and was finally assassinated in 1634 when his loyalty became suspect. The governmental role in recruitment and logistics was less than is the case today, but the system of military entrepreneurship did not weaken political or operational direction to the extent that had occurred in the West during the Thirty Years' War (1618–48) and as happened in Turkey in 1730. The argument that the larger Western military forces of the late seventeenth and early eighteenth centuries[35] contributed to a lack of effectiveness is dubious, and not least if the frame of reference is set by Western navies, as well as by China and Russia.

In the West, continuing a process that had developed markedly from the mid-seventeenth century, the nobility became a more reliable support of the Crown, strengthening the state and notably its military arm, while urban autonomy was replaced by a greater degree of government control.[36] The domestic backing of the nobility proved a vital support in waging war, both politically and organisationally.[37] The assistance of the nobility made it far easier to ensure backing from the bulk of the population for whatever level of militarisation was deemed appropriate, for the local sway of the nobility was significant.[38] Moreover, organised violence was rationalised in terms of a monopolisation of violence by the state and its use for appropriate activities.[39] In turn, the nobility could be defended and extolled in terms of service to the state, as with Russia, Savoy-Piedmont and elsewhere, while positive ideas of service could also be expanded to more inclusive views of the nation.[40] These trends clashed with the continuing reality of troops and, in particular, officers serving foreign rulers.

Where the process of state monopolisation of violence failed, notably in the elective monarchy of Poland, then both military and state were weak, for example, as a result of the crisis of the 1760s.[41] The same was true in Hungary and Slovakia, where there was a serious rising against the Habsburgs in 1703–11 in which the nobility played a key role and their dependants joined in large numbers.[42] A conspicuous case of the absence of such monopolisation was seen in Afghanistan, where the continued vitality of tribal units and the nature of the economy, society and culture, obliged rulers to wage profitable and prestigious wars abroad or to face serious opposition.

It proved easier in states where there was no monopolisation of violence for foreign powers to intervene in order to keep matters in confusion, as Count Sinzendorf, an Austrian envoy, pointed out about Poland in 1709.[43] The same was true of India. Alongside rulers who suffered from such intervention, others, in contrast, reduced the independent power of the aristocracy, for example Martanda Varma, Rajah of Travancore (r. 1729–58), who used his army to overthrow the power of the *Pillamar* or Eight Lords.

More generally, military service was linked to practices of social organisation and control, while changes, in both, reflected political developments and pressures. Denmark provided a good instance of this process.

Conscription for much of the century was very much dependent on the support of the aristocratic landowners, who, in return, gained legislation in 1733 that forbade the sons of peasants to leave the estate where they were born. Thus, the landowners had their control over the workforce enhanced. However, from 1784, a new group of ministers came to the fore in government and they self-consciously embraced reform as a means of strengthening Denmark, both socially and economically. In 1788, new legislation abolished the 1733 law imposing labour control and allocated responsibility for conscription to the government. Moreover, the nature of military service changed, being now focused not on agricultural land, but, instead, on the male farming population, thereby becoming a personal, national, patriotic duty. This change certainly represented an increase in the role of government.[44] In contrast, in Spain, Charles III failed to impose a system of conscription in 1770. In Denmark, furthermore, military reforms in the 1760s had increased governmental control over the military by integrating the militia into the army organisation.[45]

In the Turkish empire, economic, political and ethnic factors combined to ensure that the government had less control over the military system than in the seventeenth century. In part, this was because of a loss of power over the élite *janissary* forces. In part, these forces represented the significant hereditary component in the Turkish military. A similar component could be found elsewhere, with the troops in the Chinese banner forces largely hereditary, but the latter were under greater state control than their Turkish counterparts. A comparable loss of control occurred in Morocco, where the effective corps of black slave soldiers created by Sultan Mawlay Isma'il (r. 1672–1727) became, under his successor, Ahmad Adh-Dhahabi (r. 1727–9), a force for chaos trying to sell its political support.

In part, the change in the Turkish empire was due to the shrinking of imperial borders, which was linked not only to expanding foreign opponents, particularly Russia, but also to a growing independence on the part of the semi-nomadic tribal forces that had hitherto provided a key military resource. The Crimean Tatars, who had contributed greatly to Turkish strength in cavalry, became less reliable and useful, notably in the war of 1768–74 with Russia. Moreover, the staples of the Turkish army ceased to provide the force they had delivered during the seventeenth century. The *sipahis*, the cavalry, who had been rewarded with *timars*, or fiefs that were renewable but not inherited, were no longer as significant an element, in part because the economic problems of the late seventeenth and early eighteenth century eroded the value of *timars*, while many ceased to be awarded to *sipahis*. The *janissaries*, standing infantry recruited by a forced levy among Christians in the Balkans, became less important, in part because the levy raised far fewer boys, but also because of the costs and abuse of the *janissary* system: there were a large number on the *janissary* lists who did not fight (some were dead), and there were also problems with the readiness of *janissaries* to rebel. Nevertheless, *janissary* garrisons proved highly significant as a support for governmental authority, both in Constantinople and in major provincial centres and fortresses.

In order to pay for the military, the Turks, from the 1690s, increasingly relied on tax-farming. This practice permitted the anticipation of revenue, but also led to a lack of control over revenues as well as over the raising of troops. The government turned to forces, mercenaries and militia, raised by provincial governors and other notables, who increasingly appropriated government revenues to this end and who operated in an autonomous fashion.[46] Despite the use of the army to overthrow powerful local figures, such as Nasuh Pasha, the Governor of Damascus, in 1713, the ability of the central government to control this developing system was limited. Moreover, the lengthy conflicts with provincial governors seen in the Turkish empire in the 1780s and 1790s were not matched in the West or China. The new military system also failed to provide the sustained effort required for war with Russia in 1768–74 and 1787–92. Many of the new militia forces lacked persistence on the battlefield.

The Western system of recruitment and logistics was crucial to the ability to think and act effectively in strategic terms. This ability was scarcely novel, but the increase in discipline, planning, and organisational regularity and predictability that characterised Western armies and navies from the mid-seventeenth century made it less difficult to implement strategic conceptions. These characteristics also enabled Western states to show some of the features of Chinese warmaking in this period.

At the same time, it is important not to exaggerate Chinese capability or the role of the state there, a point more generally true in Chinese military history. The Chinese state held soldiers responsible for some of the costs of their equipment and weaponry. Moreover, 'to a large extent, the continuous existence of the *de facto* hereditary military household system prohibited the Qing [Manchu] state from keeping up with the global trend in further strengthening, or modernising, its military'.[47]

The greater effectiveness of armies and navies was abundantly demonstrated by the leading Western powers, notably Russia and Britain, but not only by them. As part of a more general pattern, Austria's military culture became characterised more by regulation than by improvisation. A new transport corps was created in 1771, and the supply system was centralised.[48] Hit hard in the War of the Spanish Succession (1701–14), which also became a Spanish civil war, the Spanish army and navy were revitalised so as to be able to launch effective operations in the 1710s, 1730s and 1740s, and Spain's potential and intentions were serious issues for other states.[49] Like Britain, France and the Dutch, Spain also had to face the challenges of deploying forces overseas and of maintaining colonial armies. These tasks led to serious organisational and political issues. These issues, and indeed the cost of imperial conflict, became more serious from mid-century.[50]

The effectiveness of Western forces leaves an important trace in the archives in the shape of increased documentation, certainly compared with the situation in the fifteenth century, although less than that over the last century. This increase was not only the case for Western states. For example, in Turkey, the financial administration kept more detailed inventories, which makes (and made) it possible to follow work on fortifications more easily.[51] At the same time, the reliance on local élites for government and raising troops in most of the Turkish empire's borderlands limited the extent of governmental and military standardisation, and, indeed, ensured a considerable degree of autonomy.[52] Yet, this autonomy also facilitated the raising of troops, as with Ali Pasha, Governor of Ioannina from 1787, who raised Albanian levies to fight against rebellious governors similarly able to draw on such levies, defeating Pasvanoğlu Osman, Governor of Vidin, in 1797 and besieging Vidin in 1798. Pasvanoğlu, however, saw off the attack. The extensive Chinese use of militia, notably against rebellions, can in part be seen in this context.

Enhanced Western organisational capability was not simply a matter of financing, supplying or moving armies, but also improved the organisational and operational effectiveness of individual units. Although a measure of standardisation was seen in India, the Western powers, alongside the Chinese, moved most towards a large-scale rationalisation of such units. Their army units were to have uniform sizes, armaments, clothing and command strategies. Such developments made it easier to implement drill techniques that maximised firepower. Allied and subsidised units could be expected to fight in an identical fashion with 'national' units, which was a marked contrast to the situation in those states where there were major differences between core and ancillary troops, especially Turkey where there were significant ethnic and political dimensions to this contrast. The Westerners extended their model to India, training local units to fight as they did. The Western system, of permanent regiments, *ad hoc* brigades, and a clearly-defined military hierarchy, both reached its potential with Frederick the Great and could be exported. In turn, this organisation was to be overtaken by Napoleon's corps system.

The combination of greater governmental power and developments in weaponry was not only seen in Western states and empires, but also in those willing to adopt aspects of their military system. This adoption was seen most clearly in the shadow of Western power. Thus, Sahin Giray, who became Khan of the Crimean Tatars in 1777, sought to build up a regular army that would follow his orders, so that he was no longer dependent on the goodwill of the Tatar clans. Seeking an army of 20,000 regulars, Sahin introduced conscription: one soldier from every fifth household, with the arms and horses provided by the household. The soldiers were to wear Western military dress, and to drill and organise in the Russian manner. He also began plans for constructing a powder factory and a foundry. Sahin's Westernisation policies led to rebellion in 1777, and Sahin was only able to resume control in 1778 thanks to Russian military assistance. He repeated his attempts to form a Russian-style army, but this was now a matter of 1,000 guards only. Sahin also sought to purchase arms, and in 1781 acquired 30 cannon and mortars. However, his plans were again cut short by rebellion, during which much of his army proved unreliable, and were ended in 1783 by Russian occupation and annexation.[53]

Selim III (r. 1789–1807) similarly sought to introduce changes in the Turkish army, developing a new force, the *Nizam-I Cedid* (New Order Army) organised and armed on Western lines. He faced considerable opposition, even to the army's use of supposedly more Western-style uniforms.[54]

Effectiveness was a matter not only of armaments and training, but also of loyalty. This element tends to be underplayed, but was very important in many states. For example, faced by repeated serious opposition from within his own family, Timur Shah of Afghanistan (r. 1773–93) relied heavily on a bodyguard he established of (Shi'ite) Qizilbash, which helped lead to his being seen as pro-Persian.

Order and opposition

This account deliberately focuses on direction and planning, because these were characteristics of the military forces of Adam Smith's 'opulent and civilised' states, and of what have more recently been termed 'fiscal–military states'.[55] Effectiveness was not simply a product of more developed systems of control and support, but these systems were important to the ability to discharge a range of functions. Apart from grand shifts, of territorial change and statebuilding, armies were also responsible for the maintenance of order and the defence of authority around the world, whether against brigands or against striking workers, since most states had no equivalent to a national police force. Thus, troops were used to suppress opposition to increases in the price of bread, as in Normandy in 1768.

Order was imposed by the army both within states, for example in tumultuous cities, such as Madrid in 1766 and London in 1780, and in

unruly borderlands, where ethnic minorities, smugglers and other defi-
ers of authority flourished, as in Russia.[56] In Adam Smith's Scotland, the
aftermath of the unsuccessful Jacobite rising in 1745–6 was harsh. The
Hanoverian regime had been overthrown in Scotland and the army humiliated, and the government was determined to ensure that there was no
recurrence. The Highlanders were regarded as barbarians, and the military
was used to impose not only order but also a new governmental policy. The
'pacification' of the Highlands was to be characterised by killings, rapes and
systematic devastation, and by a determined attempt to alter the political,
social and strategic structure of the Highlands. The clans were disarmed,
and the clan system broken up, while roads to open up, and forts to awe, the
Highlands were constructed. Hereditable jurisdictions were abolished, and
the wearing of Highland clothes prohibited. The rebellion and its suppression gave cause and opportunity for the sort of radical state-directed action
against inherited privilege, especially regional and aristocratic privilege,
that was so rare in Britain.

The need to maintain order was not a task placed only on Western and
Western-commanded forces. In 1791, William Lindsay, British Secretary
of Legation at St Petersburg, predicting the fall of the Turkish empire to
Russian expansion, remarked, 'Half the Turkish Empire is either in open
rebellion or, at least, independent.'[57] The Turkish army sought to suppress
risings both in the capital, Constantinople, and in rebellious provinces, for
example the opposition of Kara Mahmud, Governor of Scutari in the 1780s
and 1790s, and of Pasvanoğlu Osman, Governor of Vidin in the 1790s;[58]
although this opposition overlapped with autonomous developments in
administration and army recruitment. Furthermore, the Turkish army
was used in borderlands against, for example, the Bedouin who attacked
pilgrims on the route to Mecca, allegedly killing 20,000 of them at al-'Ula
in 1757.[59] In 1732 and 1741, expeditions were sent from Cairo to help pilgrims
whose route was blocked near Aqaba.[60] As with other Turkish operations,
such campaigning involved both regulars and provincial levies. There was
also reliance on a system of fortresses.

Similarly, the Chinese army acted in borderlands and also against risings,
both by Han Chinese, for example the large-scale White Lotus rebellion of
1796–1805, and by non-Chinese subjects, such as the Jinchuan and Miao
tribal risings. These campaigns were often on a large scale and could be
difficult, as in 1773 when Wenfu, the Grand Secretary as well as a Manchu
frontier general, was defeated and killed in a surprise attack at Muguomu
by Jinchuan forces, a formidable foe. However, the latter were eventually
defeated, the war ending in 1776. Indian rulers also faced opposition by
subject peoples, such as the Corrgis who resisted Tipu Sultan of Mysore

(r. 1782–99). His campaigns against them led to resettlement and forcible conversion to Islam. Tipu embraced similar policies against other opposing groups, including the Malabar Christians.[61]

In Japan, where the rapidly increasing population put pressure on limited resources of food and land, leading to an increase in social pressure,[62] the forces of the major lords suppressed peasant risings. These increased from the first half of the century: 724 risings have been recorded for 1716–50, but, after a further increase in and from the 1750s, there were more than fifty annually on average in the 1780s. Moreover, their scale and level of violence increased while the focus shifted from village communities pressing their feudal overlords to cut taxes or provide more rice, to attacks on the more prosperous members of the village communities. These uprisings also spread to the towns, with violent riots in Edo, Osaka and other major cities in 1787. In 1788, there were 117 separate revolts.

The Japanese government relied on the forces of the *daimyos* (regional lords). In 1738, large protests near the silver mines at Ikuno were only suppressed as a result of action by troops from thirteen *daimyos*' domains, while, in 1769, all *daimyos* were instructed to stamp out protests irrespective of the merits of the grievances. The concentration of weaponry helped the *daimyos*, as the number and type of guns and ammunition held by peasants was regulated and registered.[63]

The information and scholarship available on rebellions centres on Western states, accentuating the tendency to focus military history on them, but, as Japan shows, opposition to state control existed more generally, allowing for the frequent ambiguity of the concept of the state. This ambiguity was particularly apparent in the case of resistance to empires and major states, however each is defined, as such resistance can be seen both as opposition on the part of lower-level polities to imperial incorporation and as rebellions against governmental policies or control. This control was religious, ethnic and political, these concepts overlapping far more than they could be separated.

This process can be seen in China's south-west, where the vast area covered by the provinces of Sichuan, Yunnan, Guizhou and Guangxi posed serious problems for the emperors as these provinces were regarded as particularly prone to disorder, including banditry. The poorly-defined frontiers and administrative boundaries of this large region compounded problems in maintaining order, and led to an assertive determination to produce defined frontiers that, in turn, helped cause conflict. In a process also increasingly seen in the West, power-sharing ceased to be acceptable in China, and this change affected hitherto agreed consensuses along the Burmese and Vietnamese frontiers, as well as attitudes towards other hereditary lordlings who were at a distance from these frontiers. This process linked defeudalisation by the Chinese with the dispossession of aboriginal peoples. A similar course had led to a rebellion in Formosa (Taiwan) in 1731 by indigenous tribes that was put down the following year.[64]

In Russia, southward expansion across the steppe was related to a determination to control hitherto independent actors, as indeed was Russian expansion into Poland. Notions of civilisational superiority played a particular role in the former expansion, but there was also a practical determination to achieve strategic advantage in terms of the wider geopolitics of conflict with the Turks. The demarcation of borders was part of the process. There was resistance, notably in the case of the Don Cossacks with Kondratii Bulavin's unsuccessful rebellion in 1707–9, which was brutally suppressed. Increasing governmental authority was linked to a process of regulation, to the spread of agriculture and settlement, and to military service in Russia's armies.[65]

War and statebuilding

There is a general tendency to focus on states and the relationship between war and state transformation, with the mobilisation of resources for conflict leading to bureaucratic development. Moreover, this development was part of a process in which, according to some scholars, states accumulated coercion in order to protect and control capital. At the same time, the bureaucratic and political processes involved helped lead to the enhancement of public goods, such as better communications.[66]

This account suffers, however, from a tendency to present war as a single-purpose activity with a clear trajectory, and, in particular, from a failure to place due weight on the many significant cultural and sociological factors involved in military organisation and activity. These factors could cut across what might appear the best form of organisation in terms of bureaucratic efficiency or the accumulation of coercion and capital. For example, while rulers might seek to ensure that they would choose officers, and thus guarantee merit, the definition of the latter was partly conceived in social terms. This process was seen, for example, in the appointments made by Frederick the Great of Prussia (r. 1740–86), who proved more favourable than his father, Frederick William I (r. 1713–40), to the appointment of nobles as officers. Merit could also be conceived in terms of ethnic and religious loyalty.

Aside from the weakness of a schematic approach towards military organisation based on crude and ahistorical utilitarianism in the shape of modern-style bureaucratic processes, there are also the multiple issues posed by the question of effectiveness. One of the major difficulties is that of the sources available and used, as these tend to be those of the states. The latter have an understandable tendency to exaggerate bureaucratic regularity and to present the best case when discussing operations, notably that of the triumph over opponents. However, as work on China, in particular, has indicated, this account is often highly inaccurate. Misleading reports from generals and officials interacted with a determination at the centre to provide an appropriate gloss on campaigning.[67]

Alternative sources for operations are rare, but, where they exist, suggest a less positive situation. Andreas Ly's account of the First Jinchuan War (1747–9) highlighted the military weaknesses of the Chinese in an asymmetrical campaign in difficult terrain, prefiguring the more serious problems that were to arise for Chinese forces in Burma two decades later. At the same time, his journal, in discussing the pressure of the war, indicated the strength of the Chinese state:

> The blacksmiths of this city [Chengdu] have nearly all been occupied at forging cannon for three months (16 April 1748) … small boats have been seized in order to carry coal, and blacksmiths have been compelled to cart new cannon. The people are weighed down by many public burdens, whether tribute, taxes, or labour. Horses and mules belonging to farmers and merchants are kept … to carry rice, wheat, and lima beans as food, first for the soldiers and then for pack animals in war (19 July 1748).[68]

Spreading power, increasing authority, and overcoming opposition, both absorbed military efforts and were important aspects of military capability because of the major strains that this capability and, even more, war placed on states. Serious financial constraints arose from the nature of economic and fiscal systems and from the size of the forces that had to be supported; and lengthy wars exacerbated the problem. Financial problems hit logistics and also led to troop mutinies, for example among the Austrian force in Spain in 1711. As a result of a shortage of money, the Spanish army destined for Italy in 1741 faced multiple difficulties, including problems with the artillery. The Chinese force sent against the Gurkhas of distant Nepal in 1791 included few bannermen in part because of the cost of operations. It was less expensive to send more local militia; but, even so, the size of the force was limited.

Furthermore, innovations that have been praised, nevertheless still had important limitations. The magazines (stores) developed to support French forces in the late seventeenth century generally only contained supplies able to support initial operations, which caused problems if the conflict was a lengthy one and it proved impossible to transfer the cost by operating in foreign states. The more financially secure British state also faced serious problems in supplying its military. Furthermore, there were key cultural issues affecting the response to apparent advances in weaponry and doctrine. For example, there was a tension between scientific ideas and the prestige of the attack, notably in sieges, as in the War of the Spanish Succession (1701–14) when French and other generals proved willing to abandon ideas and practices of deliberate siegecraft and, instead, to focus on assaults on fortresses, which promised a more rapid conclusion but involved heavy losses of manpower.[69]

Conclusions

These points qualify Adam Smith's contrast between advanced polities and primitive peoples, and need to be borne in mind when there is a stress on state power. The contrast between transformation, training, doctrine, weapons specifications and planning, and the realities of warmaking was enhanced by the very extent to which military activity was bureaucratised, for that process was both a response to the contrast and provided a measure of it. Thus, with Peter the Great (r. 1689–1725), it is possible to emphasise the transition in the Russian military, but also the extent to which practice did not match the new system he sought to enforce. The Seven Years' War (1756–63) saw a major and sustained projection of power against Prussia but also demonstrated serious weaknesses in Russian logistics.[70]

It is possible to emphasise the degree to which casualties and costs reduced the military effectiveness of the combatants in that war,[71] and the Prussian army was certainly chewed-up in repeated campaigning.[72] At the same time, the ability to continue campaigning and mounting offensives was highly important to the politics of the early 1760s, notably the collapse of the Austro-Russian alliance in 1762 and the coming of peace. Moreover, Britain retained an ability to launch major expeditions, while the French army continued campaigning against Britain's allies in western Germany.

Russia also exemplifies Adam Smith's point about change. The development and success of its military rested on broader currents of Russian economic growth and governmental improvement.[73] Despite major costs, financial and social, and an inability to meet the expenses of war, which led to a heavy and repeated reliance on foreign subsidies and loans,[74] it was possible for Russia, as also with China and Britain, to see an effectiveness that was very different from the situation in the mid-seventeenth century.[75] The essential theme, therefore, is one of continuity, a continuity in which longer-term changes overlapped with those from the mid-seventeenth century. To describe either set of changes in terms of military revolution is unhelpful,[76] but the net consequence was a significant enhancement in military capability for Smith's 'opulent and civilised'.

9 Conclusions

Our men, arranged in military order, fired ... the greater part
of them ['licentious savages'], after a feeble resistance with their
bows, arrows, and swords, giving way to our superior courage
and discipline, fled ... two hundred ... prisoners ... severely
punished for their crimes.

Dean Mahomet, 1772.[1]

The significance of change

War was central to the history of the period and to the experience of
its peoples, and the wars of the century were far from inconsequential.
However, the classic focus in scholarly attention for this period is Western,
and the eighteenth century there, prior to the French Revolution and, more
particularly, the outbreak of the French Revolutionary Wars in 1793, is
commonly regarded as a period of military conservatism, indecisiveness
and stagnation, part of an interlude between periods of alleged military
revolution in 1560–1660 and 1792–1815. The sole major alternative to this
approach suggests that the latter revolution began with the outbreak of the
War of American Independence in 1775. That conflict is then linked to the
French Revolutionary Wars.

The standard account goes on being reiterated, explicitly and implicitly,
despite scholarly criticism. However, whichever of the wars is seen as the
alleged tipping point into modernity, this account is a mistaken account
for the world as a whole in that, in this classic account, much of the world's
military history is excluded or treated as secondary and subordinate to this
theme and chronology. Moreover, the standard account is also misleading
for the West, both in terms of the alleged revolutions and with respect to
the intervening period. The latter two issues are linked, as qualifying the
supposed revolutions helps to provide a new context for this intervening period. Ironically, if military revolutions are sought, then nothing
in the West in the period 1560–1815 matched the early sixteenth-century
deployment of gunpowder weaponry in long-range warships and on the

battlefield, nor the sweeping organisational and technological changes of the last half of the nineteenth century.

But that does not mean that wartime in the meantime was static. It is not a case of revolution or nothing. There were developments in weaponry that were significant, notably, at the outset of the eighteenth century, the deployment of flintlock muskets equipped with bayonets as the infantry weaponry in Western armies. This deployment, and the associated abandonment of the pike, led to an important increase in infantry firepower that helped to lessen the value of cavalry, but that lessening was not a new process and, indeed, can be traced back several centuries. Instead, developments in weaponry, both on land and at sea, essentially took place within existing military structures and did not change the nature of warfare nor the relevant organisational structures.

Yet, this situation did not mean a limitation in perspectives. Indeed, the notion that systems that can be categorised as conservative are incapable of significant change (and, as a corollary, have to be overthrown for such change to occur) is mistaken. In the eighteenth century, armies and navies, both Western and non-Western, competed for major goals. The Chinese greatly extended their power over non-Chinese peoples, while the Mughal (Indian) and, even more, Safavid (Persian) dynasties collapsed, and the fate of North America was largely settled, as, essentially, was the struggle between Britain and France in India. The claim that supply problems made achieving strategic objectives only rarely possible,[2] is not vindicated by the campaigning, much of which delivered results in terms of victories won and territory conquered. Russia became a great power, the Turks were pushed back in Europe, and, in the 1790s, French hegemony in Western Europe was restored, albeit temporarily. War led to the rise of a number of other powers, including Afghanistan under the Durranis, Burma under 'Alaungpaya, and Gurkha Nepal. The means available could deliver many of the results required.

Some of the consequences of this military activity have lasted until today. British success over France ensured that North America would have a political culture derived from Britain. A French-dominated trans-oceanic world would have looked to Catholicism, civil law, French culture and language, and to different notions of representative government and politics from those of Britain. Thus, the eighteenth century was important not only for the relative position of the West, but also to the question, 'Which West?'

This result was not inevitable. If, in 1815, Britain was the strongest state in the world ruling the most powerful empire, the situation had been very different seventy years earlier, as Jacobite forces under Bonnie Prince

Charlie (Charles Edward Stuart) advanced on Derby, outmanoeuvring the regular armies sent to defeat them, while the British government feared a supporting French invasion of southern England, which indeed was planned. If, by 1815, Britain was the dominant military power in India, in 1746 the British had lost Madras (Chennai) to the French, who were then the leading Western power in India and who seemed most likely to win co-operation from Indian rulers. There was nothing inevitable in the British triumph. Indeed, a Jacobite success in 1745–6 would have altered Britain's position in the world, and the character of the 'West', not only with regard to political alignments but also with reference to the nature of public culture, economic interest and social dynamics.

There was also the important question of 'Which East?' In practice, this question was less central an issue than in other periods as there was no real challenge to the unity and cohesion of the Chinese state, although the situation was very different as far as the wider Manchu empire was concerned for the Zunghar challenge threatened Manchu control over the eastern Mongols. The Chinese defeat of the Zunghars helped settle the related questions of China's conflict with challengers from the steppe and its dominance of 'near-China'. Japan's complete quiescence in international relations meant that the crisis of the 1590s over control of Korea did not recur.

South Asia passed through more profound changes, notably with the near-total collapse of the Mughal empire. Whereas, in the sixteenth and seventeenth centuries, the Mughals, Ottomans and Safavids had been generally successful in linking their frontier areas with their imperial objectives, and also in controlling interregional trade routes, in the eight-eenth century they failed to meet the challenge.[3] By 1740, the Marathas had become a major power in India; although not further afield and not across all of India. They remained a key force in 1800, but were now joined, in eastern and southern India, by Britain. Furthermore, Britain's total victory over Tipu Sultan of Mysore in 1799 demonstrated the extent of change since 1740, and indeed the early 1780s when the British were under heavy pressure from Mysore.

At the same time, as throughout this book, there is the question of relative significance, both to contemporaries and in terms of subsequent developments. For example, was this victory over Tipu Sultan more or less significant than other developments in the 1790s, notably the White Lotus rebellion in China, or the suppression of Polish independence, or the successful rising against French rule in Saint-Domingue, or the conflicts in Western Europe? This question should be seen as implicit throughout this book and for every period, as there is no inherently obvious way to assess significance and allocate space. Indeed, one of the pedagogic purposes of this book is that of emphasising to readers that they need to consider the allocation of space and to decide whether it is appropriate within and between chapters.

Alongside developments came the question of how change was understood by contemporaries. There was a long-term tendency to see firepower as a decisive shift towards effectiveness, and, indeed, a condition of military modernity. This tendency was especially pronounced in the West, but other societies also had to adapt. Many, however, had an uneasiness with change that reflected attitudes to morality and legitimacy. In the Chinese novel *Nüxian waishi* (1711) by Lü Xiong, the Moon Queen condemned the impact of cannon:

> At midnight, Moon Queen, together with Instructress Pao and Instructress Man, went and had a look at the situation of Pei-P'ing so she might point out a strategy. She saw that cannon without number had been placed on top of all the city-walls: Red-Barbarians' [Portuguese] cannon, shrapnel-cannon, Heaven-exploding cannon and Divine Mechanism cannon ... Moon Queen said ... 'Such things are not meant for use against people! They turn all who dare to be soldiers into a pulp of flesh. There is no use anymore for the six tactics and three strategies.'

Moon Queen then used an amulet to make the cannon ineffective.

Whatever the response, the sense of a revolutionary new potential focused in the West on gunpowder weaponry,[4] while, in India, there was also an important development of infantry forces. These processes, however, left the evaluation of other, subsequent, and apparently less significant, changes, far less clear; and this is the case both for contemporary and for more modern views. Challenging the notion of military revolution, especially by embracing new technology, a classic means of evaluation was to look, instead, for renewed effectiveness by returning, in whole or in part, to earlier patterns of behaviour. In particular, echoing the idea that firepower had somehow compromised courage, if not masculinity, came the interest in returning to the tactics of shock, both in order to build up, sustain and use fighting quality and in order to inflict harm on the enemy.

These tactics took a number of forms, but the culture of print makes it possible to follow Western suggestions in the field in a way that is not so readily possible for elsewhere in the world. At the same time, the contested and contingent nature of views in that culture has to be underlined. These views, which extended to the idea of resuming 'the arms in use before the invention of gunpowder',[5] reflected in part the difficulties of linking mobility to firepower as well as the quest for a margin of decisive advantage.

This varied and widely-diffused set of assumptions has sometimes been focused on French thought prior to the outbreak of the French Revolution in 1789, and on the subsequent military changes stemming from both thought and Revolution;[6] but this approach misunderstands the wider context. In particular, the inherent dynamism of *ancien régime* warmaking, both in the West and further afield, requires consideration. Moreover, the extent of this dynamism makes it difficult to use conservatism as an explanation for failure. Instead, it may be more helpful both to refer to less successful dynamism and to emphasise continuity.[7] As far as fighting methods were concerned, Western warfare reflected the standard action–reaction pattern of development, with leaders creating opportunities and responding to deficiencies in a dynamic fashion, but within a fundamental continuity in fighting systems. If Marlborough smashed through the French centre in successive victories in the 1700s, from Blenheim, and Frederick the Great successfully devised and introduced the tactic of the oblique attack in the 1740s, then they did so with essentially the same forces as their opponents.

Similarity, however, can conceal important contrasts. The tactical flexibility displayed by eighteenth-century Western generals, in comparison with their seventeenth-century predecessors, owed much to the replacement of the musket/pike combination by flintlock-bayonet soldiers. In place of the chequerboard formations, came linear ones. By the 1790s, these formations were to seem rigid and inflexible in comparison with the columns of the Revolutionary French, but that perspective underplays the ability of generals in the 1700s and 1740s (during the Wars of the Spanish and Austrian Successions as well as the other conflicts of the period), especially, but not only, Marlborough, Eugene, Frederick the Great and Saxe, to deliver victories in a way that had not proved possible in the 1690s.

Similarly at sea, where, within the continuing powerful constraints of sail as the motive system, winds, currents and the need to rely on direct gunfire, and the particular difficulties of ascertaining the moves of opponents[8] and of forcing battle, warships were employed more effectively, in both tactical and operational terms, by Western navies than in the late seventeenth century. Design improvements, not least based on a greater understanding of hydrostatics and ship stability, enhanced seaworthiness, while better guns and gun-drill increased firepower.

There were also major advances in the West in artillery: in the understanding of ballistics, in gunfounding, and in organisation, especially in the standardisation of cannon. The application of new knowledge was a key theme in Western military development. To try to measure its impact in comparison with, say, maritime primacy, or the significance of Western sources of bullion, or Western investment in the military,[9] is not possible, but they each contributed to military development, as well as interacting to that end to at least some extent.

Government and the military

Turning anew to common themes, rather than ones that divide West and non-West, this study leaves a large role to chance and to consequential decisions taken by individuals. The account offered reveals discontinuities and reversals in the familiar narrative of a march of technological, administrative and martial progress. The overall impression, therefore, is of events driven by local contingencies, rather than of overarching global forces and trends (military, bureaucratic, fiscal, scientific revolutions) influencing and directing developments on the international, national, regional or local level. This was the case not only beyond the West, for example against indigenous forces, but also in the West, for example in the Jacobite rebellions in Britain.

However, the assessment of administration and logistics offers a note of caution. In the cases of China, Russia and Britain, while the course and result of tactical engagements cannot fit into neat and deterministic models of Western or technological progress, administrative centralisation and effectiveness did offer governments men, *matériel* and staying power that their opponents lacked. At the same time, states frequently contracted out aspects of their military system, notably logistics. Of the three just mentioned, this was particularly true of Britain.[10] Turning to politics as well as administration, the relationship between war and statebuilding remained significant, each being an important condition of the other; although Japan showed that it was possible to have a state without war.

The revolutionary period of the last decades of the century exemplified the relationship between war and statebuilding as new governments sought military power in order both to secure their own position and to enforce their views. Thus, in the USA, Shays's Rebellion in 1786–7 encouraged Edmund Randolph to open the Constitutional Convention in 1787 by calling for the federal government to have the power to suppress rebellions. Subsequently, the Federalists, notably Alexander Hamilton, the Secretary to the Treasury from 1789 to 1795, pressed for a shift of power from the states to the federal government, and, in rejecting the views of those who felt that the militias were more effective than regulars, sought to develop the professional army as a strong permanent force able to unite America against internal subversion and foreign threat. In 1798, the army was expanded, while in 1799 Hamilton suggested using it to conquer Louisiana and Florida from Spain.[11]

Revolutionary France can be seen as a more vigorous example of the same process, but, again, it was scarcely a new departure. Ideology, state-building and the military were also linked characteristics of the *ancien régime*, for example with the Pietism, or activist Protestantism, in the army of Frederick William I of Prussia (r. 1713–40), who built up the army that Frederick the Great used.[12] This linkage was also seen elsewhere in the world. If the conscription of Revolutionary and Napoleonic France is regarded by some commentators as harnessing nationalism and leading towards modernity, representing a revolution in both military affairs and the state,[13] conscription was scarcely a monopoly of modern and modernising states, or at least of the conventional listing of these states. A wider global perspective makes this clear as conscription can be seen in the case of states not regarded as modern, for example in Burma.

Ironically, moreover, Western states after the defeat of Napoleon in 1815 preferred to rely on professional long-service regulars rather than large numbers of conscripts; while, throughout, this proved the pattern for the British army, the most successful multi-purpose force of the period. Indeed, features other than conscription can be seen as equally, if not more, 'modern', namely those of capitalist professionalism. In particular, the combination, in India, of a large-scale military labour market, able to respond to new challenges and opportunities in tasks and training, with the finances of a dynamic sector of the world economy, produced a volatile situation in which new outcomes were readily generated. British campaigns drew on the resources of the East India Company, the British government, British 'Agency Houses' (local trading and finance establishments), such as John Palmer and Co., and Alexander and Co., and Asian financial networks.

In the end, the military fiscalism of British India was to triumph,[14] although the earlier development, on strong local foundations,[15] of effective new forms and units of native infantry and artillery both challenged this outcome and revealed a capacity for change that many other non-Westerners did not emulate to this degree, not least the Turks. Moreover, this development was particularly challenging when, as with Mir Qasim, Nawab of Bengal in the early 1760s, the military system, which included the establishment of a gun-making centre at Patna, rested on impressive fiscal fundamentals. He turned against British dominance in 1764 and his troops fought well at Buxar before being defeated. Mysore moved in the same direction toward a more effective military.[16]

Developments in the world economy in the eighteenth century can certainly be understood in terms of modernisation, but their contribution to the idea of an early-modern military revolution closing in the eighteenth century, let alone a new military revolution beginning in the 1790s, is less sure. In part, this is because the key element in the supposed early-modern military revolution was not so much the general world economy, but, rather, the strength of individual states' military–fiscal systems, the latter referred to as 'military fiscalism'. This strength was not a new element of the eighteenth-century world and, instead, can be seen over previous centuries, both during the so-called early-modern military revolution and earlier. This argument opens the door to a discussion about administrative 'progress', and concerning the role of the military and war in paving the way for the formation of modern states throughout the globe in the nineteenth and twentieth centuries.

Military fiscalism rested not only on government institutions, but also on broader social, economic and political patterns,[17] notably with naval strength. This strength was the product of co-operation between interest groups. Thus, British naval power was located in a different pattern of response from that affecting Britain's rivals. Governmental support for other navies could be extensive, but tended to lack the political, social and institutional grounding seen in Britain, where institutional practices and political assumptions drew on linked constituencies of support. As a consequence, elsewhere there could be a mismatch between governmental decisions to expand resources and build up naval strength and, on the other hand, a more limited achievement in terms of the delivery of effective naval power.

The West and the Rest

Military effectiveness and capability should not be assessed solely in Western terms. Warfare in much of the world was planned and waged quite effectively without reference to Western methods, technology and politics. Moreover, conflict between Western and non-Western powers proved the basis for mutual innovations that shaped warmaking in later centuries. By the end of the eighteenth century, a range of effective and dynamic military systems were present around the world. It was far from inevitable in 1800 that the systems of the Marathas and Revolutionary/Napoleonic France were to succumb speedily, while, by 1860, but certainly not 1800, the Chinese understood that their system was in need of radical change. However, Britain and Russia were clearly impressive powers by 1800. They and China were the key military successes of the eighteenth century, and that helps attract attention to the period, because, albeit with the USA succeeding Britain as the leading maritime force, this triumvirate remain the world's leading military powers, having seen off a series of challenges and adapted successfully to a number of key changes.

Thus, the eighteenth century excites attention, not only as the last age of a truly diverse and varied global military situation, a point that takes precedence over any supposed rise of the West, but also because the century sees the onset of a modern international system. In contrast to China, the Turks, the Safavids and their successors in Persia, and the Mughal successor states, all lagged in creating the infrastructure of institutional politics and in establishing stable civil–military relations.

Military revolution?

At the same time, if a common pattern is to be discerned across the world, it is one in which there was also a considerable measure of continuity with earlier circumstances and practices. Moreover, if military revolution means an abrupt change and a fundamental development in capabilities, organisation or goals, then none occurred in this period; but such revolutions anyway are much less common than is frequently argued. Rather, it is more common for change to occur incrementally, not least in response to the pressure of circumstances. Partly as a consequence, it is foolish to neglect periods that did not apparently have military revolutions and, instead, to focus on those that allegedly did.

If periods with revolutions are in fact infrequent and assume some of their meaning in terms of longer-lasting circumstances and developments, then these conditions deserve more attention. This direction encourages a focus on the *ancien régime* period because it is with reference to those years that the significance of supposedly revolutionary developments in the preceding and following eras can be assessed. In each case, this focus suggests a downplaying of such significance. Western armies and navies developed more in the period 1660–1725 than they had earlier in the seventeenth century, the classic period of the early-modern military revolution. This focus on 1660–1725 is the case for numbers, organisation, and political support and governmental systems able to sustain a powerful military. Military change, which has typically been taken as a catalyst of the development of administrative centralisation and increasing state power and reach, was actually a consequence of these changes. What made the transformation in warfare in the later seventeenth and early eighteenth centuries so spectacularly greater than anything that had gone before was the fact that Western states had already passed through various organisational thresholds, whether in improving the standards and quality of administration, or, as is now increasingly recognised, in managing to co-opt the support and resources of their socio-political élites more successfully than before. Combined with tactical changes in land and sea combat, especially the use of the bayonet and of line-ahead tactics at sea, these advances ensured that, *if* the problematic notion of an early-modern military revolution is to be applied, it is better devoted to the later period, 1660–1725, than to the years conventionally considered, 1450–1660.[18]

At the same time, it is important to note the problems encountered in 1660–1725. To take naval organisation and governmental support, two elements that are commonly stressed, it is instructive to read a dispatch of 7 January 1718 from Charles Whitworth, the experienced British envoy in the United Provinces: 'The States [Parliament] of Holland were assembled today for several hours. All the great towns have consented to the equipping of a fleet, but one or two of very small note, as the Brill, Schiedam etc still making some difficulty, the deliberations have been deferred.' In the event, it took months to obtain agreement.[19] On the other hand, a different impression can be given if opposition is shown as arising from concern about government policy, notably that the fleet was in practice designed for war in the developing international crisis and not, as alleged, to protect trade.[20]

Turning to the other end chronologically, any emphasis on changes arising in, and from, French Revolutionary warfare is qualified by a consideration of earlier circumstances, and notably the diversity, flexibility, and rate of change seen over the previous three decades. As far as earlier circumstances are concerned, a degree of popular engagement affecting conflict, a theme correctly advanced for the French Revolutionary and Napoleonic period, had been noted in earlier struggles such as the Spanish stage of the War of Spanish Succession.[21] Moreover, far from starting military modernity in 1792, with the outbreak of the French Revolutionary Wars, the changes of the 1760s–80s included important organisational developments, notably with the division, and tactical innovations such as the interest in column advances, as well as the Austrians' and Russians' development of more effective formations for conflict with the Turks.

Furthermore, the development of a reform-minded intellectual climate within Western armies (albeit not formal in any modern sense) did not begin with the French Revolution but was one of the Enlightenment period's hallmarks. There would have been no Clausewitz without the Saxes, Lloyds, Guiberts, and Schaumburg-Lippes of the eighteenth century.[22] Change was seen as a possibility to be encouraged, exploited, and harnessed, as well as a problem to overcome. Change covered not only military techniques but also attitudes towards the treatment of other Western civilians in wartime.

There was also change in the West's capability on the world scale. From the 1750s, the ability to deploy substantial forces in North America was a significant example of enhanced force projection, as was the struggle between British and French fleets off India's coast in the early 1780s. In terms of naval and trans-oceanic capability and warfare, however, it is difficult to see any evidence of revolutionary change in the 1790s and 1800s. As far as technology is concerned, changes in 1815–65, including steam, iron and shell guns, were more influential than anything from the previous fifty years or indeed the previous three centuries.

Yet again, as is the argument of the two preceding volumes,[23] the notion of an early-modern military revolution appears misleading. Any attempt to include the period 1792–1815 in this period and process does not significantly alter the situation. In addition, much of the above discussion is focused on the West, rather than covering the entire world, in part because the work has not yet been done to provide a comprehensive (or even partial) global account of military modernisation. Indeed, debate is required over how best to assess effectiveness, over the extent to which change was needed in order to achieve effectiveness, and over the role of modernisation in this account. This book ends by suggesting the open-ended nature of the necessary conclusions, the requirement for additional work, and the conceptual and methodological flexibility that a departure from an analysis and chronology focused on the West will, hopefully, lead to. Far from being 'done', the military history of the period remains incomplete, but this incompleteness is itself a cause and consequence of intellectual enquiry and the welcome broadening out of the subject.

List of Abbreviations

Add.	Additional Manuscripts
AE	Paris, Archives du Ministère des Relations Extérieures
Ang.	Angleterre
BL	London, British Library, Department of Manuscripts
BN	Paris, Bibliothèque Nationale
CP	Correspondance Politique
IO	India Office
NA	London, National Archives
NAF	Nouvelles Acquisitions Françaises

Notes

Preface

1. The latter are defined as Europeans other than the Turks, the term used to describe the Ottomans.
2. R. Muir, *Salamanca 1812* (New Haven, Connecticut, 2001); P. Lenihan, *1690: Battle of the Boyne* (Stroud, 2003).
3. For a lack of reliable information on Sind west of the Indus delta, H.T. Lambrick, *Sind: A General Introduction* (Hyderabad, Sind, 1964), p. 197.
4. For a critique of the looseness of this idea, B.L. Davies, 'Introduction', in Davies (ed.), *Warfare in Eastern Europe, 1500–1800* (Leiden, 2012), pp. 13–14.
5. S. Conway, 'British Soldiers at Home: The Civilian Experience in Wartime, 1740–1783', and D.A. Bell, 'The Limits of Conflict in Napoleonic Europe – And Their Transgression', in E. Charters, E. Rosenhaft and H. Smith (eds), *Civilians and War in Europe, 1618–1815* (Liverpool, 2012), pp. 129, 203. However, the absence of a term does not mean the lack of a concept, as is also shown by the cases of geopolitics and strategy.

1: Introduction

1. P. Porter, *Military Orientalism: Eastern War Through Western Eyes* (London, 2009).
2. J. Black, *Rethinking Military History* (London, 2004).
3. J. Black, 'The Napoleonic Wars in Global Perspective', in F.C. Schneid (ed.), *The Projection and Limitations of Imperial Powers 1680–1850* (Leiden, 2012), pp. 149–69.
4. J. Black, *The Age of Total War 1860-1945* (Westport, Connecticut, 2006).
5. J. Black, *War and the New Disorder in the 21st Century* (London, 2004) and *War Since 1990* (London, 2009).
6. R. McCullough, *Coercion, Conversion and Counterinsurgency in Louis XIV's France* (Leiden, 2007).
7. See B. Davies, *Empire and Military Revolution in Eastern Europe: Russia's Turkish Wars in the Eighteenth Century* (London, 2011).

8. P. Bianchi, 'La guerra franco-piemontese e le Valli valdesi (1792–1799)', in G.P. Romagnani (ed.), *La Bibbia, la coccarda e il tricolore. I Valdesi fra due emancipazioni, 1798–1848* (Turin, 2001), pp. 73–117. On the 1740s, S. Wilkinson, *The Defense of Piedmont, 1742–1748: A Prelude to the Study of Napoleon* (Oxford, 1927).

9. G. Parker, *The Military Revolution: Military Innovation and the Rise of the West, 1500–1800* (2nd edn, Cambridge, 1996).

10. W.H. McNeill, *The Age of Gunpowder Empires, 1450–1800* (Washington, 1989); C.J. Rogers (ed.), *The Military Revolution Debate: Readings on the Military Transformation of Early Modern Europe* (Boulder, Colorado, 1995).

11. J. Black, *Beyond the Military Revolution: War in the Seventeenth-Century World* (Basingstoke, 2011).

12. J. Black, *War in the Nineteenth Century, 1800–1914* (Cambridge, 2009).

13. R. Tapper (ed.), *The Conflict of Tribe and State in Iran and Afghanistan* (London, 1983).

14. J. Black (ed.), *The Origins of War in Early Modern Europe* (Edinburgh, 1987); J. Black, *Why Wars Happen* (London, 1998).

15. G. Jordan and N. Rogers, 'Admirals as Heroes: Patriotism and Liberty in Hanoverian England', *Journal of British Studies*, 28 (1989), pp. 201–22.

16. R.E. Glass, 'The Image of the Sea Officer in English Literature, 1660–1710', *Albion*, 26 (1994), pp. 583–99; A. McNairn, *Behold the Hero: General Wolfe and the Arts in the Eighteenth Century* (Liverpool, 1997).

17. Philip V of Spain to Max Emmanuel, 10 Sept. 1702, 12 Oct. 1704, BN. NAF. 486 fols 78, 89.

18. P. Spalding, *Lafayette: Prisoner of State* (Columbia, South Carolina, 2010).

19. F.J. Baumgartner, *Declaring War in Early Modern Europe* (Basingstoke, 2011), p. 114.

20. P. Mansel, 'Monarchy, Uniform and the Rise of the Frac, 1760–1813', *Past and Present*, 96 (1982), pp. 103–32.

21. Marquis de Clermont d'Ambolise, French envoy, to Vergennes, French foreign minister, 19 April, 14 June 1777, Paris, Archives Nationales, KK 1393.

22. V.G. Kiernan, *The Duel in European History: Honour and the Reign of Aristocracy* (Oxford, 1989).

23. R.J.B. Muir and C.J. Esdaile, 'Strategic Planning in a Time of Small Government: the Wars against Revolutionary and Napoleonic France, 1793–1815', in C.M. Woolgar (ed.), *Wellington Studies* (3 vols, Southampton, 1996), I, 80.

24. J. Waley-Cohen, *The Culture of War in China: Empire and the Military under the Qing Dynasty* (London, 2006).

25. J. Ruff, *Violence in Early Modern Europe, 1500–1800* (Cambridge, 2001).

26. H. Carl, 'Restricted Violence? Military Occupation during the Eighteenth Century', in E. Charters, E. Rosenhaft and H. Smith (eds), *Civilians and War in Europe, 1618–1815* (Liverpool, 2012), pp. 116–26.

27. Thomas Robinson, British envoy in Vienna, to William, Earl of Harrington, British Secretary of State, reporting views of Austrian minister Bartenstein, 22 Feb. 1741, NA. SP. 80/144.

28. R. Bonney (ed.), *The Rise of the Fiscal State in Europe, c. 1200–1815* (Oxford, 1999).

29. J. Black, *War Since 1945* (London, 2004) and *Avoiding Armageddon: From the Great War to the Fall of France, 1918–40* (London, 2012).

30. J. Black, *Great Powers and the Quest for Hegemony: The world order since 1500* (London, 2008), e.g. pp. 57–60.

2: 1700–1720

1. J. Black, *Beyond the Military Revolution: War in the Seventeenth-Century World* (Basingstoke, 2011), pp. 134–50.

2. For weapons development in Tibet, see D.J. LaRocca (ed.), *Warriors of the Himalayas: Rediscovering the Arms and Armor of Tibet* (New Haven, Connecticut, 2006).

3. L. Petech, *China and Tibet in the Early Eighteenth Century: History of the Establishment of the Chinese Protectorate in Tibet* (Leiden, 1950), pp. 32–73; T.W.D. Shakabpa, *Tibet: A Political History* (New York, 1984), pp. 135–57.

4. T.J. Barfield, *The Perilous Frontier: Nomadic Empires and China* (Oxford, 1989), p. 290.

5. J. Needham, *Military Technology: The Gunpowder Epic* (Cambridge, 1987), pp. 393–8; J. Waley-Cohen, 'China and Western Technology in the Late Eighteenth Century', *American Historical Review*, 98 (1993), pp. 1531–2.

6. Y. Dai, *The Sichuan Frontier and Tibet: Imperial Strategy in the Early Qing* (Seattle, Washington, 2009), p. 79.

7. T. Saguchi, 'The Formation of the Turfan Principality under the Qing Empire', *Acta Asiatica*, 41 (1981), pp. 76–94.

8. M.E. Lewis, *China's Cosmopolitan Empire: The Tang Dynasty* (Cambridge, Massachusetts, 2010).

9. F.W. Bergholz, *The Partition of the Steppe: The Struggle of the Russians, Manchus, and the Zunghar Mongols for Empire in Central Asia, 1619–1758: A Study in Power Politics* (New York, 1993).

10. M.W. Charney, *Southeast Asian Warfare, 1300–1900* (Leiden, 2004).

11. J.R. McNeill, *Mosquito Empires: Ecology and War in the Greater Caribbean, 1620–1914* (Cambridge, 2010).

12. J. Black, *War and Technology* (Bloomington, Indiana, 2013).

13. N.K. Wagle and R.G.S. Cooper, 'The Battle of Dabhoi', in A.R. Kulkarni, M.A. Nayeem and T.R. de Souze (eds), *Mediaeval Deccan History* (Mumbai, 1996), pp. 268–96.

14. P. Barua, *The State at War in South Asia* (Lincoln, Nebraska, 2005), p. 321.

15. S. Subrahmanyam, *Penumbral Visions: Making Polities in Early Modern South India* (Ann Arbor, Michigan, 2001).

16. N. Ülker, 'The Political Aspects of the Campaign of the Pruth in 1711', *Cultura Turcia*, 3 (1966), pp. 202–16; B. Davies, *Empire and Military Revolution in Eastern Europe: Russia's Turkish Wars in the Eighteenth Century* (London, 2011).

17. D. McKay, *Prince Eugene of Savoy* (London, 1977).

18. G. Ágoston, 'The Ottoman Wars and the Changing Balance of Power along the Danube in the Early Eighteenth Century', in C. Ingrao, N. Samardžić and J. Pešalj (eds), *The Peace of Passarowitz, 1718* (West Lafayette, Indiana, 2011), pp. 95–6.

19. J. Pitts, *A Faithful Account of the Religion and Manners of the Mahometans* (3rd edn, London, 1731), p. 171.

20. C. Finkel and V. Ostapchuk, 'Outpost of Empire: an Appraisal of Ottoman Building Registers as Sources for the Archaeology and Construction History of the Black Sea Fortress of Özi [Ochakov]', *Muquarnas*, 22 (2005), pp. 150–88, esp. 161–80.

21. P. Englund, *The Battle of Poltava* (London, 1992).

22. A. Konstam, *Peter the Great's Army* (London, 1993).

23. J. Cracraft, *The Petrine Revolution in Russian Culture* (Cambridge, Massachusetts, 2004), pp. 140–2.

24. M. Hochedlinger, *Austria's Wars of Emergence: War, State and Society in the Habsburg Monarchy, 1683–1797* (Harlow, 2003).

25. J. Thornton, 'Warfare, Slave Trading and European Influence: Atlantic Africa 1450–1800', in J. Black (ed.), *War in the Early Modern World* (London, 1999), pp. 129–46.

26. R.C. Padden, 'Cultural Change and Military Resistance in Araucanian Chile, 1550–1730', *Southwestern Journal of Anthropology*, 13 (1957), pp. 103–21.

27. J. Hemming, *Red Gold: The Conquest of the Brazilian Indians, 1500–1760* (2nd edn, London), 1995).

28. J. Higginbotham, *Old Mobile: Fort Louis de la Louisiane 1702–1711* (Mobile, Alabama, 1977).

29. M. Giraud, *A History of French Louisiana, I: The Reign of Louis XIV, 1698–1715* (Baton Rouge, Louisiana, 1974).

30. D. Weber, *The Spanish Frontier in North America* (New Haven, Connecticut, 1992).

31. N. Sheidley, 'Hunting and the Politics of Masculinity in Cherokee Treaty-Making, 1763–75', in M. Daunton and R. Halpern (eds), *Empire and Others: British Encounters with Indigenous Peoples, 1600–1850* (London, 1999), pp. 167–85.

32. D.H. Dye, 'The Transformation of Mississippian Warfare: Four Case Studies from the Mid-South', in E.N. Arkush and M.W. Allen (eds), *The Archaeology of Warfare: Prehistories of Raiding and Conquest* (Gainesville, Florida, 2006), pp. 101–47.

33. C.S. Keener, 'An Ethnohistorical Analysis of Iroquois Assault Tactics Used against Fortified Settlements of the Northeast in the Seventeenth Century', *Ethnohistory*, 46 (1999), pp. 777–807.

34. B.J. Oatis, *A Colonial Complex: South Carolina's Frontiers in the Era of the Yamasee War, 1680–1730* (Lincoln, Nebraska, 2004).

35. A. Gallay, *The Indian Slave Trade: The Rise of the English Empire in the American South, 1670–1717* (New Haven, Connecticut, 2002), p. 337; W.L. Ramsey, *The Yamasee War: A Study of Culture, Economy, and Conflict in the Colonial South* (Lincoln, Nebraska, 2008).

36. A. Lyons, *The 1711 Expedition to Quebec* (London, 2013).

37. J.S. Pritchard, *In Search of Empire: The French in the Americas, 1670–1730* (Cambridge, 2004), pp. 420–42.

38. A. Balisch, 'Infantry Battlefield Tactics in the Seventeenth and Eighteenth Centuries on the European and Turkish Theatres of War: the Austrian Response to Different Conditions', *Studies in History and Politics*, 3 (1983–4), p. 44; J.A. Lynn, *Giant of the Grand Siècle: The French Army, 1610–1715* (Cambridge, 1997), p. 476.

39. R. Gobetti, 'Le armi bianche all'inizio del Settecento', in R.S. Giachino et al. (eds), *Torino 1706* (Turin, 2006), pp. 75–82.

40. P. Levrau, 'Crippled by a Musket Shot and a Sabre Slash', in D. Money (ed.), *1708: Oudenarde and Lille* (Cambridge, 2008), p. 70.

41. B.P. Hughes, *Firepower: Weapons Effectiveness on the Battlefield, 1630–1850* (London, 1974).

42. D. Chandler, *The Art of Warfare in the Age of Marlborough* (London, 1976); C. Jorgensen et al., *Fighting Techniques of the Early Modern World* (Steeplehurst, 2005).

43. J. Black, *European International Relations 1648–1815* (Basingstoke, 2002).

44. J. Ostwald, 'The "Decisive" Battle of Ramillies, 1706: Prerequisites for Decisiveness in Early Modern Warfare', *Journal of Military History*, 64 (2000), pp. 668–77.

45. C. Sturgill, *Marshal Villars and the War of the Spanish Succession* (Lexington, Kentucky, 1965).

46. D. Chandler, *Marlborough as Military Commander* (London, 1973).

47. Memorandum on Anglo-Portuguese meeting, 16 Sept. 1705, BL. Add. 61122 fol. 64.
48. Instructions for Charles, 3rd Earl of Peterborough and Admiral Sir Clowdisley Shovell, commanders of the English force sent to the Mediterranean, 10 Sept. 1705, BL. Add. 61122 fol. 13.
49. Charles Hedges, envoy in Turin, to Marlborough, 28 Sept. 1705, BL. Add. 61264 fol. 84.

3: 1720–1740

1. T.J. Barfield, *The Perilous Frontier: Nomadic Empires and China* (Oxford, 1989).
2. R. Matthee, *Persia in Crisis: Safavid Decline and the Fall of Isfahan* (London, 2011), pp. 217–41.
3. E.V. Ansimov, *The Reforms of Peter the Great: Progress through Coercion in Russia* (Moscow, 1993), pp. 255–61.
4. D.J. Taylor, *Russian Foreign Policy, 1725–39: The Politics of Stability and Opportunity* (PhD, University of East Anglia, 1983), pp. 191–2, 201.
5. C. Ingrao, 'Habsburg Strategy and Geopolitics During the Eighteenth Century', in B. Király, G.E. Rothenberg and P. Sugar (eds), *East Central European Society and War in the Pre-Revolutionary Eighteenth Century* (New York, 1982), pp. 49–66; J.P. LeDonne, *The Grand Strategy of the Russian Empire, 1650–1831* (Oxford, 2004).
6. J. Sarkar, *Nadir Shah in India* (Calcutta, 1973), pp. 40–51.
7. *Ibid.*
8. L. Lockhart, *Nadir Shah* (London, 1938); M. Axworthy, *Sword of Persia: Nader Shah, from Tribal Warrior to Conquering Tyrant* (London, 2006).
9. M. Axworthy, 'The Army of Nader Shah', *Iranian Studies*, 40 (2007), pp. 635–46.
10. Born in 1711, the fourth son of the Yongzheng emperor, he became emperor in October 1735 and ruled until he died in the beginning of 1799. However, his reign title was only in use from 1736 to 1796, when his son, the Jiaqing emperor, was enthroned.
11. C.R. Bawden, *The Modern History of Mongolia* (New York, 1968), p. 114.
12. P.C. Perdue, 'Empire and Nation in Comparative Perspective: Frontier Administration in Eighteenth-Century China', in H. Islamoğlu and P.C. Perdue (eds), *Shared Histories of Modernity: China, India and the Ottoman Empire* (New Delhi, 2009), p. 36.
13. L. Petech, *China and Tibet in the Early Eighteenth Century* (Leiden, 1972), pp. 116–44.
14. M. Zelin, *The Magistrates' Tael: Rationalising Fiscal Reform in Eighteenth-Century Ch'ing China* (Berkeley, California, 1984).

15. J.E. Herman, *Amid the Clouds and Mist: China's Colonization of Guizhou, 1200–1700* (Cambridge, Massachusetts, 2007).

16. A.S. Donnelly, *The Russian Conquest of Bashkiria, 1552–1740* (New Haven, Connecticut, 1968); M. Khodarkovsky, *Russia's Steppe Frontier: The Making of a Colonial Empire, 1500–1800* (Bloomington, Indiana, 2002); W. Sunderland, *'Taming the Wild Field': Colonization and Empire on the Russian Steppe* (Ithaca, New York, 2004).

17. M. Edwardes (ed.), *Major John Corneille, Journal of my Service in India* (London, 1966), p. 35.

18. J.K. Thornton, *The Kingdom of Kongo: Civil War and Transition, 1641–1718* (Madison, Wisconsin, 1983).

19. J. Hemming, *Red Gold: The Conquest of the Brazilian Indians, 1500–1760* (2nd edn, London, 1995).

20. G.D. Jones, *The Conquest of the Last Maya Kingdom* (Stanford, California, 1998), pp. 300–35.

21. M. Giraud, *A History of French Louisiana, V: The Company of the Indies, 1723–1731* (Baton Rouge, Louisiana, 1991), p. 317.

22. E.J. Cashin, *Guardians of the Valley: Chickasaws in Colonial South Carolina and Georgia* (Columbia, South Carolina, 2009).

23. C. Radding, 'Forging Cultures of Resistance on Two Colonial Frontiers: Northwestern Mexico and Eastern Bolivia', in J. Smolenski and T.J. Humphrey (eds), *New World Orders: Violence, Sanction, and Authority in the Colonial Americas* (Philadelphia, Pennsylvania, 2005), p. 169.

24. J. Cerdá Crespo, *Conflictos Coloniales: la Guerra de los Nueve Años 1739–1748* (Alicante, 2010).

4: 1740–1760

1. For an effective recent account of the oceanic and colonial dimension, see D.A. Baugh, *The Global Seven Years War 1754–1763* (Harlow, 2011).

2. S. van Schaik, *Tibet: A History* (New Haven, Connecticut, 2011), pp. 143–5.

3. P. Lococo, 'The Qing Empire', in D.A. Graff and R. Higham (eds), *A Military History of China* (Boulder, Colorado, 2002), p. 129; M. Courant, *L'Asie centrale aux XVIIe et XVIIIe siècles: Empire Kalmouk ou Empire Mantchou?* (Lyon, 1912).

4. P.C. Perdue, 'Military Mobilization in Seventeenth- and Eighteenth-century China, Russia, and Mongolia', *Modern Asian Studies*, 30 (1996), pp. 757–93.

5. M. Zelin, *The Magistrate's Tael: Rationalising Fiscal Reform in Eighteenth Century Ch'ing China* (Berkeley, California, 1992).

6. Y. Dai, 'The Qing State, Merchants, and the Military Labor Force in the Jinchuan Campaigns', *Late Imperial China*, 22 (2001), pp. 35–90.

7. Y. Dai, '*Yingyun Shengxi*: Military Entrepreneurship in the High Qing Period: 1700–1800', *Late Imperial China*, 26 no. 2 (2005), pp. 1–67; and 'Military Finance in the High Qing Period: An Overview', in N. Di Cosmo (ed.), *Military Culture in Imperial China* (Cambridge, Massachusetts, 2009), pp. 296–316, 380–2.

8. *Re* stopping Genoese remittances of money to French troops in Italy, instructions to John Chetwynd, British diplomat, 3 Aug. 1706, BL. Add. 61525 fol. 3.

9. P.C. Perdue, *China Marches West: The Qing Conquests of Central Eurasia* (Cambridge, Massachusetts, 2005), pp. 270–89.

10. *Ibid.*, pp. 289–92.

11. J.A. Millward, *Beyond the Pass: Commerce, Ethnicity, and Empire in Qing Central Asia, 1759–1864* (Stanford, California, 1998).

12. J. Waley-Cohen, 'Religion, War, and Empire-building in Eighteenth-century China', *International History Review*, 20 (1998), pp. 336–52.

13. R. Entenmann, 'Andreas Ly on the First Jinchuan War in Western Sichuan, 1747–1749', *Sino-Western Cultural Relations Journal*, 19 (1997), pp. 7–8.

14. Y. Dai, *The Sichuan Frontier and Tibet: Imperial Strategy in the Early Qing* (Seattle, Washington, 2009), p. 129.

15. R. Greatrex, 'A Brief Introduction to the First Jinchuan War', in P. Kvaerne (ed.), *Tibetan Studies* (Oslo, 1994), I, 247–63.

16. R.W. Olson, *The Siege of Mosul and Ottoman–Persian Relations, 1718–1743: A Study of Rebellion in the Capital and War in the Provinces of the Ottoman Empire* (Bloomington, Indiana, 1975).

17. E. Tucker, *Nadir Shah's Quest for Legitimacy in Post-Safavid Iran* (Gainesville, Florida, 2006).

18. R. Murphey, *Ottoman Warfare 1500–1700* (London, 1999), p. xiv.

19. C.A. Bayly, 'India and West Asia, c. 1700–1830', *Asian Affairs*, 19 (1988), pp. 3–19.

20. V. Aksan, 'Ottoman Military Power in the Eighteenth Century', in B. Davies (ed.), *Warfare in Eastern Europe 1500–1800* (Leiden, 2012), p. 321.

21. J.J. Gommans, *The Rise of the Indo-Afghan Empire, c. 1710–1780* (Leiden, 1995).

22. J.J. Gommans, 'Indian Warfare and Afghan Innovation during the Eighteenth Century', *Studies in History*, 11 (1995), pp. 261–80.

23. M. Alam, *The Crisis of Empire in Mughal North India: Awadh and the Punjab, 1707–1748* (Delhi, 1986).

24. C.A. Bayly, *Rulers, Townsmen, and Bazaars: North Indian Society in the Age of British Expansion, 1770–1870* (Cambridge, 1983).

25. M. Vigié, *Dupleix* (Paris, 1993).

26. B.J. Gupta, *Sirajuddaullah and the East India Company, 1756–1757: Background to the Foundation of British Power in India* (Leiden, 1966), pp. 116–26.

27. G. Singh, *Ahmad Shah Abdali* (Lahore, 1993).

28. A.D. Gupta, *Indian Merchants and the Decline of Surat, c. 1700–1750* (Wiesbaden, 1979).

29. M. Edwardes (ed.), *Major John Corneille, Journal of my Service in India* (London, 1966), pp. 53, 66.

30. Ibid., pp. 121, 124.

31. C. Wickremesekera, *'Best Black Troops in the World': British Perceptions and the Making of the Sepoy, 1746–1805* (New Delhi, 2002).

32. Edwardes (ed.), *Corneille*, pp. 39, 50, 63.

33. G.E. Harvey, *History of Burma* (London, 1925), p. 341.

34. J.J. Ewald, *Soldiers, Traders, and Slaves: State Formation and Economic Transformation in the Greater Nile Valley, 1700–1885* (Madison, Wisconsin, 1990), pp. 45–6.

35. S. Brumwell, *Redcoats: The British Soldier and War in the Americas, 1755–1763* (Cambridge, 2002).

36. D. Syrett, *Shipping and Military Power in the Seven Years War: The Sails of Victory* (Exeter, 2008).

37. A.J.B. Johnston, *Endgame 1758: The Promise, the Glory, and the Despair of Louisbourg's Last Decade* (Lincoln, Nebraska, 2008); H. Boscawen, *The Capture of Louisbourg, 1758* (Norman, Oklahoma, 2011).

38. M. Ward, *Breaking the Backcountry: The Seven Years' War in Virginia and Pennsylvania, 1754–1765* (Pittsburgh, Pennsylvania, 2003).

39. Guy Dickens, British envoy in Berlin, to William, Earl of Harrington, Secretary of State, 4 Feb. 1741, NA. SP. 90/49 fol. 85.

40. M. Anderson, *The War of the Austrian Succession, 1740–1748* (Harlow, 1995).

41. J.M. Hill, 'The Distinctiveness of Gaelic Warfare, 1400–1750', *European History Quarterly*, 22 (1992), pp. 340–1.

42. C. Duffy, *The '45* (London, 2003).

43. D. Showalter, *The Wars of Frederick the Great* (Harlow, 1996).

44. F.A.J. Szabo, *The Seven Years War in Europe, 1756–63* (Harlow, 2008), p. 428; C.J. Duffy, *Instrument of War: The Austrian Army in the Seven Years War* (Chicago, Illinois, 2000).

45. J. Oates, *The Jacobite Campaigns: The British State at War* (London, 2011).

46. T. Andrade, *Lost Colony: The Untold Story of China's First Great Victory over the West* (Princeton, New Jersey, 2011), p. 15.

47. P.C. Perdue, 'Fate and Fortune in Central Eurasian Warfare: Three Qing Emperors and their Mongol Rivals', in N. Di Cosmo (ed.), *Warfare in Inner Asian History, 500–1800* (Leiden, 2002), pp. 390, 394.

5: 1760–1780

1. C.R. Pandit, *An Account of the Last Battle of Panipat*, trans. J. Browne, intro. H.G. Rawlinson (Oxford, 1926); T.S. Shejwalkar, *Panipat 1761* (Poona, 1946); H.R. Gupta (ed.), *Marathas and Panipat* (Chandigarh, 1961).

2. P.M. Joshi (ed.), *Selections from the Peshwa Daftar (New Series), Revival of Maratha Power, 1761–72* (Bombay, 1962).

3. Call to Clive, 25 May 1763, John Pybus to Clive, 22 Mar. 1763, BL. IO. Mss. Eur. G37 Box 30 fols 70–1, 37; S.C. Hill, *Yusuf Khan: The Rebel Commandant* (London, 1914).

4. Paterson diary, July 1770, BL. IO. Mss. Eur. E379/1, p. 268.

5. G.J. Bryant, 'The Cavalry Problem in the Early British Indian Army, 1750–1785', *War in History*, 2 (1995), pp. 1–21.

6. J. Sarkar, 'Haidar Ali's Invasion of the Eastern Carnatic, 1780', in I. Habib (ed.), *Resistance and Modernization under Haidar Ali and Tipu Sultan* (New Delhi, 1999), pp. 21–34; G. Kaliamurthy, *Second Anglo-Mysore War: 1780–84* (Delhi, 1987).

7. G.J. Bryant, 'British Logistics and the Conduct of the Carnatic Wars, 1746–1783', *War in History*, 11 (2004), pp. 278–306; and 'Asymmetric Warfare: The British Experience in Eighteenth-Century India', *Journal of Military History*, 68 (2004), pp. 431–69.

8. A. Abeydeera, 'Mapping as a Vital Element of Administration in the Dutch Colonial Government of Maritime Sri Lanka, 1658–1796', *Imago Mundi*, 45 (1993), pp. 103–4.

9. D. Martin, 'Bonpo Canons and Jesuit Cannons: On Sectarian Factors Involved in the Ch'ien-lung Emperor's Second Gold Stream Expedition of 1771 to 1776, Based Primarily on Some Tibetan Sources', *Tibet Journal*, 15, 2 (1990), pp. 3–28.

10. Y. Dai, '*Yingyun Shengxi*: Military Entrepreneurship in the High Qing Period, 1700–1800', *Late Imperial China*, 26 (2005), pp. 50–1.

11. S. Naquin, *Shantung Rebellion: The Wang Lun Uprising of 1774* (New Haven, Connecticut, 1981).

12. M.G. Chang, *A Court on Horseback: Imperial Touring and the Construction of Qing Rule, 1680–1785* (Cambridge, Massachusetts, 2007).

13. G.H. Luce, 'Chinese Invasions of Burma in the Eighteenth Century', *Journal of the Burma Research Society*, 15 (1925), pp. 115–28; L.K. Jung,

'The Sino-Burmese War, 1766–1770: War and Peace under the Tributary System', *China Papers*, 24 (1971), pp. 74–103.

14. Y. Dai, 'A Disguised Defeat: The Myanmar Campaign of the Qing Dynasty', *Modern Asian Studies*, 38 (2004), p. 183 fn. 124.

15. J.R. Perry, *Karim Khan Zand: A History of Iran, 1747–1779* (Chicago, Illinois, 1979).

16. B. Davies, *Empire and Military Revolution in Eastern Europe: Russia's Turkish Wars in the Eighteenth Century* (London, 2011), p. 279.

17. G. Ágoston, *Guns for the Sultan: Military Power and the Weapons Industry in the Ottoman Empire* (Cambridge, 2005), p. 199.

18. B. Menning, 'Russian Military Innovation in the Second Half of the Eighteenth Century', *War and Society*, 2 (1984), pp. 33–5.

19. V. Aksan, *Ottoman Wars 1700–1870: An Empire Besieged* (Harlow, 2007), pp. 145–58.

20. S.H. Hemsley, *A Short History of Eritrea* (Oxford, 1945), p. 79.

21. M.W. Aregay, 'A Reappraisal of the Impact of Firearms in the History of Warfare in Ethiopia, *c*. 1500–1800', *Journal of Ethiopian Studies*, 14 (1976–9), pp. 87–122.

22. J. Marshall, *Travels*, vol. 3 (London, 1772), pp. 136–7.

23. P. Longworth, *The Cossacks* (New York, 1970), pp. 185–6.

24. T.E. Hall, *France and the Eighteenth-Century Corsican Question* (New York, 1971), pp. 187–204.

25. A.J. Kuethe, 'The Pacification Campaign on the Riohacha Frontier, 1772–1779', *Hispanic American Historical Review*, 50 (1970), pp. 467–81.

26. M. Craton, *Testing the Chains: Resistance to Slavery in the British West Indies* (Ithaca, New York, 1982).

27. E.J. Cashin, *William Bartram and the American Revolution on the Southern Frontier* (Columbia, South Carolina, 2000), pp. 141–2.

28. A. Smith, 'Lectures on Jurisprudence 1762–63', note in *An Inquiry into the Nature and Causes of the Wealth of Nations* (1776; Oxford, 1976 edn), p. 692 fn. 9.

29. R. Middleton, *Pontiac's War* (New York, 2007), p. 201.

30. G.E. Dowd, *War under Heaven: Pontiac, the Indian Nations, and the British Empire* (Baltimore, Maryland, 2002).

31. J. Titus, *The Old Dominion at War: Society, Politics, and Warfare in Late Colonial Virginia* (Columbia, South Carolina, 1991); F. Anderson, *Crucible of War: The Seven Years' War and the Fate of Empire in British North America, 1754–1766* (New York, 2000).

32. P. Way, 'The Cutting Edge of Conflict: British Soldiers Encounter Native Americans in the French and Indian War', in M. Daunton and R. Halpern (eds), *Empire and Others: British Encounters with Indigenous Peoples, 1600–1850* (Philadelphia, Pennsylvania, 1999).

33. M.N. McConnell, *Army and Empire: British Soldiers on the American Frontier, 1758–1775* (Lincoln, Nebraska, 2004), p. 147.

34. M.L. Wortman, *Government and Society in Central America, 1680–1840* (New York, 1982).

35. S.J. and B.H. Stein, *Apogee of Empire: Spain and New Spain in the Age of Charles III, 1759–1789* (Baltimore, Maryland, 2003).

36. D. Cahill, 'The Long Conquest: Collaboration by Native Andean Elites in the Colonial System, 1532–1825', in G. Raudzens (ed.), *Technology, Disease and Colonial Conquests, Sixteenth to Eighteenth Centuries* (Leiden, 2001), pp. 86, 106.

37. D. Stoker, K.J. Hagan and M.T. McMaster (eds), *Strategy in the American War of Independence: A Global Approach* (Abingdon, 2010).

38. AE. CP. Ang. 429 fol. 15.

39. R. Middlekauff, 'Why Men Fought in the American Revolution', *Huntington Library Quarterly*, 43 (1980), pp. 135–48.

40. D.R. Cubbison, *Burgoyne and the Saratoga Campaign: His Papers* (Norman, Oklahoma, 2012).

41. J. Tiedemann, 'Patriots by Default: Queens Country, New York, and the British Army, 1776–1783', *William and Mary Quarterly*, 43 (1986), pp. 35–63.

42. J.R. McNeill, *Mosquito Empires: Ecology and War in the Greater Caribbean, 1620–1914* (Cambridge, 2010).

43. J.A. Nagy, *Rebellion in the Ranks: Mutinies of the American Revolution* (Yardley, Pennsylvania, 2008).

44. For the remainder of the war, see pp. 149–50.

45. D. Higginbotham, 'The Early American Way of War: Reconnaissance and Appraisal', in D. Higginbotham (ed.), *War and Society in Revolutionary America: The Wider Dimension of Conflict* (Columbia, South Carolina, 1988), pp. 260–312; W.E. Lee, 'Early American Ways of War: A New Reconnaissance, 1600–1815', *Historical Journal*, 44 (2001), pp. 269–89.

46. S. Brumwell, *Redcoats: The British Soldier and War in the Americas, 1775–1763* (Cambridge, 2002); R. Middleton, *Amherst and the Conquest of Canada* (London, 2003); M. Ward, *Breaking the Backcountry: The Seven Years' War in Virginia and Pennsylvania, 1754–1765* (Pittsburgh, Pennsylvania, 2003) and *The Battle for Quebec, 1759: Britain's Conquest of Canada* (Stroud, 2005).

6: 1780–1800

1. T.B. Lam, 'Intervention versus Tribute in Sino-Vietnamese Relations, 1788–1790', in J.K. Fairbank (ed.), *The Chinese World Order: Traditional China's Foreign Relations* (Cambridge, Massachusetts, 1968), pp. 165–79.

2. S. van Schaik, *Tibet: A History* (New Haven, Connecticut, 2011), pp. 156–9.
3. I would like to thank Yingcong Dai for letting me use a copy of her unpublished paper 'Reaching the Empire's Limits: The Qing Invasion of Nepal in 1792'.
4. Y. Dai, 'Civilians Go into Battle: Hired Militias in the White Lotus War, 1796–1805', *Asia Major*, 3rd ser., 22 (2009), pp. 145–78.
5. W.J. Koening, *The Burmese Polity, 1752–1819: Politics, Administration and Social Organisation in the Early Kon-baung Period* (Ann Arbor, Michigan, 1990), pp. 22–5.
6. E.W. Thompson, *The Last Siege of Seringapatnam* (Delhi, 1990).
7. N.P. Sahai, *Politics of Patronage and Protest: The State, Society and Artisans in Early Modern Rajasthan* (New York, 2006).
8. G.T. Kulkarni and M.R. Kantak, *Battle of Kharda: Challenges and Responses* (Pune, 1980).
9. G.J. Bryant, 'Asymmetric Warfare: The British Experience in Eighteenth-Century India', *Journal of Military History*, 68 (2004), p. 469.
10. I. Habib, *State and Diplomacy under Tipu Sultan: Documents and Essays* (Delhi, 2001).
11. S. Gordon, *Marathas, Marauders and State Formation in Eighteenth-Century India* (Delhi, 1994).
12. R.G.S. Cooper, *The Anglo-Maratha Campaigns and the Contest for India: The Struggle for Control of the South Asian Military Economy* (Cambridge, 2003).
13. H. Fasa'i, *History of Persia under Qajar Rule* (New York, 1972), pp. 52–4.
14. M. Axworthy, *A History of Iran: Empire of the Mind* (New York, 2008), p. 171.
15. A.K.S. Lambton, 'The Tribal Resurgence and the Decline of the Bureaucracy in the Eighteenth Century', in T. Naff and R. Owen (eds), *Studies in Eighteenth-Century Islamic History* (Carbondale, Illinois, 1977), pp. 109–29.
16. F. Charles-Roux, *Le Projet français de conquête de l'Égypte sous le règne de Louis XVI* (Cairo, 1929); Francis, Marquess of Carmarthen, Foreign Secretary, to Duke of Dorset, envoy in Paris, 26 Mar. 1784, NA. FO. 27/11 fols 262–3.
17. D. Crecelius, 'Egypt in the Eighteenth Century', in M.W. Daly (ed.), *The Cambridge History of Egypt, II: Modern Egypt, from 1517 to the End of the Twentieth Century* (Cambridge, 1999), pp. 59–70.
18. A. Balisch, 'Infantry Battlefield Tactics in the Seventeenth and Eighteenth Centuries on the European and Turkish Theatres of War: the Austrian Response to Different Conditions', *Studies in History and Politics*, 3 (1983–4), pp. 55–9.

19. C. Finkel, *Osman's Dream: The Story of the Ottoman Empire, 1300–1923* (New York, 2006), p. 386.

20. J.P. LeDonne, 'Geopolitics, Logistics, and Grain: Russia's Ambitions in the Black Sea Basin, 1737–1834', *International History Review*, 28 (2006), pp. 1–41.

21. J.R. Cole, *Napoleon's Egypt: Invading the Middle East* (New York, 2007).

22. P. Mackesy, *British Victory in Egypt, 1801* (London, 1995).

23. A. Vassiliev, *The History of Saudi Arabia* (London, 1998), pp. 88–98.

24. M.B. Broxup, 'Russia and the North Caucasus', and P.B. Henze, 'Circassian Resistance to Russia', in M.B. Broxup (ed.), *The North Caucasus Barrier: The Russian Advance towards the Muslim World* (London, 1992), pp. 3, 73–6.

25. J.K. Thornton, 'Firearms, Diplomacy, and Conquest in Angola', in W.E. Lee (ed.), *Empires and Indigenes: Intercultural Alliance, Imperial Expansion, and Warfare in the Early Modern World* (New York, 2011), p. 187.

26. J.D. Popkin, *A Concise History of the Haitian Revolution* (Chichester, 2012), p. 42.

27. G.M. Berg, 'The Sacred Musket: Tactics, Technology and Power in Eighteenth-century Madagascar', *Comparative Studies in Society and History*, 27 (1985), pp. 263, 278–9.

28. S. Tenkorang, 'The Importance of Firearms in the Struggle between Ashanti and the Coastal States, 1708–1807', *Transactions of the Historical Society of Ghana*, 9 (1968), pp. 1–16.

29. J.E. Inikori, 'The Import of Firearms into West Africa', *Journal of African History*, 18 (1977), pp. 339–68; W. Richards, 'The Import of Firearms into West Africa in the Eighteenth Century', *Journal of African History*, 21 (1980), pp. 43–59.

30. R.L. Roberts, *Warriors, Merchants, and Slaves: The State and the Economy in the Middle Niger Valley, 1700–1914* (Stanford, California, 1987); S.P. Reyna, *Wars Without End: The Political Economy of a Precolonial African State* (Hanover, New Hampshire, 1990).

31. D. Sweet, 'Native Resistance in Eighteenth-century Amazonia: the "Abominable Muras" in War and Peace', *Radical History Review*, 53 (1992), pp. 49–80.

32. P. Hämäläinen, *The Comanche Empire* (New Haven, Connecticut, 2008), p. 135.

33. P. Silver, *Our Savage Neighbors: How Indian War Transformed Early America* (New York, 2008), pp. 288–90.

34. J. Sugden, *Blue Jacket: Warrior of the Shawnees* (Lincoln, Nebraska, 2000).

35. A.D. Gaff, *Bayonets in the Wilderness: Anthony Wayne's Legion in the Old North-West* (Norman, Oklahoma, 2004).

36. P. Griffin, *American Leviathan: Empire, Nation, and Revolutionary Frontier* (New York, 2007).

37. G.F. Williams, *Year of the Hangman: George Washington's Campaign Against the Iroquois* (Yardley, Pennsylvania, 2005).

38. C. Saunt, *A New Order of Things: Property, Power, and the Transformation of the Creek Indians, 1733–1816* (New York, 1999).

39. J. Piecuch, *Three Peoples, One King: Loyalists, Indians, and Slaves in the Revolutionary South, 1775–1782* (Columbia, South Carolina, 2008).

40. J. Ferling, *Almost a Miracle: The American Victory in the War of Independence* (New York, 2007), p. 573.

41. G.E. Fehlings, 'America's First Limited War', *Naval War College Review*, 53 (2000), pp. 101–44.

42. T.P. Slaughter, *The Whiskey Rebellion: Frontier Epilogue to the American Revolution* (New York, 1986).

43. S. White, *The Little Ice Age Crisis of the Ottoman Empire: Ecology, Climate and Rebellion, 1550–1770* (Cambridge, 2011).

44. S.T. Ross, 'The Development of the Combat Division in Eighteenth-Century French Armies', *French Historical Studies*, 1 (1965), p. 86.

45. P. Bianchi, *Onore e Mestiere. Le Riforme Militari nel Piemonte del Settecento* (Turin, 2002), pp. 233–46, 296.

46. M. Price, 'The Dutch Affair and the Fall of the *Ancien Régime, 1784–1787*', *Historical Journal*, 38 (1995), pp. 875–905.

47. B. Stone, *The Genesis of the French Revolution: A Global Historical Interpretation* (Cambridge, 1994).

48. J.C. Riley, *The Seven Years' War and the Old Regime in France: The Economic and Financial Toll* (Princeton, New Jersey, 1987).

49. D.A. Bell, *The First Total War: Napoleon's Europe and the Birth of Warfare as We Know It* (Boston, Massachusetts, 2007). For serious flaws in Bell's work, see E.C. Kiesling, '"Total War, Total Nonsense" or "The Military Historian's Fetish"', in M.S. Neiberg (ed.), *Arms and the Man: Military History Essays in Honor of Dennis Showalter* (Leiden, 2011), pp. 223–7.

50. F. Dendena, 'A New Look at Feuillantism: the Triumvirate and the Movement for War in 1791', *French History*, 26 (2012), pp. 6–33.

51. U. Planert, 'Innovation or Evolution? The French Wars in Military History', in R. Chickering and S. Förster (eds), *War in an Age of Revolution, 1775–1815* (Cambridge, 2010), p. 84.

52. K.A. Roider, *Baron Thugut and Austria's Response to the French Revolution* (Princeton, New Jersey, 1987), pp. 153–4.

53. E.M. Vovsi, '"Brevet to the Scaffold or to Glory": the High Command of the French Army and Revolutionary Government, 1792–94', *Napoleonic Scholarship*, 4 (Nov. 2011), pp. 142–53.

54. P. Dwyer, *Napoleon: The Path to Power* (New Haven, Connecticut, 2008).

55. P. Paret, *The Cognitive Challenge of War: Prussia 1806* (Princeton, New Jersey, 2009).

56. W. Cobbett, (ed.), *Parliamentary History of England*, 3 (London, 1818), cols 226–7.

57. J.A. Olsen and M. v. Creveld (eds), *The Evolution of Operational Art from Napoleon to the Present* (Oxford, 2011).

58. J. Lynn, 'The Evolution of Army Style of the Eighteenth Century', *War and Society*, 2 (1984), pp. 23–41; and 'The Evolution of Army Style in the Modern West, 800–2000', *International History Review*, 18 (1996), pp. 505–45.

59. J. Lukowski, *The Partitions of Poland 1772, 1793, 1795* (Harlow, 1999), pp. 163–74.

60. D. Keogh and N. Furlong (eds), *The Mighty Wave: The 1798 Rebellion in Wexford* (Blackrock, 1996).

61. B.W. Menning, 'The Imperial Russian Army, 1725–1796', in F.W. Kagan and R. Higham (eds), *The Military History of Tsarist Russia* (Basingstoke, 2002), p. 73.

62. D.E. Showalter, 'Tactics and Recruitment in Eighteenth Century Prussia', *Studies in History and Politics*, 3 (1983–4), p. 36.

63. A.W. Fisher, *The Russian Annexation of the Crimea, 1772–1783* (Cambridge, 1970).

64. John Chetwynd, envoy in Turin, to Charles Hedges, 13 Nov. 1706, BL. Add. 61525 fol. 8.

65. J.W. Hall (ed.), *The Cambridge History of Japan, IV: Early Modern Japan* (Cambridge, 1991), p. 475.

66. B.W. Menning, 'Military Institutions and the Steppe Frontier in Imperial Russia, 1700–1861', *Acta* of the 1980 Conference of the International Commission of Military History (Bucharest, 1981), pp. 174–94; and 'Russian Military Innovation in the Second Half of the Eighteenth Century', *War and Society*, 2 (1984), pp. 31–6.

67. S.N. Sen, *The Military System of the Marathas* (2nd edn, Calcutta, 1958), pp. 109–18.

68. P.A. Lorge, *The Asian Military Revolution: From Gunpowder to the Bomb* (Cambridge, 208), p. 135.

69. BL. Add. 57313 fol. 13.

70. K. Roy, *War, Culture and Society in Early Modern South Asia, 1740–1849* (Abingdon, 2011), pp. 78–9.

71. S. Gordon, 'The Limited Adoption of European-style Military Forces by Eighteenth Century Rulers in India', *Indian Economic and Social History Review*, 35 (1998), pp. 229–45; and 'Symbolic and Structural Constraints on the Adoption of European-style Military Technologies in the

Eighteenth Century', in R.B. Barnett (ed.), *Rethinking Early Modern India* (New Delhi, 2002), pp. 155–78.

72. B.P. Lenman, 'The Weapons of War in Eighteenth-Century India', *Journal of the Society for Army Historical Research*, 46 (1968), pp. 33–43; P.J. Marshall, 'Western Arms in Maritime Asia in the Early Phases of Expansion', *Modern Asian Studies*, 14 (1980), pp. 13–28.

73. S. Bidwell, *Swords for Hire: European Mercenaries in Eighteenth Century India* (London, 1971).

74. J.N. Sarkar, *Sindhia as Regent of Delhi* (Bombay, 1953).

75. P. Barua, 'Military Developments in India, 1750–1850', *Journal of Military History*, 58 (1994), p. 616.

76. S. Sen, *Empire of Free Trade: The East India Company and the Making of the Colonial Marketplace* (Philadelphia, Pennsylvania, 1998).

77. C.A. Bayly, 'The British Military–Fiscal State and Indigenous Resistance: India 1750–1820', in L. Stone (ed.), *An Imperial State at War: Britain from 1689 to 1815* (London, 1994), pp. 324–49; S. Alavi, *The Sepoys and the Company: Tradition and Transition in Northern India, 1770–1830* (Delhi, 1995), p. 4.

78. Roy, *War, Culture and Society*, pp. 57–8; A. Webster, *The Twilight of the East India Company – The Evolution of Anglo-Asian Politics, 1790–1860* (Woodbridge, 2009), p. 52.

79. J. Cuenca-Esteban, 'The British Balance of Payments, 1772–1820: India Transfers and War Finance', *Economic History Review*, 54 (2001), p. 67.

80. R. Bin Wong, *China Transformed: Historical Change and the Limits of European Experience* (Ithaca, New York, 1997); K. Pomeranz, *The Great Divergence: China, Europe and the Making of the Modern World Economy* (Berkeley, California, 1999).

81. John Methuen, envoy in Lisbon, to James Craggs, Secretary of State, 19 Sept. 1705, BL. Add. 61122 fol. 47.

82. E. Ingram, *Commitment to Empire: Prophecies of the Great Game in Asia, 1797–1800* (Oxford, 1981); and *The British Empire as a World Power* (London, 2001), pp. 178–83; R.W. Beachey, *A History of East Africa, 1592–1902* (London, 1996), pp. 14–15.

83. T. Potgieter and A. Grundlingh, 'Admiral Elphinstone and the Conquest and Defence of the Cape of Good Hope, 1795–96', *Scientia Militaria*, 35 (2007), p. 55.

84. P. Macdougall, 'British Seapower and the Mysore Wars of the Eighteenth Century', *Mariner's Mirror*, 97 (2011), p. 306.

85. P.K. O'Brien, 'The Political Economy of British Taxation, 1660–1815', *Economic History Review*, 2nd ser., 41 (1988), pp. 1–32; J. Brewer, *The Sinews of Power: War, Money and the English State, 1688–1783* (London, 1989).

86. J. Black, 'Britain and the "Long" Eighteenth Century, 1688–1815', in J.A. Olsen and C.S. Gray (eds), *The Practice of Strategy from Alexander the Great to the Present* (Oxford, 2011), p. 172.
87. G. Chet, *The Ocean is a Wilderness: Atlantic Piracy and the Limits of Governmental Legitimacy in the Modern State, 1688–1856* (New York, 2012).

7: Naval Capability and Warfare

1. R.W. Beachey, *A History of East Africa, 1592–1902* (London, 1996), pp. 14–15.
2. M. Edwardes (ed.), *Major John Corneille, Journal of my Service in India* (London, 1966), p. 118.
3. D. McNab, B.W. Hodgins and D.S. Standen, '"Black with Canoes": Aboriginal Resistance and the Canoe: Diplomacy, Trade and Warfare in the Meeting Grounds of Northeastern North America, 1600–1821', in G. Raudzens (ed.), *Technology, Disease and Colonial Conquests, Sixteenth to Eighteenth Centuries* (Leiden, 2001), p. 245.
4. Y. Dai, 'A Disguised Defeat: The Myanmar Campaign of the Qing Dynasty', *Modern Asian Studies*, 38 (2004), p. 166.
5. P. Lococo, 'The Qing Empire', in D.A. Graff and R. Higham (eds), *A Military History of China* (Boulder, Colorado, 2002), p. 125.
6. B.A. Elleman, 'The Neglect and Nadir of Chinese Maritime Policy under the Qing', in A.S. Erickson, L. Goldstein and C. Lord (eds), *China Goes to Sea: Maritime Transformation in Comparative Historical Perspective* (Annapolis, Maryland, 2009).
7. R.J. Antony, *Like Froth Floating on the Sea: The World of Pirates and Seafarers in Late Imperial South China* (Berkeley, California, 2003).
8. Edwardes (ed.), *Corneille*, p. 67; A. Deshpande, 'The Politics and Culture of Early Modern Warfare on the Konkan Coast of India during the Seventeenth and Eighteenth Centuries', in Y. Sharma (ed.), *Coastal Histories: Society and Ecology in pre-Modern India* (Delhi, 2010), pp. 43–73.
9. P. Macdougall, 'British Seapower and the Mysore Wars of the Eighteenth Century', *Mariner's Mirror*, 97 (2011), pp. 299–314.
10. A.C. Hess, 'The Forgotten Frontier: the Ottoman North African Provinces during the Eighteenth Century', in T. Naff and R. Owen (eds), *Studies in Eighteenth Century Islamic History* (Carbondale, Illinois, 1977), pp. 74–87; C. Heywood, 'What's in a Name? Some Algerine Fleet Lists, 1686–1714, from British Libraries and Archives', *Maghreb Review*, 31 (2006), pp. 103–28; L. Merouche, *Recherches sur l'Algérie à l'époque ottomane, II: La Course: mythes et réalité* (Paris, 2007).

11. Manchester to Sunderland, 23 Mar. 1708, Huntingdon, County Record Office DD M36/8, p. 93.
12. I would like to thank Chris Storrs for letting me read his unpublished paper 'State Formation in Early Modern Europe: The Savoyard Navy *c.* 1713–98'.
13. A. DeGroot, 'The Ottoman Mediterranean since Lepanto: Naval Warfare during the Seventeenth and Eighteenth Centuries', *Anatolica*, 20 (1994), pp. 269–93.
14. Harley to George Stepney, envoy in The Hague, 10 Dec., reply 28 Dec. 1706, BL. Add. 7059 fols 119, 228.
15. L. Thys-Şenocak et al., 'Understanding Archaeology and Architecture through Archival Records: The Restoration Project of the Ottoman Fortress of Seddülbahir on the Gallipoli Peninsula of Turkey', in A.C.S. Peacock (ed.), *The Frontiers of the Ottoman World* (London, 2009), p. 207.
16. T. Freller, 'In Search of a Mediterranean Base: The Order of St John and Russia's Great Power Plans during the Rule of Tsar Peter the Great and Tsarina Catherine II', *Journal of Early Modern History*, 8 (2004), pp. 3–30.
17. S.J. Shaw, 'Selim III and the Ottoman Navy', in R. Harding (ed.), *Naval History, 1680–1850* (Aldershot, 2006), pp. 280–1.
18. R. Matthee, *Persia in Crisis: Safavid Decline and the Fall of Isfahan* (London, 2012), pp. 229–31.
19. R.D. Bathurst, 'Maritime Trade and Imamate Government: Two Principal Themes in the History of Oman to 1728', in D. Hopwood (ed.), *The Arabian Peninsula: Society and Politics* (London, 1972), pp. 89–106.
20. L. Lockhart, 'Nadir Shah's Campaigns in Oman, 1733–1744', *Bulletin of the School of Oriental and African Studies*, 8 (1935–7), pp. 157–73.
21. P. Auchterlonie, *Encountering Islam. Joseph Pitts: An English Slave in 17th-Century Algiers and Mecca* (London, 2012), pp. 23, 25.
22. N.A.M. Rodger, 'Form and Function in European Navies, 1660–1815', in L. Akveld et al. (eds), *In het Kielzog* (Amsterdam, 2003), pp. 85–97.
23. S. Willis, 'Fleet Performance and Capability in the Eighteenth Century Royal Navy', *War in History*, 11 (2004), pp. 373–92.
24. Memorandum on state of French navy [1706–7], NA. SP. 78/154 fol. 46.
25. J.R. Bruijn, 'A Little Incident in 1707: The Demise of a Once Glorious Dutch Naval Organisation', in A.M. Forssberg et al. (eds), *Organising History* (Lund, 2011), p. 121.
26. J.B. Hattendorf, '"To Aid and Assist the Other": Anglo-Dutch Naval Cooperation in Coalition Warfare at Sea, 1689–1714', in A.F. de Jongste and A.J. Veenendaal (eds), *Anthonie Heinsius and the Dutch Republic, 1688–1720: Politics, War, and Finance* (The Hague, 2002), pp. 177–98.

27. Charles, 4th Earl of Manchester, British envoy in Venice, to Charles, Earl of Sunderland, Secretary of State, 27 Ap. 1707, Huntingdon, County Record Office DD M36/8 p. 10.

28. R. Harding, *The Emergence of Britain's Global Naval Supremacy: The War of 1739–1748* (Woodbridge, 2010).

29. N.A.M. Rodger, *The Insatiable Earl: A Life of John Montagu, Fourth Earl of Sandwich, 1718–1792* (London, 1993).

30. J.P. Merino Navarro, *La armada Española en el siglo XVIII* (Madrid, 1981).

31. J.R. Bruijn, *The Dutch Navy of the Seventeenth and Eighteenth Centuries* (Columbia, South Carolina, 1993).

32. S. Willis, *The Glorious First of June: Fleet Battle in the Reign of Terror* (London, 2011), esp. p. 325.

33. N.A.M. Rodger, *The Command of the Ocean: A Naval History of Britain, 1649–1815* (London, 2004); C. Wilkinson, *The British Navy and the State in the Eighteenth Century* (Woodbridge, 2004); R. Mackay and M. Duffy, *Hawke, Nelson and British Naval Leadership, 1747–1805* (Woodbridge, 2009).

34. J.R. Dull, *The Age of the Ship of the Line: The British and French Navies, 1650–1815* (Lincoln, Nebraska, 2009).

35. R. Morriss, *Naval Power and British Culture, 1760–1850: Public Trust and Government Ideology* (Farnham, 2004); and *The Foundations of British Maritime Ascendancy: Resources, Logistics and the State, 1755–1815* (Cambridge, 2011).

36. D.A. Baugh, 'Naval Power: What Gave the British Naval Superiority', in L. Prados de la Escosura (ed.), *Exceptionalism and Industrialisation: Britain and its European Rivals, 1688–1815* (Cambridge, 2004), p. 257.

37. E. Gibbon, *The History of the Decline and Fall of the Roman Empire*, ed. J.B. Bury (7 vols, London, 1896–1900), IV, 166–7.

38. Wych to John, Lord Carteret, Secretary of State for the Northern Department, 10 Ap. 1742, NA. SP. 91/31.

39. James Craggs, British Secretary of State, to John, 2nd Earl of Stair, envoy in Paris, 10, 14, 21 Sept. 1719, NA. SP. 104/30.

40. Charles Whitworth, envoy in The Hague, to Earl of Sunderland, 18 Jan. 1718, NA. SP. 84/261 fols 52–3.

41. S.F. Gradish, 'The Establishment of British Seapower in the Mediterranean, 1689–1713', *Canadian Journal of History* (1975), pp. 1–16.

42. Chetwynd, outletter book, 25 Jan. 1704, Stafford, Staffordshire Record Office, D 649/8/2 p. 56.

43. Daniel, 2nd Earl of Nottingham to Anthonie Heinsius, leading Dutch politician, 24 Mar. 1704, in A.J. Veenendaal (ed.), *De Briefwisseling van Anthonie Heinsius 1702–1720*, vol. 3 (The Hague, 1980), p. 108.

44. A.R. Wadia, *The Bombay Dockyard and the Wadia Master Builders* (Bombay, 1957).

45. Edwardes (ed.), *Corneille*, pp. 95–9.

46. D. Syrett, *Shipping and Military Power in the Seven Years War: The Sails of Victory* (Exeter, 2008); R. Knight and M. Wilcox, *Sustaining the Fleet, 1793–1815: War, the British Navy and the Contractor State* (Woodbridge, 2010); M. Wilcox, '"This Great Complex Concern": Victualling the Royal Navy on the East Indies Station, 1780–1815', *Mariner's Mirror*, 97 (2011), pp. 32–49.

47. G. Cole, *Arming the Royal Navy, 1793–1815: The Office of Ordnance and the State* (London, 2012).

48. Newcastle to Vernon, 26 Mar. 1740, BL. Add. 32693 fols 109–13.

49. Edwardes (ed.), *Corneille*, p. 55.

50. J. Glete, *Navies and Nations: Warships, Navies and State Building in Europe and America, 1500–1860* (2 vols, Stockholm, 1993), I, 311.

51. T. Zorlu, *Innovation and Empire in Turkey: Sultan Selim III and the Modernisation of the Ottoman Navy* (London, 2011).

52. W.J. Morgan, 'American Privateering in America's War for Independence, 1775–1783', *American Neptune*, 36, 2 (Apr. 1976), pp. 79–87.

53. W.M. Fowler, *Rebels Under Sail: The American Navy During the Revolution* (New York, 1976).

54. J.B. Hattendorf, 'The Formation and the Roles of the Continental Navy, 1775–1785', in J.B. Hattendorf, *Talking about Naval History* (Newport, Rhode Island, 2011), p. 200.

55. F.C. Leiner, *Millions for Defense: The Subscription Warships of 1798* (Annapolis, Maryland, 2000); M.A. Palmer, *Stoddart's War: Naval Operations during the Quasi-War, 1798–1801* (Columbia, South Carolina, 1987).

8: War and Society

1. A. Smith, *Inquiry into the Nature and Causes of the Wealth of Nations* (London, 1776), pp. 699, 708.

2. R. Entenmann, 'Andreas Ly on the First Jinchuan War in Western Sichuan, 1747–1749', *Sino-Western Cultural Relations Journal*, 19 (1997), p. 12.

3. P.T. Hoffman, 'Prices, the Military Revolutions and Western Europe's Comparative Advantage in Violence', *Economic History Review*, 64, special issue (2011), pp. 56–7.

4. J.W. Frey, 'The Indian Saltpeter Trade, the Military Revolution and the Rise of Britain as a Global Superpower', *Historian*, 71 (2009), pp. 507–54.

5. W.E. Lee, 'Fortify, Fight, or Flee: Tuscarora and Cherokee Defensive Warfare and Military Culture Adaptation', *Journal of Military History*, 68 (2004), pp. 713–70.

6. M. Husain (ed.), *Fath-ul-Mujahideen: A Treatise on the Rules and Regulations of Tipu Sultan's Army and His Principles of Strategy* (Karachi, 1950).

7. J.H. von Landsberg, *Nouveaux Plans et Projets, pour fortifier, défendre, et attaquer les places* (The Hague, 1758).

8. P. Speelman, *Henry Lloyd and the Military Enlightenment of Eighteenth-Century Europe* (Westport, Connecticut, 2002); and P. Speelman (ed.), *War, Society and Enlightenment: The Works of General Lloyd* (Leiden, 2005).

9. D.A. Neill, 'Ancestral Voices: The Influence of the Ancients on the Military Thought of the Seventeenth and Eighteenth Centuries', *Journal of Military History*, 62 (1998), pp. 487–520.

10. I.D. Gruber, *Books and the British Army in the Age of the American Revolution* (Chapel Hill, North Carolina, 2010); S. Powers, 'Studying the Art of War: Military Books Known to American Officers and Their French Counterparts during the Second Half of the Eighteenth Century', *Journal of Military History*, 70 (2006), pp. 781–814.

11. M. Wishon, *Interaction and Perception in Anglo-German Armies, 1689–1815* (University College, London, PhD, 2011).

12. *Observator*, 11 Oct. 1704; T.C.W. Blanning, *The Culture of Power and the Power of Culture: Old Regime Europe, 1660–1789* (Oxford, 2002).

13. J. Bennett and S. Johnston, *The Geometry of War, 1500–1750* (Oxford, 1996); A.W. Crosby, *The Measure of Reality: Quantification and Western Society, 1250–1600* (Cambridge, 1997).

14. Sotheby's Catalogue, *The Library of the Earls of Macclesfield, Part 10: Applied Arts and Sciences* (London, 2007), pp. 90–1; for earlier experiments, see p. 172.

15. B.D. Steele, 'Muskets and Pendulums: Benjamin Robins, Leonhard Euler, and the Ballistics Revolution', *Technology and Culture*, 35 (1994), pp. 345–82.

16. T. Andrade, *Lost Colony: The Untold Story of China's First Great Victory over the West* (Princeton, New Jersey, 2011), pp. 326–7.

17. J. Langins, *Conserving the Enlightenment: French Military Engineering from Vauban to the Revolution* (Cambridge, Massachusetts, 2004).

18. H.W. Dickinson, *Educating the Royal Navy: Eighteenth and Nineteenth Century Education for Officers* (Abingdon, 2007).

19. C. Farinella, *L'Accademia repubblicana. La Società dei Quaranta e Anton Mario Lorgna* (Milan, 1993).

20. L.D. Ferreiro, *Ships and Science: The Birth of Naval Architecture in the Scientific Revolution, 1600–1800* (Cambridge, Massachusetts, 2007).

21. R.P. Multhauf, 'The French Crash Program for Saltpeter Production, 1776–94', *Technology and Culture*, 12 (1971), pp. 163–81; P. Bret, 'The Organization of Gunpowder Production in France, 1775–1830', in

B.J. Buchanan (ed.), *Gunpowder: The History of an International Technology* (Bath, 1996), pp. 261–745.

22. R. Donkin, *Military Collections and Remarks* (London, 1777), p. 190; E. Venn, *Pox Americana: Great Smallpox Epidemic of 1775–83* (New York, 2001); A. Becker, 'Smallpox in Washington's Army: Strategic Implications of the Disease during the American Revolutionary War', *Journal of Military History*, 68 (2004), pp. 381–430.

23. E. Lund, *War for the Every Day: Generals, Knowledge, and Warfare in Early Modern Europe, 1680–1740* (Westport, Connecticut, 1999); and 'The Generation of 1683: The Scientific Revolution and Generalship in the Habsburg Army, 1686–1723', an essay that is more wide-ranging than its title, in B. Davies (ed.), *Warfare in Eastern Europe, 1500–1800* (Leiden, 2012), pp. 199–248.

24. P. Bianchi, *Onore e Mestiere. Le Riforme Militari nel Piemonte del Settecento* (Turin, 2002), pp. 88–100; C. Ingrao, *The Hessian Mercenary State: Ideas, Institutions, and Reform under Frederick II, 1760–1785* (Cambridge, 1987); P.K. Taylor, *Indentured to Liberty: Peasant Life and the Hessian Military State, 1688–1815* (Ithaca, New York, 1994).

25. P.H. Wilson, 'Early Modern German Military Justice', in D. Maffi (ed.), *Tra Marte e Astrea. Giustizia e giurisdizione militare nell'Europa della prima età moderna, secc. XVI–XVIII* (Milan, 2012), pp. 43–85, esp. p. 85.

26. J. Lynn, 'The Battle Culture of Forbearance, 1660–1789', in W.E. Lee (ed.), *Warfare and Culture in World History* (New York, 2011), p. 94.

27. F. Andújar Castillo, *El Sonido del Dinero. Monarquía, Ejército y Venalidad en la España del siglo XVIII* (Madrid, 2004).

28. D. Bien, 'The Army in the French Enlightenment: Reform, Reaction, and Revolution', *Past and Present*, 85 (1979), pp. 68–98; W. Doyle, *Venality: The Sale of Offices in Eighteenth-Century France* (Oxford, 1996), pp. 134–6, 166–7.

29. P.H. Wilson, 'Violence and the Rejection of Authority in Eighteenth-Century Germany: The Case of the Swabian Mutinies in 1757', *German History*, 12 (1994), pp. 1–26.

30. H. Kleinschmidt, 'Using the Gun: Manual Drill and the Proliferation of Portable Firearms', *Journal of Military History*, 63 (1999), pp. 601–29.

31. C. Duffy, *The Military Experience in the Age of Reason* (2nd edn, London, 1998).

32. J. Pringle, *Observations on the Diseases of the Army* (London, 1752); D. Monro, *An Account of the Diseases Which Were Most Frequent in the British Military Hospitals in Germany, From January 1761 to the Return to the Troops to England in March 1763* (London, 1764); C. Storrs, 'Health, Sickness, and Medical Services in Spain's Armed Forces c. 1665–1700', *Medical History*, 50 (2006), pp. 325–50.

33. M. Hochedlinger, 'Mars Ennobled: The Ascent of the Military and the Creation of a Military Nobility in Mid-Eighteenth-Century Austria', *German History*, 17 (1991), pp. 141–76.

34. D. Parrott, *The Business of War: Military Enterprise and Military Revolution in Early Modern Europe* (Cambridge, 2012), pp. 293–300.

35. For figures, see J. Luh, *Kriegskunst in Europa, 1650–1800* (Cologne, 2004), p. 17; J. Glete, *Navies and Nations: Warships, Navies and State-Building in Europe and America, 1500–1860* (2 vols, Stockholm, 1993).

36. M. Wolfe, *Walled Towns and the Shaping of France: From the Medieval to the Early Modern Era* (Basingstoke, 2009).

37. C. Storrs and H.M. Scott, 'The Military Revolution and the European Nobility, c. 1600–1800', *War in History*, 3 (1996), pp. 1–41, esp. p. 40; H.M. Scott (ed.), *The European Nobilities in the Seventeenth and Eighteenth Centuries* (2nd edn, Basingstoke, 2007).

38. P.H. Wilson, 'Social Militarisation in Eighteenth-Century Germany', *German History*, 18 (2000), pp. 1–39.

39. P.H. Wilson, 'War in German Thought from the Peace of Westphalia to Napoleon', *European History Quarterly*, 28 (1998), pp. 37–8.

40. J.M. Smith, *Nobility Reimagined: The Patriotic Nation in Eighteenth-Century France* (Ithaca, New York, 2005).

41. D. Stone, 'Patriotism and Professionalism: The Polish Army in the Eighteenth Century', *Studies in History and Politics*, 3 (1983–4), p. 63.

42. A. Markó, 'Upper Hungary and Rákóczi II', *Hungarian Quarterly*, 3 (1938), pp. 278–301.

43. Sinzendorf to Count Wratislau, 2 Oct. 1709, Vienna, Haus-, Hof-, und Staatsarchiv, Grosse Korrespondenz, vol. 64 fol. 106.

44. K.J.V. Jespersen, 'Conscription and Deception: The Statute of Conscription 1788 and its Role as Political Instrument in Non-Revolutionary Denmark', in J. Delmas (ed.), *L'Influence de la révolution française sur les armées en France, en Europe et dans le Monde* (2 vols, Vincennes, 1991), I, 307–16.

45. K.J.V. Jespersen, 'Claude Louis, Comte de Saint-Germain (1707–1778): Professional Soldier, Danish Military Reformer, and French War Minister', in *Actes du 7ᵉ Colloque International d'Histoire Militaire* (Manhattan, Kansas, 1984).

46. V. Aksan, 'Whatever Happened to the Janissaries? Mobilization for the 1768–1774 Russo-Ottoman War', *War in History*, 5 (1998), pp. 23–36; and 'Ottoman Military Recruitment Strategies in the Late Eighteenth Century', in E.J. Zürcher (ed.), *Arming the State: Military Conscription in the Middle East and Central Asia, 1775–1925* (London, 1999), pp. 21–39; A. Anastasopoulos and E. Kolovos (eds), *Ottoman Rule and the Balkans,*

1760–1850: Conflict, Transformation, Adaptation (Rethymno, 2007). I have benefited greatly from hearing a paper delivered by Virginia Aksan at the 2011 Gunther E. Rothenberg seminar.

47. Y. Dai, 'Yingyun Shengxi: Military Entrepreneurship in the High Qing Period, 1700–1800', *Late Imperial China*, 26 (2005), p. 57.

48. M. Hochedlinger, *Austria's Wars of Emergence: War, State and Society in the Habsburg Monarchy, 1683–1797* (Harlow, 2003), p. 304.

49. Report from Spain, 23 July 1738, Lucca, Archivio di Stato, Anziani al Tempo della Libertà 634 fol. 59.

50. A. Kuethe and J. Marchena (eds), *Soldados del Rey. El ejército borbónico en América colonial en vísperas de la Independencia* (Castelló de la Plana, 2005); C. Marichal, *Bankruptcy of Empire: Mexican Silver and the Wars between Spain, Britain and France, 1760–1810* (Cambridge, 2007).

51. V. Ostapchuk and S. Bilyayeva, 'The Ottoman Northern Black Sea Frontier at Akkerman Fortress: The View from a Historical and Archaeological Project', in A.C.S. Peacock (ed.), *The Frontiers of the Ottoman World* (London, 2009), pp. 153–5.

52. M. Hickok, *Ottoman Military Administration in Eighteenth-Century Bosnia* (Leiden, 1997); Anastasopoulos and Kolovos (eds), *Ottoman Rule and the Balkans, 1760–1850: Conflict, Transformation, Adaptation.*

53. A.W. Fisher, *The Russian Annexation of the Crimea 1772–1783* (Cambridge, 1970), pp. 86–8, 117, 126.

54. V. Aksan, 'Breaking the Spell of the Baron de Tott: Reframing the Question of Military Reform in the Ottoman Empire, 1760–1830', *International History Review*, 24 (2002), pp. 253–77.

55. C. Storrs (ed.), *The Fiscal–Military State in Eighteenth-Century Europe* (Farnham, 2009).

56. P. Avrich, *Russian Rebels, 1600–1800* (New York, 1972).

57. Lindsay, memorandum, 31 Aug. 1791, Bland Burges Deposit, Bodleian Library, Oxford, vol. 58, p. 19.

58. R. Zens, 'Pasvanoğlu Osman Paşa and the Paşalık of Belgrade, 1791–1807', *International Journal of Turkish Studies*, 8 (2002), pp. 89–104; R. Gradeva, 'Osman Pazvantoğlu of Vidin: Between Old and New', in F. Anscombe (ed.), *The Ottoman Balkans, 1750–1830* (Princeton, New Jersey, 2006), pp. 89–104.

59. K. Barbir, *Ottoman Rule in Damascus, 1708–1758* (Princeton, New Jersey, 1980), pp. 200–1.

60. D. Pringle, '"Aqaba Castle in the Ottoman Period, 1517–1917', in A.C.S. Peacock (ed.), *The Frontiers of the Ottoman World* (London, 2009), p. 103.

61. K. Roy, *War, Culture and Society in Early Modern South Asia, 1740–1849* (Abingdon, 2011), pp. 73–4.

62. C. Totman, *Early Modern Japan* (Berkeley, California, 1994).

63. J.W. Hall (ed.), *The Cambridge History of Japan, IV: Early Modern Japan* (Cambridge, 1991), pp. 459, 465–7, 483, 573.

64. A Woodside, 'The Ch'ien-Lung Reign', in W.J. Peterson (ed.), *The Cambridge History of China, Vol. 9, pt 1: The Ch'ing Empire to 1800* (Cambridge, 2002), p. 253; J.R. Shepherd, *Statecraft and Political Economy on the Taiwan Frontier, 1600–1800* (Stanford, California, 1998).

65. T. Barrett, *At the Edge of Empire: The Terek Cossacks and the North Caucasus Frontier, 1700–1860* (Boulder, Colorado, 1999); W. Sunderland, *Taming the Wild Field: Colonisation and Empire on the Russian Steppe* (Ithaca, New York, 2004); B.J. Boeck, *Imperial Boundaries: Cossack Communities and Empire-Building in the Age of Peter the Great* (Cambridge, 2009).

66. S.P. Reyna, 'The Force of Two Logics: Predatory and Capital Accumulation in the Making of the Great Leviathan, 1415–1763', in S.P. Reyna and R.E. Downs (eds), *Deadly Developments: Capitalism, States and War* (Amsterdam, 1999), pp. 23–68; C. Tilly, 'States, State Transformation, and War', in J.H. Bentley (ed.), *The Oxford Handbook of World History* (Oxford, 2011), pp. 190–1.

67. J. Waley-Cohen, 'Commemorating War in Eighteenth-Century China', *Modern Asian Studies*, 30 (1996), pp. 869–99; Y. Dai, 'A Disguised Defeat: the Myanmar Campaign of the Qing Dynasty', *Modern Asian Studies*, 38 (2004), pp. 145–89, esp. 167–85.

68. R. Entenmann (ed.), 'Andreas Ly on the First Jinchuan War in Western Sichuan, 1747–1749', *Sino-Western Cultural Relations Journal*, 19 (1997), pp. 11, 15.

69. J. Ostwald, *Vauban under Siege: Engineering Efficiency and Martial Vigor in the War of the Spanish Succession* (Leiden, 2007).

70. J. Keep, 'Feeding the Troops: Russian Army Supply Policies during the Seven Years War', *Canadian Slavonic Papers*, 29 (1987), pp. 24–44.

71. T.C.W. Blanning, *The French Revolutionary Wars, 1787–1802* (London, 1996), p. 16.

72. C. Duffy, *The Army of Frederick the Great* (Newton Abbot, 1974), pp. 189–91; D. Showalter, *The Wars of Frederick the Great* (London, 1996), pp. 260–2.

73. R. Hellie, 'The Petrine Army: Continuity, Change, and Impact', *Canadian-American Slavic Studies*, 8 (1974), p. 250.

74. J.M. Hartley, *Russia, 1762–1825: Military Power, the State and the People* (Westport, Connecticut, 2008).

75. C.B. Stevens, *Russia's Wars of Emergence, 1460–1730* (Harlow, 2007), pp. 287–303.

76. J. Black, *Beyond the Military Revolution: War in the Seventeenth-Century World* (Basingstoke, 2011).

9: Conclusions

1. M.H. Fisher (ed.), *The Travels of Dean Mahomet: An Eighteenth-Century Journey Through India* (Berkeley, California, 1997), p. 55.
2. J. Luh, '"Strategie und Taktike" in Ancien Régime', *Militargeschichtliche Zeitschrift*, 64 (2005), pp. 101–31.
3. J.L.L. Gommans, *The Rise of the Indo-Afghan Empire c. 1710–1780* (Leiden, 1995), p. 3.
4. C.J. Rogers, 'The Idea of Military Revolutions in Eighteenth and Nineteenth-Century Texts', *Revista de História das Ideias*, 30 (2009), pp. 397–9.
5. C. Dalrymple, *A Military Essay* (London, 1761), p. 56.
6. D.A. Bell, *First Total War: Napoleon's Europe and the Birth of Warfare as We Know It* (Boston, Massachusetts, 2007).
7. C. Paoletti, 'War, 1688–1812', in P. Wilson (ed.), *A Companion to Eighteenth-Century Europe* (Oxford, 2008), p. 475.
8. James Craggs, British Secretary of State, to John, 2nd Earl of Stair, envoy in Paris, 2, 9, 16 Ap. 1719, NA. SP. 104/30.
9. P.T. Hoffman, 'Prices, the Military Revolution, and Western Europe's Comparative Advantage in Violence', *Economic History Review*, 64 (2011), pp. 39–59.
10. G. Bannerman, *Merchants and the Military in Eighteenth-Century Britain: British Army Contracts and Domestic Supply, 1739–1763* (London, 2008).
11. R.H. Kohn, *Eagle and Sword: The Beginnings of the Military Establishment in America* (New York, 1975).
12. B. Marschke, *Absolutely Pietist: Patronage, Factionalism, and State Building in the Early Eighteenth-Century Army Chaplaincy* (Tübingen, 2005).
13. D. Stoker, F.C. Schneid and H.D. Blanton (eds), *Conscription in the Napoleonic Era: A Revolution in Military Affairs?* (Abingdon, 2009).
14. D.M. Peers, 'Revolution, Evolution, or Devolution: The Military and the Making of Colonial India', in W.E. Lee (ed.), *Empires and Indigenes: Intercultural Alliance, Imperial Expansion, and Warfare in the Early Modern World* (New York, 2011), p. 8.
15. R.G.S. Cooper, 'Culture, Combat, and Colonialism in Eighteenth- and Nineteenth-Century India', *International History Review*, 27 (2005), p. 539.
16. S. Subrahmanyam, 'Profiles in Transition: Of Adventurers and Administrators in South India, 1750–1810', *Indian Economic and Social History Review*, 39 (2002), pp. 197–232.
17. J. Brewer, *The Sinews of Power: War, Money, and the English State, 1688–1783* (London, 1989); J.A.F. de Jongste and A.J. Veenendaal (eds), *Anthonie Heinsius and the Dutch Republic, 1688–1720: Politics, War and Finance* (The

Hague, 2002); C. Storrs (ed.), *The Fiscal–Military State in Eighteenth-Century Europe* (Farnham, 2009).

18. J. Black, *Beyond the Military Revolution: Warfare in the Seventeenth-Century World* (Basingstoke, 2011).

19. Whitworth to Charles, 3rd Earl of Sunderland, Secretary of State, 7, 11, 14, 18, 21, 25, 28 Jan., 4, 8, 11 Mar. 1718, NA. SP. 84/261.

20. Whitworth to Sunderland, 25 Jan. 1718, NA. SP. 84/261 fols 80–1.

21. Henri, Earl of Galway, British general in Spain, to Charles, 3rd Earl of Peterborough, 12 Nov. 1706, BL. Add. 61264 fol. 128.

22. E. Krimmer and P.A. Simpson (eds), *Enlightened War: German Theories and Cultures of Warfare from Frederick the Great to Clausewitz* (Woodbridge, 2011) offers little for the subject of this book.

23. J. Black, *War in the World, 1450–1600* (Basingstoke, 2011) and *Beyond the Military Revolution: Warfare in the Seventeenth Century* (Basingstoke, 2011).

Selected Further Reading

The notes of this book and of the books listed here provide details of other relevant works. It is also very useful to read current issues of the leading journals, notably the *Journal of Military History*. Published original sources are also very valuable, although those available tend to focus on Western warfare.

General

Black, J. *Rethinking Military History* (2004)

McNeill, W.H. *The Pursuit of Power: Technology, Armed Force, and Society since AD 1000* (1983)

McNeill, W.H. *The Age of Gunpowder Empires, 1450–1800* (1989)

Parker, G. *The Military Revolution: Military Innovation and the Rise of the West, 1500–1800* (2nd edn, 1996)

Asia

Alam, M. *The Crisis of Empire in Mughal North India: Awadh and the Punjab, 1707–1748* (1986)

Alavi, S. *The Sepoys and the Company: Tradition and Transition in Northern India 1770–1830* (1995)

Barfield, T.J. *The Perilous Frontier: Nomadic Empires and China, 221 BC to AD 1757* (1989)

Dai, Y. *The Sichuan Frontier and Tibet: Imperial Strategy in Early Qing* (2009)

Gommans, J. *The Rise of the Indo-Afghan Empire, c. 1710–1780* (1995)

Gommans, J. and Kolff, D.H.A. (eds) *Warfare and Weaponry in South Asia, 1000–1800* (2001)

Khordarkovsky, M. *Where Two Worlds Met: The Russian State and the Kalmyk Nomads, 1600–1771* (1992)

Kolff, D.H.A. *Naukar, Rajput and Sepoy: The Ethnohistory of the Military Labour Market in Hindustan, 1450–1850* (1990)

Millward, J.A. *Beyond the Pass: Economy, Ethnicity, and Empire in Qing Central Asia, 1759–1864* (1998)

Olson, R.W. *The Siege of Mosul and Ottoman–Persian Relations 1718–1743: A Study of Rebellion in the Capital and War in the Provinces of the Ottoman Empire* (1975)

Perdue, P.C. *China Marches West: The Qing Conquest of Central Eurasia* (2005)

Roy, K. *War, Culture and Society in Early Modern India* (2011)

Waley-Cohen, J. *The Culture of War in China: Empire and the Military under the Qing Dynasty* (2006)

Africa

Thornton, J. *Warfare in Atlantic Africa, 1500–1800* (1999)

Oceania

Dukas, N.B. *A Military History of Sovereign Hawai'i* (1998)

Taylor, A. *The Maori Warrior* (1998)

Tregaskis, R. *The Warrior King: Hawaii's Kamehameha the Great* (1973)

America

Baugh, D.A. *The Global Seven Years War 1754–1763* (2011)

Starkey, A. *European and Native American Warfare, 1676–1815* (1998)

Europe

Barker, T.M. *Army, Aristocracy, Monarchy: Essays on War, Society and Government in Austria, 1618–1780* (1982)

Chickering, R. and Förster, S. (eds) *War in an Age of Revolution, 1775–1815* (2010)

Duffy, C. *The Military Experience in the Age of Reason* (2nd edn, 1998)

Tallett, F. and Trim, D.J.B. (eds) *European Warfare, 1350–1750* (2010)

Naval

Glete, J. *Navies and Nations: Warships, Navies, and State-Building, I: Europe and America, 1500–1860* (1993)

Harding, R. *Seapower and Naval Warfare, 1650–1830* (1999)

Rodger, N.A.M. *The Command of the Ocean: A Naval History of Britain, 1649–1815* (2004)

War and society

Lynn, J. *Women, Armies, and Warfare in Early Modern Europe* (2008)
Ruff, J. *Violence in Early Modern Europe, 1500–1800* (2001)
Steele, B.D. and Dorland, T (eds) *The Heirs of Archimedes: Science and the Art of War through the Age of Enlightenment* (2005)
Storrs, C. (ed.) *The Fiscal–Military State in Eighteenth-Century Europe* (2009)

Index